MANGIA

SOUPS, SALADS, SANDWICHES, ENTRÉES,
AND BAKED GOODS

From the Renowned New York City Specialty Shop

Ricardo Diaz and Nancy Jessup

INTRODUCTION BY
Sasha Muniak

HarperCollins*Publishers*

HarperCollins books may be purchased for educational, business,
or sales promotional use. For information, please write: Special Markets
Department, HarperCollins Publishers Inc., 10 East 53rd Street,
New York, NY 10022.

FIRST EDITION

Designed by Joel Avirom and Jason Snyder

Printed on acid-free paper

Library of Congress Cataloging-in-Publication Data
Diaz, Ricardo.
    Mangia / by Ricardo Diaz and Nancy Jessup; introduction by
Sasha Muniak.—1st ed.
        p. cm.
    Includes index.
    ISBN 0-06-019989-X
1. Cookery. I. Muniak, Sasha. II. Mangia (Bakery). III. Title.
TX714 .D535 2001
641.5—dc21   00-053903

01 02 03 04 05 ❖/RRD 10 9 8 7 6 5 4 3 2 1

*To our customers, with a cupful
of gratitude for their loyalty*

———————

ACKNOWLEDGMENTS

We wish to thank all the chefs and staff at Mangia, past and present, for their passion and commitment.

With special thanks specifically to: Henry Ahle, for his advice and encouragement; Curtis Crystal, for his support; Roger Hockett, for his help in our bakery; Evie Righter for her patience, guidance, and unfailing good humor.

Susan Friedland, our editor, showed us the way, and Carla Glasser, our literary agent, helped us stay the course through trying times—our sincere gratitude.

Last, to Alicia Hallahan Ghadouani, for keeping us all under control.

The Salad Table 187

The Entrée Table 303

The Accents Table 351

MANGIA

INTRODUCTION

When we were in the earliest stages of planning Mangia, long before we opened our door on West Fifty-sixth Street, the choices for lunch were few in midtown Manhattan for the thousands of busy working professionals who poured out of the skyscrapers and office buildings at midday during the week. They could choose among coffee shops, delicatessens, food carts, and restaurants. Those were the basic options. But what if you did not have the time for a formal lunch or were not in the mood for a pastrami sandwich? What if you wanted to eat something different back at your desk?

We imagined what we ourselves might like for lunch to get us through the long afternoons: a cup of homemade soup, a salad, a piece of crusty bread, a glass of freshly squeezed juice. We realized we were imagining the types of foods you see in Europe, in the charcuteries in France, on the antipasto tables in Italy, among the mezze in Greece, and the tapas in Spain. We were envisioning uncomplicated dishes made with fresh and wholesome ingredients: freshly prepared food that would be served at room temperature—that, in fact, tasted best at room temperature.

For as much as we tried, we could not discount the importance of sandwiches in our emerging business plan. Sandwiches are the perfect finger food, a very practical solution for lunch. A sandwich literally and figuratively packs all the components of a meal between two slices of bread and, when done correctly, succeeds in a totally satisfying way. The beauty of a sandwich for anyone who is busy, and this includes office and field workers alike, is that, if need be, it can be eaten with only one hand.

Sandwiches became part of our plan. Not just any sandwiches. It took a good deal of thinking about sandwiches, in general, and their individual components, in particular, before we concluded that the filling is only one of the important parts of a sandwich; the bread is the other, and it is no less important. With that uppermost in mind, we decided to offer a variety of sandwiches. There were two caveats, though: We would make our sandwiches with the best breads we could buy, and not cut it until the order for the sandwich was in hand.

The concept for Mangia had crystallized. We would buy fresh, wonderful ingredients, and prepare and present them at room temperature as authentically as possible as lunch to the businesspeople of Manhattan in a location accessible to them. We would clean up, go home, come in at dawn the next morning, and begin all over again.

We opened our door in February 1982. Our success was immediate and caught us off guard and completely unprepared. The kitchen was too small, the selling space on Fifty-sixth Street too crowded. Our upstairs neighbors complained about the smells—what we liked to think of as aromas!—and our refrigeration failed. But the lines of customers were long, and our customers were faithful and outspoken. We learned on the spot what worked, and just as definitively what did not. The criticism went straight to our hearts. It was a humbling experience.

What we took away from opening was manifold. First of all, we lost our fear of making mistakes. Many wonderful dishes evolved from mistakes, and quite a few other ones emerged totally different from their original concepts. Our customers seemed to understand that our efforts, whatever the outcome, came from a vision, a passion for plain, good-tasting food. We came face-to-face with the hundreds of details a business needs to attend to simply to operate in New York City five out of seven days a week fifty-two weeks a year. We also made two fundamental realizations that govern how we operate today, nineteen years later. The first is that you can never know enough; the second is that our kitchen had to resemble a laboratory for experimentation and renewal.

From the very beginning, we knew we wanted to present the food we prepared at Mangia buffet style. It was part of our original concept and for me hit an especially nostalgic note. I am of Polish descent. Europe has always been an important place for me. Ricardo Diaz, Mangia's head of food design for the past eleven years, is Mexican and has traveled extensively in Europe. Nancy Jessup, our executive chef, is 100 percent American and well-traveled in Europe and the Middle East, too. Together we made quite a team! Presenting food as mezze, antipasto, or tapas, we all agreed, provides a subliminal welcome and suggests anticipation, arrival—an implicit "this is for you." Most of all, a buffet allows for a great deal of choice. It is also practical. From our point of view, we could be ready for lunch service ahead of time. From a staff point of view, our chefs would not be under the kind of duress that comes with finishing dishes *à la minute*. From a service point of view, it was supremely efficient: it was self-serve.

For the customer, a buffet was eminently practical, too. The choices were accessible, service would be easy. The time needed to flag down a waiter or waitress invariably bent on serving someone else no longer had to be factored in. A busy working person could be in and out in no time. The only part of the equation that wasn't in some way predictable was how long it might take that customer to decide on what to choose.

Presenting our dishes in this style also allowed us to use ice tables, something we had always wanted to do. All of us loved their old-fashioned appeal. We wanted the immediacy and impact of the food that only ice tables allow. It was like setting our platters on diamonds!

Which bring us directly to the food that Mangia serves. It is freshly prepared. Our scones, muffins, and buns are baked in our bakery the night or morning before they are served for breakfast. If you are among the first in line in the morning, you might even be lucky enough to find the Chelsea Bun you want still warm. Our selections of salads—the foods we place on our "antipasto table," as we call it—were made, assembled, and plated just prior to serving. We all know now that freshly prepared food is the goal.

The recipes on the pages that follow are the ones that we make on any given day at the three Mangias we now run in New York City. Because we are all about freshly prepared food served at room temperature, some of the recipes have been slightly adapted for the home cook. We don't expect you to be draining pasta, or chopping herbs, or washing salad greens an hour or so before company comes. For that reason, we have included information on what can be made in advance and for how long. Similarly, at the end of many of the recipes, we have indicated in a note whether or not a certain preparation keeps. As I mentioned earlier in this introduction, we don't keep leftovers and never have. If a salad contains raw ingredients, for example, tomatoes or cucumbers, we do not recommend that you keep it. The raw ingredients fade and leach water. In short, that salad barely resembles what it was like fresh. Pasta and grain salads that contain no raw ingredients at all will often keep for about twenty-four hours. If stored longer than that, both texture and flavors will change.

Freezing has never been part of our plan, either. We have, however, included freezing instructions for some of our breakfast baked goods—the scones, muffins, and loaf cakes. We watch as many dozens of muffins disappear in a morning, but many home cooks cannot count on even a dozen muffins vanishing from the breakfast table. And, anyway, they are wonderful to have on hand, only an arm's length away.

We have organized the recipes that follow according to how they are displayed at Mangia every day—on "tables." We have the sandwich and panini table, salads table, and so on; in other food shops these might be called "stations." From the earliest days of Mangia, we have had an entrée table, a limited selection of seafood, poultry, and meats that pair seamlessly with almost any one of our salads. There you may find Grilled Orange-Marinated Salmon (page 310), Pan-Fried Cajun Swordfish (page 313), or Sea Scallops with Spicy Peanut Butter Sauce (page 322); or Stewed Chicken with Tomatoes, Green Olives, and Raisins (page 330) or Roast Filet of Beef with Peppercorn Crust (page 345). Like our salads, we serve our entrées at room temperature. If you elect to serve these entrées hot, they will still be delicious, but they are served at Mangia within one hour of reaching room temperature. The only exception to this rule are our soups: they are served hot or chilled, not tepid.

At Mangia, the platters on our tables are continually replenished at lunchtime, so the issue of food actually standing for any amount of time is not a concern. Of course, at home, where you do not have the benefit of the ice tables, as we do at Mangia, you will want to take precautions in hot weather. Be especially cautious with foods containing mayonnaise: do not leave them out.

One of the great pleasures of walking into Mangia at lunchtime is the number of choices that greet you, that dazzle the eye. You can decide on a little of this, with a little of that. You can forego the salads and opt for a lovely fresh sandwich instead. Or you can enjoy one item, and only that. It is for you to decide.

That is how you should pair the recipes in this book as well. Begin with what you like, with what appeals to you. Exercise choice. Always take risks, and no matter what you make, taste as you go. When it comes to pairing foods buffet style, remember that there are no written rules. We can tell you that there should be a protein by way of a fish or meat selection, a grain, a vegetable dish, and so on. You may be vegetarian, though. Of course, taste, texture, and color all factor in, but start with what you find appealing and go from there. The mix and ultimate match is up to you.

As interpretive, or undisciplined, as that approach may be, there should be no such leeway with the ingredients you use. Buy the very best you can. If you have a green market or farmer's market near you, take advantage of it during the summer months, just as we do at the Union Square market in New York City.

Learn about ingredients. Remember that certain vegetables, like tomatoes, are not at their best, and never will be, if they have been refrigerated. Experiment with different kinds of olive oils and vinegars. We use extra-virgin olive oil at Mangia because it is the most flavorful. We also use a variety of vinegars because there are many different types, and while they are similar, they are not the same. Experiment and you will see what we mean. There is no substitute for freshly ground pepper. It is a wonderful culinary weapon. Have the courage to season the food you prepare. Don't be timid. Aside from the above mentioned, we have no list of recommended standard pantry ingredients. It comes down to this: Use the best and freshest ingredients you can.

When presenting the food you make, let it speak for itself. Surrender to the beauty of the ingredients. Do not feel as if you have to "decorate." The main purpose of food is to be eaten; decorated food, the decorations that is, frequently are not, and serve only to distract. You want the integrity of the ingredients to show through.

One of the most appealing examples is a platter of roasted tomatoes. According to Ricardo, our head of food design at Mangia, "It is better than a painting. The color, the caramelization around the edges from the heat, the shape of the tomatoes themselves, their juiciness, the fact that you can recognize what they are—it is the entire image that appeals." What is striking when you really think about it, is how little has been done to them. Similarly, when you plate the food you have prepared, remember that simple backgrounds, like a white platter, tend to work best.

Mangia is a result of the creativeness of many people, beginning with Ricardo Diaz and Nancy Jessup. Chefs, bakers, cooks, dishwashers, managers, sales clerks, and customers have helped to shape the recipes that follow. To all, our gratitude.

Sasha Muniak

The Bakery Table

BREAKFAST

DESSERT

While there is no bakery table per se at Mangia, on any given morning our customers are very aware of our breakfast offerings—scones, muffins, and buns. The counters are piled high with them. Baskets are filled to overflowing. You look around, and that is what you see. There is an aroma of coffee in the air. The juice bar hums. Breakfast is a busy time.

We begin baking our breakfast items the night before and continue into the early morning of the day they are served, which helps explain their appeal: They are fresh. For some of our earliest-arriving customers, they are even warm. Our baked goods share an old-fashioned look: The scones are squared off and rustic; the muffins also appear handmade. The unsalted butter and buttermilk we use in all our scones ensure the tenderest crumb. Mascarpone, which is baked into several of our muffins, makes them so moist you can have them for breakfast or tea. Our two buns harken back to a simpler time when home cooks used to make yeast doughs without batting an eye. Those buns were delicious then, and they are just as tempting now. They are challenging, but fun to make, too.

We have included a handful of dessert selections, namely, loaf cakes and cookies, in this grouping. Why just those? They were among the first products we made when we opened in early 1982, and they are, hands down, still among our most popular. Like our traditional breakfast offerings, each has lasting appeal. A great chocolate chip or peanut butter cookie (pages 58 and 62), or a slice of moist, spicy carrot zucchini cake (page 52) is a treat, whether you are enjoying it at Mangia or at home.

Use the finest ingredients you can in all of the recipes that follow, and take pleasure in making them. The pleasure of a really good baked product, for both cook and consumer, is immeasurable.

BREAKFAST

Scones

Buttermilk Scones

Cheddar Scones

Whole-Wheat Scones

Pecan Cinnamon Oat Scones

Pumpkin Cranberry Scones

Rock Cakes

Prosciutto and Black Pepper Scones

Muffins

Banana Muffins

Blueberry Muffins

Three-Berry Corn Muffins

Carrot Muffins

Cheddar Muffins

Coconut Muffins

Gingerbread Muffins

Honey Bran Muffins

Lemon and Poppyseed Mascarpone Muffins

Strawberry Mascarpone Muffins

Peanut Butter Muffins

Buns

Chelsea Buns

Walnut Sticky Buns

SCONES

Buttermilk Scones

This classic scone, one of the first we ever made when we opened in 1982, is still one of our most popular. Buttermilk, which we use in all our scone recipes, creates a more tender crumb than regular milk does and adds a slightly tangy flavor. The golden raisins make them just sweet enough and add visual appeal. Fresh out of the oven, these are irresistible topped with softened butter, a fruit preserve, or, for a special treat, mascarpone cheese at room temperature.

3½ cups all-purpose flour

1 tablespoon plus ¾ teaspoon baking powder

½ teaspoon salt

½ pound (2 sticks) cold unsalted butter

1¼ cups golden raisins

3 large eggs

½ cup sugar

¾ cup buttermilk

FOR THE GLAZE

1 egg yolk

1 tablespoon milk

1. Preheat the oven to 400 degrees F. Have ready a large ungreased baking sheet.

2. In a large bowl, combine the flour, baking powder, and salt; stir to blend.

3. Cut the butter into small pieces. Add to the dry ingredients, working it in with the tips of your fingers or a pastry blender until the mixture resembles coarse crumbs. Stir in the golden raisins.

4. In a medium bowl, beat the eggs lightly. Add the sugar and buttermilk and stir until combined. Add the wet ingredients to the dry ones, stirring just until incorporated. (The dough will be wet and sticky, with visible streaks of flour.)

5. Turn the dough out onto a lightly floured surface and knead it 6 or 7 times, until uniform and soft. Divide the dough into 3 equal pieces. Pat each piece, one at a time, into a 4-inch square. With a knife, quarter the square. Place the quarters, 1 inch apart, on the baking sheet. Repeat with the remaining pieces of dough.

6. Make the glaze. In a small bowl, beat the egg yolk and milk. Brush the tops of the scones with the egg glaze.

7. Bake the scones about 20 minutes, until golden. The scones are best served warm, with your favorite spread. Store them in an airtight container or, tightly wrapped in plastic, in the refrigerator or freezer (see box below).

MAKES 1 DOZEN SCONES

Variations

Fresh Blueberry Scones

Omit the golden raisins and substitute 1 cup picked-over fresh blueberries, rinsed and dried. Shape, bake, and serve the scones as directed above.

Date Scones

Omit the golden raisins and substitute 1½ cups chopped pitted dried dates. Add 2 teaspoons freshly grated orange zest to the wet ingredients. Shape, bake, and serve the scones as directed above.

TO STORE AND REFRESH SCONES

Scones can be stored in an airtight container for up to 8 hours. To store them overnight, refrigerate them, tightly wrapped in plastic. Reheat before serving: Remove the plastic wrap; then wrap them in aluminum foil, and place in a preheated 350 degree F oven for 15 minutes until hot.

You can also freeze scones with excellent results. Wrap them well in plastic wrap and store them in the freezer for no more than 2 months—longer than that and they lose their flavor. To reheat, let the scones defrost for 15 minutes. Then proceed as you would for refrigerated scones, but heat them for about 20 minutes.

Cheddar Scones

While these rich-tasting, golden scones are a natural accompaniment to either a bowl of soup or a salad at lunch, they also happen to be wonderful for breakfast, with crisp bacon and eggs. They are also excellent, as are the Gruyère and Parmigiano-Reggiano variations on this theme, served with baked ham and assorted mustards and chutneys. You can substitute smoked Cheddar for the sharp that is called for, but whichever Cheddar you use, it should be of good quality—not orange, which indicates that it has been dyed.

2½ cups all-purpose flour

1 tablespoon baking powder

¼ teaspoon salt

Pinch of cayenne

12 tablespoons (1½ sticks) cold unsalted butter

2 large eggs

¾ cup buttermilk

4 ounces sharp Cheddar cheese, grated

1. Preheat the oven to 400 degrees F. Have ready a large ungreased baking sheet.

2. In a large bowl, combine the flour, baking powder, salt, and cayenne; stir to blend.

3. Cut the butter into small pieces. Using the tips of your fingers or a pastry blender, work the butter into the dry ingredients until the mixture resembles coarse crumbs.

4. In a medium bowl, beat the eggs lightly, then stir in the buttermilk. Add the mixture to the dry ingredients, add the grated Cheddar, and fold together until the flour is moistened. The mixture will be wet with streaks of flour throughout.

5. Turn the dough out onto a lightly floured surface and knead 4 or 5 times, until uniform. Shape into a 9-inch square. With a knife, cut the dough into 12 equal squares. Place them, 2 inches apart, on the baking sheet.

6. Bake the scones about 20 minutes, until golden brown. Let cool 10 minutes before serving. Store the scones in an airtight container or, tightly wrapped in plastic, in the refrigerator or freezer (see page 13).

MAKES 1 DOZEN SCONES

Variations

Gruyère Scones

Substitute 4 ounces of grated Gruyère cheese for the Cheddar. Shape, bake, and cool the scones as directed above.

Parmigiano-Reggiano Scones

Substitute 1 cup of coarsely grated Parmigiano-Reggiano cheese (a 3½-ounce piece) for the Cheddar. Shape, bake, and cool the scones as directed above.

Whole-Wheat Scones

We like the rustic look of scones in general, and these, in particular. They are just plain inviting—rich brown in color and shot through with lots of dark raisins, some of which poke through the top. The small amount of whole-wheat flour adds a hint of nutty flavor. A drizzle of honey makes these especially good.

You can also serve them for lunch or at tea. Halve and top the scones with thinly sliced prosciutto or shavings of manchego cheese—two possibilities, among lots of others, that play nicely off the sweetness of all those raisins.

2 cups all-purpose flour

½ cup whole-wheat flour

⅓ cup firmly packed light brown sugar

1 tablespoon baking powder

½ teaspoon salt

12 tablespoons (1½ sticks) cold unsalted butter

1¼ cups dark raisins

2 large eggs

¾ cup buttermilk

1. Preheat the oven to 400 degrees F. Have ready a large ungreased baking sheet.

2. In a large bowl, combine both flours, the brown sugar, baking powder, and salt; stir until blended.

3. Cut the butter into small pieces. Using the tips of your fingers or a pastry blender, work the butter into the dry ingredients until the mixture resembles coarse crumbs. Stir in the raisins.

4. In a small bowl, beat the eggs lightly; then stir in the buttermilk. Add the wet ingredients to the dry ones, stirring until just blended.

5. Turn the dough out onto a lightly floured surface and knead 6 or 7 times, until soft and uniform. Shape into a 9-inch square. With a knife, cut the dough into 12 equal pieces and place them, 2 inches apart, on the baking sheet.

6. Bake the scones for about 20 minutes, until golden. They are best served warm with softened butter, your favorite jam or jelly, or honey. Store the scones in an airtight container or, tightly wrapped in plastic wrap, in the refrigerator or freezer (see page 13).

MAKES 1 DOZEN SCONES

Pecan Cinnamon Oat Scones

When you bake a batch of these, your kitchen, perhaps even your whole house, will be perfumed with the aroma of cinnamon. Lots of pecans make these rich and crunchy. While we consider these one of our "everyday" scones, they are special enough for holiday mornings. Thick strawberry jam, the kind with chunks of berries, makes a superb topping.

1. Preheat the oven to 400 degrees F. Have ready a large ungreased baking sheet.

2 cups all-purpose flour

½ cup old-fashioned rolled oats (not the instant variety)

⅓ cup firmly packed light brown sugar

2 tablespoons ground cinnamon

1 tablespoon baking powder

1¼ cups pecan pieces

12 tablespoons (1½ sticks) cold unsalted butter

2 large eggs

¾ cup buttermilk

2. In a large bowl, combine the flour, oats, brown sugar, cinnamon, baking powder, and pecan pieces; stir until blended.

3. Cut the butter into small pieces. Using the tips of your fingers or a pastry blender, work the butter into the dry ingredients until the mixture resembles coarse crumbs.

4. In a medium bowl, beat the eggs until blended; then stir in the buttermilk. Add the wet ingredients to the dry ones, mixing until no streaks of flour show.

5. Turn the dough out onto a lightly floured surface and knead 6 or 7 times, until soft and cohesive. Shape into a 9-inch square. With a knife, cut the square into 12 equal pieces and place them, 2 inches apart, on the baking sheet.

6. Bake the scones for about 20 minutes, until golden brown. Store them in an airtight container or, tightly wrapped in plastic, in the refrigerator or freezer (see page 13).

MAKES 1 DOZEN SCONES

Pumpkin Cranberry Scones

When autumn arrives, and with it pumpkins ripening in the fields, we like to offer these seasonal scones. You don't have to prepare fresh pumpkin to make them: Canned pumpkin works just fine. Moist and not too sweet, these are tasty in the morning, especially on Thanksgiving. Or serve them with the turkey.

3¾ cups all-purpose flour

1½ tablespoons baking powder

½ teaspoon salt

¼ teaspoon ground ginger

¼ teaspoon ground cinnamon

¼ teaspoon ground cardamom

¼ teaspoon ground allspice

½ pound (2 sticks) cold unsalted butter

4 large eggs

⅔ cup sugar

¾ cup buttermilk

½ cup pumpkin puree (not pumpkin pie filling)

1 cup cranberries, picked over, rinsed, and drained

1. Preheat the oven to 400 degrees F. Have ready a large ungreased baking sheet.

2. In a large bowl, combine the flour, baking powder, salt, and spices and stir until blended.

3. Cut the butter into small pieces. With the tips of your fingers or a pastry blender, cut the butter into the dry ingredients until the mixture resembles coarse crumbs.

4. In a medium bowl, beat the eggs lightly; then stir in the sugar, buttermilk, and pumpkin puree until thoroughly combined. Add the liquid ingredients and the cranberries to the dry ones, and mix just until the dry ingredients are moistened. (The dough will be wet, with visible streaks of flour.)

5. Turn the dough out onto a lightly floured surface and knead 6 or 7 times, until soft and cohesive. Divide the dough into 3 equal pieces. Pat each piece, one at a time, into a 4-inch square. Using a knife, quarter the square and place the pieces on the baking sheet 2 inches apart.

6. Bake the scones for 15 minutes, or until golden. Let cool 10 minutes; then serve. Store the scones in an airtight container or, tightly wrapped in plastic, in the refrigerator or freezer (see page 13).

MAKES 1 DOZEN SCONES

Rock Cakes

The name comes from the appearance, not the texture, which happens to be lovely—a tender crumb studded with currants, golden raisins, and candied lemon peel. The sprinkling of granulated sugar before baking ensures a handmade, old-fashioned finish. A basket of these, with a jar of jam or honey, makes a wonderful gift, especially during the holidays.

1. Preheat the oven to 400 degrees F. Have ready a large ungreased baking sheet.

2. In a large bowl, combine the flour, baking powder, ginger, mace, and salt; stir until combined.

3 cups all-purpose flour

1½ tablespoons baking powder

½ teaspoon ground ginger

½ teaspoon ground mace

½ teaspoon salt

12 tablespoons (1½ sticks) cold unsalted butter

½ cup dried currants

¼ cup golden raisins

¼ cup diced candied lemon peel

3 large eggs

¼ cup sugar plus 2 tablespoons for sprinkling

½ cup buttermilk

2 large egg whites

3. Cut the butter into small pieces. Using the tips of your fingers or a pastry blender, work it into the dry ingredients until the mixture resembles coarse crumbs. Stir in the dried currants, golden raisins, and candied lemon peel until evenly distributed.

4. In a medium bowl, beat the eggs lightly, then add the ¼ cup sugar and buttermilk, stirring until combined. Pour the wet ingredients into the dry ones and stir until just incorporated. (The dough will be somewhat wet.)

5. Turn the dough out onto a lightly floured surface and knead 5 or 6 times, until soft and cohesive. Pat the dough into a 9 x 12-inch rectangle and with a knife, cut it into 12 equal squares. Place the squares, 2 inches apart, on the baking sheet.

6. Beat the egg whites until combined; then brush the dough with them. Sprinkle the tops of the cakes with the remaining 2 tablespoons of sugar.

7. Bake the cakes about 20 minutes, until golden. They are best served warm, with softened butter or jam. Store in an airtight container or, tightly wrapped in plastic, in the refrigerator or freezer (see page 13).

Makes 1 dozen cakes

Prosciutto and Black Pepper Scones

These are elegant and sophisticated, and just peppery enough to make a fine accompaniment to soups (two particularly good matchings are suggestions below), vegetable salads, or cut-up sweet fruits. These and the smoked salmon and chive variation are also excellent with omelets or frittatas, making them ideal choices for brunch or grown-up lunches.

If you are looking for a savory scone that is more family-friendly, try the bacon variation that follows this recipe. We're keen on those topped with a rough-cut marmalade, like orange or ginger. A drizzle of maple syrup on a still-warm split bacon scone is very good, too.

3½ cups all-purpose flour

1 tablespoon plus ¾ teaspoon baking powder

1 tablespoon freshly ground black pepper

3 ounces prosciutto, sliced

½ pound (2 sticks) cold unsalted butter

3 large eggs

¾ cup buttermilk

SERVE WITH: Fresh Vegetable Soup with Orzo (page 114) or Chicken Soup with Mushrooms and Sun-Dried Tomatoes (page 82).

1. Preheat the oven to 400 degrees F. Have ready a large ungreased baking sheet.

2. In a large bowl, combine the flour, baking powder, and black pepper; stir to combine.

3. Finely chop the prosciutto. (You should have ¾ cup.)

4. Cut the butter into small pieces. With the tips of your fingers or a pastry blender, work the butter into the dry ingredients until the mixture resembles coarse crumbs. Stir in the chopped prosciutto.

5. In a small bowl, lightly beat together the eggs; then stir in the buttermilk. Add the wet ingredients to the dry ones, mixing just until the flour is moistened. (The dough will be wet and sticky, with visible streaks of flour.)

6. Turn the dough out onto a lightly floured surface and knead 6 or 7 times, until cohesive. With a rolling pin, roll the dough into a 9-inch square. With a knife, cut the dough into 12 equal squares and place, 1 inch apart, on the baking sheet.

7. Bake the scones 15 to 20 minutes, until golden. Let cool 10 minutes; then serve while still warm. Store in an airtight container or, tightly wrapped in plastic, in the refrigerator or freezer (see page 13).

MAKES 1 DOZEN SCONES

Variations

Smoked Salmon and Chive Scones

Omit the prosciutto and pepper. Replace the prosciutto with 3 ounces of finely chopped smoked salmon and ¼ cup minced fresh chives. Shape, bake, and serve the scones as directed above.

Bacon Scones

Cook 4 ounces of hickory-smoked bacon until crisp, drain on paper towels, and cool. Make the dough for the scones, omitting the prosciutto and pepper. Crumble the bacon, add it to the dough, and work it in until incorporated. Shape, bake, and serve the scones as directed above.

MUFFINS

Banana Muffins

Our banana muffins are bestsellers and have been from the day Mangia opened in February 1982. They are filled with golden raisins and pecan pieces, but the real twist is the walnut oil we add for flavor. It is an extravagance, but well worth it. If you don't have walnut oil, use safflower or canola oil. The flavor of the muffins won't be the same, but the moist crumb will be every bit as tender. For maximum flavor, use bananas that have ripened until the skins have become black; they are unsightly, but also very sweet.

4 cups all-purpose flour

2 tablespoons baking powder

4 very ripe bananas
(about 4 ounces each)

12 tablespoons (1½ sticks)
unsalted butter, at room temperature

½ cup sugar

½ cup dark corn syrup

½ cup walnut oil

2 tablespoons vanilla extract

3 large eggs

1 cup pecan pieces

1 cup golden raisins

1. Preheat the oven to 400 degrees F. Grease and flour 18 (½-cup) muffin cups.

2. Into a medium bowl, sift together the flour and baking powder. Mash the bananas in a small bowl. (You should have 1 cup of puree.)

3. In the bowl of a standing electric mixer, cream together the butter, sugar, corn syrup, walnut oil, and vanilla on medium speed until the mixture is light. Scrape down the bowl. Add the eggs, one at a time, scraping down the bowl after each addition.

4. Reduce the mixer speed to low and add the dry ingredients in two parts, beating each time until no flour shows. By hand, fold in the pecan pieces, golden raisins, and mashed bananas until well combined.

5. Spoon the batter into the prepared muffin cups, filling each three-quarters full. Bake about 20 to 25 minutes, until the tops are golden. Let the muffins cool in the pan and serve warm or at room temperature. Store, well wrapped in plastic, at room temperature or in the freezer (see box below).

MAKES 1 1/2 DOZEN MUFFINS

To Store and Refresh Muffins

If you are storing muffins for 1 day or less, wrap them well in plastic and keep at room temperature. To reheat, remove the plastic wrap; then wrap the muffins in aluminum foil and place in a preheated 350 degree F oven for 10 minutes.

Like scones, muffins freeze well. Wrap them securely in plastic wrap and store them in the freezer for no more than 2 months. Reheat while still frozen: Remove the plastic wrap, then reheat as instructed above, but for 15 minutes.

Blueberry Muffins

We make our blueberry muffins with fresh blueberries only. So earmark this recipe for early summer, when the first crop of berries comes into the markets. You might be wondering what an apple is doing in the batter. It's adding moisture to an unusual muffin batter—one with two kinds of flour, both brown and white sugar, buttermilk, and the subtle flavor of mace. These are tender and luscious. You won't even need butter.

2½ cups all-purpose flour

½ cup whole-wheat flour

1 tablespoon baking powder

½ teaspoon ground mace

½ teaspoon salt

1 small Granny Smith apple

12 tablespoons (1½ sticks) unsalted butter, at room temperature

½ cup firmly packed light brown sugar

⅓ cup granulated sugar

¼ cup soy oil or safflower oil

2 large eggs

1 teaspoon vanilla extract

1¼ cups buttermilk

1 cup fresh blueberries, picked over, rinsed, and dried

1. Preheat the oven to 350 degrees F. Grease and flour 12 (½-cup) muffin cups.

2. Into a small bowl, sift together both flours, the baking powder, mace, and salt.

3. Peel, core, and grate the apple.

4. In the bowl of a standing electric mixer, cream together the butter, both sugars, and soy oil on medium speed for 4 minutes. Scrape down the bowl. Add the eggs, one at a time, scraping down the bowl after each addition. Beat in the grated apple and vanilla.

5. Reduce the mixer speed to low and add half the dry ingredients. Beat in the buttermilk, then the remaining dry ingredients, and continue beating until no flour shows. By hand, gently fold in the blueberries.

6. Spoon the batter into the prepared muffin cups, filling each three-quarters full. Bake 20 to 25 minutes, until the tops are golden and they spring back when lightly touched. Let the muffins cool in the pan and serve warm or at room temperature. They will store, well wrapped in plastic, at room temperature or in the freezer (see page 25).

MAKES 1 DOZEN MUFFINS

Three-Berry Corn Muffins

These are the perfect summer muffin, delicious and pretty, with a juice-stained golden crumb. In berry season, make several batches of these; then freeze the overrun (see page 25 for freezing instructions). You will be happy you did, especially when the season, so short lived, has come and gone. Luxe as is, these become decadent with a dab of mascarpone on top. And don't limit them just to breakfast. They are special any time of day.

1. Preheat the oven to 400 degrees F. Grease and flour 12 (½-cup) muffin cups.

12 tablespoons (1½ sticks) unsalted butter

2 cups all-purpose flour

2 cups yellow cornmeal

⅔ cup sugar

1½ tablespoons baking powder

½ teaspoon salt

2 large eggs

2 cups buttermilk

1 cup mixed fresh berries (blueberries, raspberries, and blackberries)

2. Melt the butter in a small saucepan; set aside to cool.

3. Into a medium bowl, sift together the flour, cornmeal, sugar, baking powder, and salt.

4. In a large bowl, stir together the melted butter, eggs, and buttermilk until combined. Stir in the dry ingredients and continue stirring until incorporated. By hand, gently fold in the mixed berries, being careful not to crush.

5. Spoon the batter into the prepared muffin cups, filling each about three-quarters full. Bake 20 to 25 minutes, until the tops are golden and spring back when touched. Let the muffins cool in the pan and serve warm or at room temperature. Store, well wrapped in plastic, at room temperature or in the freezer (see page 25).

MAKES 1 DOZEN MUFFINS

Carrot Muffins

There are no nuts or raisins—no distractions, in other words—in these carrot muffins. Lots of carrots, spices, honey, and even apples enliven this batter. We have customers who, unfailingly, have one of these and a coffee to go day after day, week after week. That said, we can also attest to the fact that these are popular with soup or salad at lunch and as an afternoon treat. For that reason, the recipe makes a lot: 18. These are tasty toasted, too, with a little cream cheese, if you dare. Because they are moist to start off with, they also happen to freeze well.

4 tablespoons (½ stick) unsalted butter

2 cups all-purpose flour

1½ cups whole-wheat flour

1 tablespoon baking powder

¾ teaspoon baking soda

1½ teaspoons ground cinnamon

½ teaspoon ground nutmeg

¼ teaspoon ground cloves

½ teaspoon salt

About 5 small carrots

3 small Granny Smith apples

1 cup honey

1 cup peanut oil

½ cup sugar

4 large eggs

1. Preheat the oven to 350 degrees F. Grease and flour 18 (½-cup) muffin cups.

2. Melt the butter in a small saucepan; set aside to cool.

3. Into a large bowl, sift together both flours, the baking powder, baking soda, cinnamon, nutmeg, cloves, and salt.

4. Trim, peel, and grate enough carrots to measure 2 cups grated. Peel, core, and grate the apples to measure 2 cups grated.

5. In the bowl of a standing electric mixer, beat together the honey, peanut oil, melted butter, and sugar on medium speed for 2 minutes. Scrape down the bowl. Add the eggs and beat 2 minutes. Scrape down the bowl. Add the grated carrots and apples, and beat 1 minute.

6. Reduce the speed to low and add the dry ingredients; beat just until no streaks of flour show.

7. Spoon the batter into the prepared muffin cups, filling each three-quarters full. Bake for 20 to 25 minutes, until the tops are golden and spring back when touched. Let the muffins cool in the pan and serve warm or at room temperature. Store, well wrapped in plastic, at room temperature or in the freezer (see page 25).

MAKES 1 1/2 DOZEN MUFFINS

Cheddar Muffins

Like our Cheddar Scones (page 14), these muffins can be served over the course of the day, starting with breakfast. These are just the thing for a fall picnic or informal buffet. If you are looking for a simple, chic snack, split these in two, top each half with paper-thin slices of prosciutto or smoked ham, and serve a little chutney or chow-chow on the side. A reminder for whenever you plan to serve them: Make them with real Cheddar, the only acceptable kind.

I. Preheat the oven to 400 degrees F. Grease and flour 12 (½-cup) muffin cups.

2¼ cups all-purpose flour

2½ teaspoons baking powder

1 teaspoon sugar

¾ teaspoon salt

¼ teaspoon sweet paprika

6 tablespoons (¾ stick) unsalted butter

1 large egg

1 cup whole milk

2 whole scallions

1 cup coarsely grated extra-sharp Cheddar cheese (a 3-ounce piece)

2. Into a large bowl, sift together the flour, baking powder, sugar, salt, and paprika.

3. Melt the butter; let cool slightly.

4. In a small bowl, lightly beat the egg; add the milk and melted butter and stir to combine.

5. Trim, then mince both the green and white part of the scallions.

6. Add the butter and milk mixture to the dry ingredients, folding by hand until the dry ingredients are moistened. Add the Cheddar and scallions, stirring just to combine.

7. Spoon the batter into the prepared muffin cups, filling each three-quarters full. Bake for 20 minutes, or until the tops start to brown and spring back when touched. Let the muffins cool in the pans and serve warm or at room temperature. Store, well wrapped in plastic, at room temperature or in the freezer (see page 25).

MAKES I DOZEN MUFFINS

Coconut Muffins

If you think coconut muffins run a distant second to Mangia's other, more traditional muffins, like blueberry or bran, think again. These fly out the door. They are sweet and tender—a little bit of coconut cake, really, baked in a muffin pan. Special for breakfast, they are superb served alongside a pot of black tea and slices of lemon. They are also grand with a scoop of ice cream, for dessert.

3 cups all-purpose flour

1 tablespoon baking powder

¼ teaspoon salt

½ pound (2 sticks) unsalted butter, at room temperature

1 cup sugar

5 large eggs

8 ounces sweetened dried coconut flakes

1 cup buttermilk

1. Preheat the oven to 375 degrees F. Grease and flour 12 (½-cup) muffin cups.

2. Into a large bowl, sift together the flour, baking powder, and salt.

3. In the bowl of a standing electric mixer, cream the butter and sugar on medium speed until light and fluffy. Scrape down the bowl. Add the eggs in three batches, scraping down the bowl after each addition.

4. Reduce the mixer speed to low and add half the dry ingredients, beating just until combined. By hand, fold in the coconut flakes. Pour in the buttermilk; then add the remaining dry ingredients, mixing briefly until just combined.

5. Spoon the batter into the prepared muffin tins, filling each three-quarters full. Bake about 35 minutes, until the tops are golden and spring back when touched. Let the muffins cool in the pan and serve warm or at room temperature. Store, well wrapped in plastic, at room temperature or in the freezer (see page 25).

MAKES 1 DOZEN MUFFINS

Gingerbread Muffins

The dark molasses in these muffins lends a rich, burnt-sugar taste and almost chocolate-like color to the crumb. Lots of fresh ginger, plus some ground, ensure deep flavor. And even though real gingerbread contains no rum, there is light rum in this batter, making these truly unique. Remember this recipe at Thanksgiving, serve the muffins with the turkey dinner, and see if anyone can identify that hint of Caribbean flavor.

A word about grating fresh ginger: We find it easiest to grate it on a small hand-held flat grater, as opposed to the larger box grater, which tends, even when you use the side with the smallest holes, to pulverize the root. You need ¼ cup grated for this recipe, which is quite a bit. Select a firm piece of ginger. Ginger that is soft to the touch is not as young or fresh as it could be (the color of the flesh is darker), and it can be a chore to grate.

3¾ cups all-purpose flour

1½ teaspoons baking soda

1½ teaspoons ground ginger

1 teaspoon salt

¾ teaspoon ground cloves

¾ teaspoon ground cinnamon

1½ cups unsulfured molasses

¼ cup hot water

¼ cup light rum

¼ cup grated peeled fresh ginger

12 tablespoons (1½ sticks) unsalted butter, at room temperature

¾ cup sugar

1 large egg

1 large egg yolk

1. Preheat the oven to 375 degrees F. Grease and flour 12 (½-cup) muffin cups.

2. Into a large bowl, sift together the flour, baking soda, ginger, salt, cloves, and cinnamon.

3. In a medium bowl, combine the molasses with the hot water, rum, and grated ginger.

4. In the bowl of a standing electric mixer, cream the butter and sugar on medium speed until light and fluffy. Scrape down the sides of the bowl. Add the whole egg and egg yolk and beat for 1 minute; scrape down the sides of the bowl again. Add the molasses mixture and beat 2 minutes; scrape down the sides of the bowl.

5. Reduce the mixer speed to low. Beat in the dry ingredients in two parts and continue mixing until no streaks of flour show.

6. Spoon the batter into the prepared muffin cups, filling each three-quarters full. Bake for 25 minutes, or until a cake tester inserted in the center of a muffin comes out clean. Let the muffins cool in the pan and serve them warm or at room temperature. Store, well wrapped in plastic, at room temperature or in the freezer (see page 25).

MAKES 1 DOZEN MUFFINS

Honey Bran Muffins

We can't call these "healthy" muffins despite the amount of bran we use in them. We can call these good, moist, honey-flavored, and raisin-filled, though, and we know a basket of these at breakfast makes a great start to any day.

2½ cups bran (not bran cereal)

2 cups whole-wheat flour

2 teaspoons baking powder

¼ teaspoon baking soda

Pinch of salt

10 tablespoons (1¼ sticks) unsalted butter

1 small Granny Smith apple

1 large egg

1½ cups whole milk

¾ cup honey

¼ cup soy oil or safflower oil

1¼ cups dark raisins

1. Preheat the oven to 350 degrees F. Grease and flour 12 (½-cup) muffin cups.

2. Into a large bowl, sift together the bran, whole-wheat flour, baking powder, baking soda, and salt.

3. In a small saucepan, melt the butter; set aside to cool.

4. Peel, core, and grate the apple.

5. In a medium bowl, lightly beat the egg. Add the grated apple, and stir to combine. Stir in the butter, milk, honey, oil, and raisins until blended.

6. Add the wet ingredients to the dry ones and blend just until no streaks of flour show.

7. Spoon the batter into the prepared muffin cups, filling each three-quarters full. Bake about 40 minutes, until the tops spring back when lightly touched. Let the muffins cool in the pan and serve them warm or at room temperature. Store, well wrapped in plastic, at room temperature or in the freezer (see page 25).

MAKES 1 DOZEN MUFFINS

Lemon and Poppyseed Mascarpone Muffins

This muffin is a favorite of many of our customers, our literary agent, Carla Glasser, among them. The poppyseeds lend an Old World charm. There is nothing Old World about mascarpone, Italy's cream cheese, though. It's stylish and delicious, and something we like to bake with because, like the buttermilk we use in all our scones, mascarpone contributes texture and tang.

A note about poppyseeds: Like nuts, they can turn rancid if stored for too long at room temperature, or if kept at too high a temperature. To ensure freshness, keep the jar in the freezer.

¼ cup milk

2 tablespoons poppyseeds

3 cups all-purpose flour

1 tablespoon baking powder

½ teaspoon salt

1 large lemon

¾ pound mascarpone cheese

1¼ cups sugar

5 large eggs

½ teaspoon vanilla extract

1. Preheat the oven to 350 degrees F. Grease and flour 12 (½-cup) muffin cups.

2. In a small saucepan, heat the milk until warm. Remove the pan from the heat, add the poppyseeds, and let soak 10 minutes.

3. Into a large bowl, sift together the flour, baking powder, and salt.

4. Zest the lemon and set the zest aside. Squeeze the lemon to extract ⅓ cup juice.

5. In the bowl of a standing electric mixer, cream the mascarpone and 1 cup of the sugar on medium speed until light and fluffy. Add the eggs in three batches, scraping down the bowl after each addition. Stir in the vanilla.

6. Reduce the mixer speed to low. Add the dry ingredients in two parts, mixing just until no streaks of flour show. By hand, fold in the lemon zest and poppyseed and milk mixture.

7. Spoon the batter into the prepared muffin cups, filling each three-quarters full. Bake 20 to 25 minutes, until the tops are golden and spring back when touched.

8. While the muffins are baking, in a small saucepan, heat together the lemon juice and remaining ¼ cup sugar, stirring until the sugar dissolves.

9. Remove the muffins from the oven and brush the tops lightly with the lemon glaze. Let the muffins cool briefly in the pan while the glaze sets. Serve either warm or at room temperature. Store, well wrapped in plastic, at room temperature or in the freezer (see page 25).

MAKES 1 DOZEN MUFFINS

Strawberry Mascarpone Muffins

The mascarpone's creamy, buttery taste complements the strawberries that figure in both the muffins and glaze. Although mascarpone was once considered a specialty item, it is frequently sold in supermarkets now.

Serve these lovely-looking, sweet-tasting muffins for summer breakfasts, but of course, do not stop there. They make a superb dessert served with slices of fresh or roasted pineapple or topped with gelato or sorbet. These muffins will disappear as soon as you put them out. When strawberry season is in full bloom, it's a good idea to make several batches and freeze them.

3½ cups all-purpose flour

1 tablespoon baking powder

1½ cups whole fresh strawberries, ¾ cup quartered and ¾ cup sliced

1 cup plus 2 tablespoons sugar

1 tablespoon water

¾ pound mascarpone cheese

5 large eggs

½ teaspoon vanilla extract

FOR THE GLAZE

½ cup strawberry preserves

½ cup orange juice

1. Preheat the oven to 350 degrees F. Grease and flour 12 (½-cup) muffin cups.

2. Into a large bowl, sift together the flour and baking powder.

3. In a small saucepan, cook the quartered strawberries with the 2 tablespoons of sugar and 1 tablespoon of water until soft; remove from the heat and set aside.

4. In the bowl of a standing electric mixer, cream the mascarpone cheese and the remaining 1 cup sugar until light and fluffy. Beat in the eggs, one at a time, scraping down the bowl after each addition. Beat in the vanilla.

5. Reduce the mixer speed to low. Add half the dry ingredients, and beat for 30 seconds. Add the remaining dry ingredients and beat 30 seconds longer. By hand, fold in the cooked and raw strawberries.

6. Scoop the batter into the prepared muffin cups, filling each three-quarters full. Bake for about 25 minutes, until the tops of the muffins are golden and spring back when touched.

7. While the muffins are baking, make the glaze: Melt the strawberry preserves in the orange juice in a small saucepan over medium heat, stirring until well combined.

8. Remove the muffin pan from the oven and while the muffins are still hot, brush the tops with the strawberry glaze. Let cool slightly in the pan to allow the glaze to set and serve them warm or at room temperature. Store, well wrapped in plastic, at room temperature or in the freezer (see page 25).

MAKES I DOZEN MUFFINS

Peanut Butter Muffins

We were reminiscing one day about the peanut butter sandwiches of our youth, and the idea for a peanut butter muffin came into being. If you are feeling nostalgic for things past, or are simply in the mood for something that is sure to please, make a pan of these. They are really good with bacon or grape jelly.

Remember this recipe when you are putting together a lunch to go—be it a brown bag for school, picnic basket for an outing, or a picnic hamper, the kind with all the bells and whistles, for a concert in the park. Peanut butter may not be a sophisticated taste, but it is universally loved.

4 cups all-purpose flour

1 tablespoon baking powder

1 teaspoon salt

8 tablespoons (1 stick) unsalted butter, at room temperature

½ cup granulated sugar

½ cup firmly packed light brown sugar

⅓ cup smooth peanut butter

3 large eggs

½ teaspoon vanilla extract

1 cup whole milk

⅓ cup chopped unsalted roasted peanuts

1. Preheat the oven to 375 degrees F. Grease and flour 12 (½-cup) muffin cups.

2. Into a large bowl, sift together the flour, baking powder, and salt.

3. In the bowl of a standing electric mixer, cream the butter, both sugars, and peanut butter on medium speed until light and fluffy. Scrape down the bowl. Add the eggs, one at a time, scraping down the bowl after each addition. Stir in the vanilla.

4. Reduce the mixer speed to low. Beat in the dry ingredients, a quarter at a time, alternating with the milk and finishing with the last quarter of the dry ingredients. Fold in the chopped peanuts until well incorporated.

5. Spoon the batter into the prepared muffin cups, filling each three-quarters full. Bake 20 to 25 minutes, until the tops of the muffins are golden and spring back when touched. Let the muffins cool in the pan and serve them warm or at room temperature. Store, well wrapped in plastic, at room temperature or in the freezer (see page 25).

MAKES 1 DOZEN MUFFINS

BUNS

Chelsea Buns

We make Chelsea Buns every Friday—but only on Fridays—and customers literally wait in line for them. Buttery, rich, and satisfying, the buns are made with yeast dough, which takes time to prepare. You'll find the time well spent, though, when you taste one of these still warm from the oven. If baking your own is too much, come in early on a Friday morning and get in line! That said, though, we seriously recommend that you make your own, because once made, they store in the refrigerator very successfully for several days. As morning pastries go, they are definitely worth waking up for.

¼ cup warm water
(110 to 115 degrees F)

1 tablespoon active dry yeast

Pinch of granulated sugar

2 cups whole milk, plus ¼ cup for brushing the buns

¾ pound (3 sticks) unsalted butter

6 cups all-purpose flour

¾ cup firmly packed light brown sugar

2 large eggs

½ teaspoon vanilla extract

FOR THE FILLING

½ cup firmly packed light brown sugar

1 cup dried currants

1 tablespoon ground cinnamon

1. Pour the warm water into the bowl of a standing electric mixer, add the yeast and granulated sugar, and let the yeast proof until bubbly on the surface, about 10 minutes.

2. Meanwhile, in a medium saucepan, heat the 2 cups of milk until very warm (120 to 130 degrees F).

3. In another pan, melt the butter. Set aside ¼ cup for brushing the pans.

4. When the yeast is bubbly, fit the electric mixer with a dough hook or paddle. Add all of the flour, the brown sugar, warm milk, eggs, and the 1¼ cups melted butter and beat on low speed for 10 minutes.

5. Oil a large bowl and place the dough in it, turning it in the bowl to coat on all sides. Cover and let rise in a warm, draft-free place until doubled in volume, about 1½ hours.

6. Brush two 8-inch springform pans, 2 inches deep, with the reserved ¼ cup of melted butter.

7. Make the filling: In a bowl, stir together the brown sugar, currants, and cinnamon.

8. Once the dough has doubled, punch it down with your hands. Divide the dough into 2 equal portions. On a clean, dry, lightly floured surface, roll out each piece of dough into a rectangle 8 x 12 inches. Sprinkle half the filling over each piece of dough, leaving a 1-inch border on all sides. Starting with the long side of the dough closest to you, roll each piece of dough into a cylinder, pinching the seam closed. Cut each roll into 6 equal slices and place the slices, cut side up, with the sides touching, in the prepared springform pans. Brush the surface of the buns with the remaining ¼ cup of milk. Let the buns rise in the pans until almost doubled in size, about 30 minutes.

9. In the meantime, preheat the oven to 350 degrees F.

10. Bake the buns for about 45 minutes, until golden and a toothpick inserted into the center of one of the buns comes out clean. Cool in the pans 10 minutes. Serve warm. To store, wrap the buns well in plastic, then store in the refrigerator for up to 3 days. To reheat, remove the plastic wrap; then wrap the buns in aluminum foil. Reheat in a preheated 350 degree F oven for about 10 minutes, or until heated through.

MAKES 1 DOZEN BUNS

Walnut Sticky Buns

Sticky" says it all. If you love caramel, this is the recipe for you. Like Chelsea Buns (page 42) these are made from yeast dough. Letting the dough rise, then punching it down, is time-consuming. The beauty of this recipe (and Chelsea Buns, too), however, is that the yeasty, butter-rich buns can be baked the day before and reheated for a delectable breakfast treat.

1. Heat the water until warm (110 to 115 degrees F) in a cup or small saucepan. Add the yeast and granulated sugar and let the yeast proof until bubbly, about 10 minutes.

2. Pour the mixture in the bowl of a standing electric mixer fitted with the dough hook. Add 3 cups of the flour and all of the milk and beat on low speed for 4 minutes. Let the dough rest, covered, in the mixing bowl in a draft-free place for 30 minutes.

⅓ cup water

2 teaspoons active dry yeast

Pinch of granulated sugar

6 cups all-purpose flour

1 cup whole milk

2 large eggs

5 large egg yolks

½ cup firmly packed light brown sugar

1½ teaspoons salt

8 tablespoons (1 stick) unsalted butter, melted

1½ cups walnut pieces

FOR THE FILLING

12 tablespoons (1½ sticks) unsalted butter

¾ cup firmly packed light brown sugar

FOR THE GLAZE

¼ cup honey

⅓ cup firmly packed light brown sugar

8 tablespoons (1 stick) unsalted butter

3. Uncover the bowl and add the whole eggs and yolks, brown sugar, salt, butter, and remaining 3 cups of flour and beat 7 minutes. The dough will be smooth, soft, and elastic.

4. Oil a large bowl and place the dough in it, turning it to coat on all sides. Cover and let the dough rest in a warm place until doubled in size, about 1½ hours.

5. In the meantime, preheat the oven to 350 degrees F.

6. Spread the walnuts on a baking sheet and toast them lightly in the oven, stirring once, for about 10 minutes; remove and let cool.

7. Make the filling: In a saucepan, heat the butter with the brown sugar, stirring, until the butter has melted and the sugar has dissolved; set aside to cool.

8. Punch down the dough. On a clean, dry, lightly floured work surface, roll out the dough into a rectangle 8 x 16 inches. Drizzle the surface of the dough with half of the brown sugar–butter filling. Press half of the walnuts into the dough. Beginning with the long side of dough closest to you, roll the dough into a tight, even log, pressing the seam to seal it.

9. Grease two 8-inch springform pans, 2 inches deep. Drizzle the remaining filling over the bottoms of the prepared springform pans, dividing it equally. Top with the remaining walnuts.

10. Cut the log of dough into 1½-inch rounds and place the rounds, cut side down, with the sides touching, in the springform pans (6 in each pan). Cover with plastic wrap and let rise in a warm, draft-free place until doubled in size, about 30 minutes.

11. In the meantime, preheat the oven to 375 degrees F.

12. Bake the buns for about 45 minutes, until they are golden and a toothpick inserted in the center of one comes out clean.

13. While the buns are baking, make the glaze: In a small saucepan, heat the honey, brown sugar, and butter over medium heat, stirring, until the butter has melted and the sugar has dissolved.

14. Remove the pans from the oven and drizzle the glaze evenly over the surface of the buns. Let stand for several minutes, then run a knife around the inside of the pans to loosen the buns. Invert each pan onto a serving platter, release the sides of the pans, and remove them. Let the buns cool 15 minutes before serving. To store, wrap them well in plastic, and store in the refrigerator for several days. To reheat, remove the plastic wrap; then wrap the buns in aluminum foil. Heat in a preheated 350 degree F oven for 10 minutes, or until heated through.

MAKES 1 DOZEN BUNS

DESSERT

LOAF CAKES

Apricot and Dried Cherry
Loaf Cake

Low-Fat Banana Raspberry
Loaf Cake

Carrot Zucchini Loaf Cake

Chocolate Bread with
Crystallized Fruit

COOKIES

The Mangia Cookie

Mangia Chocolate Chip Cookies

Cinnamon and Clove Cookies

Granola Oatmeal Cookies

Peanut Butter Domes

White Chocolate Cherry Cookies

Espresso Bars

Strawberry Almond Rounds
and Apricot Almond Triangles

LOAF CAKES

Apricot and Dried Cherry Loaf Cake

The butter makes it rich; the cake flour makes it tender. Dried fruits lend not only lovely color but also a tart sweetness and texture. Serve this stylish loaf for breakfast, with a cup of tea in the afternoon, or à la mode for dessert. You can even toast it, if you wish. Like our other loaf cakes, this makes a great gift.

½ cup dried apricot halves

½ cup dried cherries

2 cups sifted cake flour

1½ teaspoons baking powder

½ teaspoon salt

½ teaspoon ground nutmeg

½ pound (2 sticks) unsalted butter, at room temperature

1½ cups sugar

5 large eggs

2 teaspoons vanilla extract

½ cup whole milk

1. Preheat the oven to 350 degrees F. Grease and flour an 8 x 4 x 2½-inch loaf pan. Cut a piece of wax paper to fit the bottom of the loaf pan, place it in the pan, and grease and flour it as well.

2. Soak the apricots and cherries separately in warm water to cover until softened, about 15 minutes. Drain the fruits and chop the apricots into ½-inch pieces.

3. In a large bowl, combine the flour, baking powder, salt, and nutmeg.

4. In the bowl of a standing electric mixer, cream the butter with the sugar on medium speed until light and fluffy, about 4 minutes. Scrape down the bowl.

5. Beat in the eggs in three batches, scraping down the bowl after each addition. Beat in the vanilla.

6. Reduce the mixer to low and add half of the dry ingredients, then the milk, then the remaining dry ingredients. By hand, fold in the cherries and apricots until fully incorporated.

7. Spread the batter in the prepared loaf pan and smooth the top with a spatula. Bake for 1 hour, until a cake tester inserted in the center of the loaf comes out clean. Let cool completely in the pan set on a rack; then unmold and slice. The loaf will keep, wrapped tightly in plastic, at room temperature for several days. For freezing instructions, see box below.

SERVES 8

TO FREEZE LOAF CAKES

Loaf cakes freeze well. Bake the loaf and let cool, then wrap tightly in plastic wrap. Freeze for up to 2 months. To defrost, remove the plastic wrap and let stand at room temperature.

Low-Fat Banana Raspberry Loaf Cake

Ordinarily, banana bread is not exactly low in fat! But with no butter, only a little oil, unexpected ingredients like cocoa powder and raspberry preserves, and a lot of mashed bananas, this unusual rendition of an exceedingly popular quick bread is lower in fat than more traditional recipes. You need really ripe bananas for this. Choose the ones with the skins that are almost black—in other words, the ones waiting to be thrown out. They provide the flavor, which there is a lot of in this tender cake.

A note about storing this cake. Because it is low in fat, it will dry out if stored for any length of time. If you need to hold it overnight, wrap it well in plastic wrap and keep at room temperature.

1¼ cups sifted cake flour

1½ teaspoons unsweetened cocoa powder

1 teaspoon baking soda

½ teaspoon ground nutmeg

¼ teaspoon salt

2 large eggs

¾ cup firmly packed dark brown sugar

2 tablespoons safflower oil

1 tablespoon nonfat plain yogurt

2 very ripe medium bananas (enough for 1 cup mashed)

2 tablespoons raspberry preserves

1. Preheat the oven to 350 degrees F. Butter and flour an 8 x 4 x 2½-inch loaf pan. Cut a piece of wax paper to fit the bottom of the pan, place the paper in the pan, and grease and flour it as well.

2. In a large bowl, combine the flour, cocoa powder, baking soda, nutmeg, and salt.

3. Mash the bananas.

4. In the bowl of a standing electric mixer, beat the eggs, sugar, oil, and yogurt on medium speed for 4 minutes, until smooth. Add the mashed bananas and the raspberry preserves and beat 1 minute longer.

5. Reduce the mixer to low and add the dry ingredients, beating just until moistened. (The batter should be uniform, but not overmixed.)

6. Pour the batter into the prepared pan and smooth the top with a spatula. Bake for about 1 hour, until a cake tester inserted in the center of the loaf comes out clean. Let cool completely in the pan set on a rack; then unmold and slice. The loaf is best eaten fresh, the day it is baked.

SERVES **8**

Carrot Zucchini Loaf Cake

As quick breads go, carrot is popular and zucchini bread is even more so, which makes this one, with carrot and zucchini, an odds-on favorite. Many versions of zucchini cake contain walnuts, but not this one. It does have the requisite moistness of all well-made zucchini breads and a lovely spicy taste, though. If you are looking to gild this lily, spread a little cream cheese on each slice for a smart accompaniment to any tea tray in the late afternoon.

2 cups sifted cake flour

2 teaspoons baking powder

½ teaspoon baking soda

½ teaspoon ground nutmeg

½ teaspoon salt

¼ teaspoon ground cinnamon

¼ teaspoon ground cloves

2 small zucchini
(enough for 1 cup grated)

4 medium carrots
(enough for 1 cup grated)

½ cup sugar

1 cup honey

1 cup safflower or canola oil

2 tablespoons unsalted butter,
at room temperature

5 large eggs

1 teaspoon vanilla extract

1. Preheat the oven to 350 degrees F. Grease and flour a 9 x 5 x 3-inch loaf pan. Cut a piece of wax paper to fit the bottom of the pan, place the paper in the pan, and grease and flour it as well.

2. Into a large bowl, sift together the flour, baking powder, baking soda, nutmeg, salt, cinnamon, and cloves.

3. Trim but do not peel the zucchini; grate enough to measure 1 cup. Trim the carrots, peel them, and grate enough to measure 1 cup.

4. In the bowl of a standing electric mixer, beat together the sugar, honey, oil, and butter on medium speed for several minutes until lightened and smooth. Beat in the eggs, one at a time, beating well after each addition. Add the vanilla and beat for 2 minutes.

5. Reduce the mixer speed to low. Add the dry ingredients in two batches, beating until moistened and no streaks of flour show. Scrape down the bowl. By hand, fold in the grated zucchini and carrots until well blended.

6. Pour the batter into the prepared loaf pan and smooth the top. Bake for about 1 hour, until golden and a cake tester inserted in the center of the loaf comes out clean. Let cool completely in the pan on a rack; then unmold and slice. The loaf will keep, wrapped tightly in plastic, at room temperature for several days. For freezing instructions, see page 49.

SERVES 8

Chocolate Bread
with Crystallized Fruit

Mascarpone—rich Italian cream cheese—helps to make this a tender loaf, and bittersweet chocolate and crystallized lemon or orange peel combine to make it unusual. The lemon peel–chocolate combination will get your attention because it is different; the orange peel with chocolate is more of a classic pairing of flavors, but is no less fine. Serve a slice of either version of this elegant loaf with a cup of rich coffee, and you are in for a treat.

The crystallized peel is sold in bakery supply stores. Citron, which figures in many fruitcakes (to the dismay of some otherwise dedicated fruitcake eaters), is not a substitute.

2½ cups sifted cake flour

2 teaspoons baking powder

½ teaspoon salt

4 ounces bittersweet chocolate

¾ cup mascarpone cheese

12 tablespoons (1½ sticks) unsalted butter, at room temperature

1½ cups sugar

5 large eggs

1 teaspoon vanilla extract

1 teaspoon grated orange zest

1 cup diced crystallized lemon or orange peel

1. Preheat the oven to 350 degrees F. Grease and flour an 8 x 4 x 2½-inch loaf pan. Cut a piece of wax paper to fit the bottom of the pan, place the paper in the pan, and grease and flour it as well.

2. Into a large bowl, sift together the flour, baking powder, and salt.

3. Break the chocolate into pieces and melt it, stirring occasionally, in the top of a double boiler over simmering water. When the chocolate has melted and is smooth, set it aside to cool; then fold in the mascarpone.

4. In the bowl of a standing electric mixer, cream the butter and sugar on medium speed until light and fluffy. Scrape down the bowl. Add the eggs, one at a time, scraping down the bowl after each addition. Beat in the vanilla and orange zest.

5. Reduce the mixer speed to low. Add the dry ingredients in two batches, beating until no streaks of flour show. By hand, fold in the chocolate-mascarpone mixture and crystallized fruit until combined.

6. Pour the batter into the prepared loaf pan and smooth the top. Bake for 55 to 60 minutes, until a cake tester inserted in the center of the loaf comes out clean. Let cool completely in the pan set on a rack; then unmold and slice. The loaf will keep, wrapped tightly in plastic, at room temperature for several days. For freezing instructions, see page 49.

SERVES 8

Variation

Chocolate Bread with Dried Cherries

Substitute an equal amount of dried cherries for the crystallized peel. Bake and cool the bread as directed above.

The Mangia Cookie

Lots of hazelnuts and butter, plus chocolate, explain why these cutouts are so addictive. There is no other way to say it: These fly out the door.

1. In a food processor, grind ½ cup of the hazelnuts to a paste. Scrape into a small bowl and set aside.

2. In the food processor, using the on/off button, grind the remaining 1¼ cups hazelnuts with ½ cup of the flour to make a coarse nut flour; transfer to a bowl.

1¾ cups whole hazelnuts, toasted and skinned (see page 57)

2¼ cups all-purpose flour

3 ounces semisweet chocolate, chilled in the refrigerator for 1 hour

¼ teaspoon salt

½ pound (2 sticks) unsalted butter, at room temperature

⅔ cup sugar

4 large egg yolks

1½ teaspoons vanilla extract

3. Grate the chilled chocolate in the food processor fitted with the grating blade.

4. Position a rack in the middle of the oven. Preheat the oven to 350 degrees F. Line 2 large cookie sheets with parchment paper.

5. Into a bowl, sift together the remaining 1¾ cups flour and the salt.

6. In the bowl of a standing electric mixer, cream the butter and sugar on medium speed until light and fluffy. Add the egg yolks, one at a time, beating well after each addition. Beat in the hazelnut paste and blend well. Add the vanilla, nut flour, grated chocolate, and the sifted flour, mixing well

after each addition. Gather the dough into a ball with your hands, and shape it into a disk. Wrap in plastic and chill for 1 hour.

7. On a lightly floured board, roll out the dough ¼ inch thick. With a round cookie cutter, 2¼ inches in diameter, cut out cookies and place them 1½ inches apart on the lined cookie sheets. Reroll the scraps only once; flour the rolling pin only if the dough starts to stick to it.

8. Bake the cookies for 15 to 20 minutes, turning the cookie sheets halfway through baking front to back. Remove from the oven when the edges of the cookies are just starting to brown. Cool the cookies on the sheets, set on racks. Store in an airtight container.

MAKES ABOUT 5 DOZEN COOKIES

TO TOAST AND SKIN HAZELNUTS

Preheat the oven to 350 degrees F. Spread the hazelnuts out on a dry baking sheet and toast them, stirring once, for 10 minutes. Wrap the hot hazelnuts in a kitchen towel and let steam for 5 minutes. While still in the towel, rub the hazelnuts against each other until the skins come off. (Not every last bit of skin will peel off, but most of it should.)

Mangia Chocolate Chip Cookies

These were one of the first cookies we offered when we opened in 1982, and they are still an all-time favorite. The better the chocolate, the better the cookie. Even though we call these chocolate chip cookies, the chips are chunks.

2 cups all-purpose flour

½ teaspoon baking soda

¼ teaspoon salt

½ pound (2 sticks) unsalted butter, at room temperature

1 cup firmly packed dark brown sugar

¼ cup granulated sugar

1 large egg

1 large egg yolk

1 tablespoon vanilla extract

½ cup coarsely chopped pecan pieces

½ cup chopped semisweet chocolate (about a 1½-ounce piece)

1. Position the racks in the middle and lower third of the oven. Preheat the oven to 350 degrees F. Line 3 large cookie sheets with parchment paper.

2. Into a small bowl, sift together the flour, baking soda, and salt.

3. In the bowl of a standing electric mixer, cream the butter with both sugars on medium speed until light and fluffy. Add the whole egg, egg yolk, and vanilla and beat until blended. Add the dry ingredients, 1 cup at a time, beating after each addition, but don't overbeat. By hand, stir in the pecans and chopped chocolate, mixing until evenly distributed.

4. Using a small cookie scoop or a teaspoon, spoon the dough onto the lined cookie sheets, leaving about 1½ inches between the mounds. With your fingers, flatten each cookie ½ inch thick.

5. Bake the cookies for 15 to 18 minutes, rotating the cookie sheets between the racks halfway through baking and turning them front to back as well, until the edges of the cookies start to turn golden brown. Cool the cookies on the sheets, set on racks. Store in an airtight container.

MAKES ABOUT 2 1/2 DOZEN COOKIES

Cinnamon and Clove Cookies

These cutout cookies are wonderful, particularly at Christmastime, when you can use prized seasonal cookie cutters. You will not believe how wonderful your house will smell when you bake these. Another plus is that the dough can be prepared in advance. Make it up to 1 week ahead and freeze. Defrost it overnight in the refrigerator, then let it stand at room temperature for 15 minutes before rolling.

Crystal sugar has larger granules than granulated sugar and is used for decorating. While optional, it makes these look pretty. The sugar can be purchased at baking supply stores and some supermarkets.

2 cups all-purpose flour

1¾ teaspoons baking soda

2 teaspoons ground cinnamon

1 teaspoon ground cloves

Pinch of salt

10 tablespoons (1¼ sticks) unsalted butter, at room temperature

1 cup sugar

1 large egg

2 tablespoons grated orange zest

2 tablespoons dark corn syrup

Crystal sugar, for sprinkling (optional)

1. Position the rack in the middle of the oven. Preheat the oven to 350 degrees F. Line 2 large cookie sheets with parchment paper.

2. Into a large bowl, sift the flour, baking soda, cinnamon, cloves, and salt.

3. In the bowl of a standing electric mixer, cream the butter and sugar on medium speed until light and fluffy. Add the egg and beat until incorporated. Beat in the orange zest and corn syrup.

4. Add the dry ingredients in two batches, beating until the dough is well mixed. With your hands, shape the dough into a disk, wrap it in plastic, and chill for 1 hour.

5. On a lightly floured board, roll out the dough ¼ inch thick. With a cookie cutter of your choice, cut out cookies and place them 1½ inches apart on the lined cookie sheets. If you wish, sprinkle the cookies with crystal sugar. Reroll the scraps only one time, or the dough will become tough.

6. Bake the cookies for 12 minutes, turning the sheets halfway through baking, front to back. Cool the cookies on the sheets, set on racks. Store in airtight containers.

MAKES 40 COOKIES, 2¼ INCHES IN DIAMETER

Granola Oatmeal Cookies

These were on our menu when we opened in February 1982, and are still a great favorite. Lots of butter, sugar, currants, *and* granola, in addition to rolled oats, make these rich and satisfying. They look fabulous in a glass cookie jar, if you can keep them around long enough to store them. Fortunately, they are drop cookies and therefore easy to make.

1. Position the racks in the middle and lower third of the oven. Preheat the oven to 350 degrees F. Line 3 large cookie sheets with parchment paper.

2. Into a bowl, sift together the flour, baking soda, cinnamon, nutmeg, and salt.

1½ cups plus 2 tablespoons all-purpose flour

¾ teaspoon baking soda

2 teaspoons ground cinnamon

¾ teaspoon grated nutmeg

¼ teaspoon salt

½ pound (2 sticks) unsalted butter, at room temperature

1 cup firmly packed dark brown sugar

½ cup granulated sugar

2 large eggs

1 teaspoon vanilla extract

1½ cups old-fashioned rolled oats

1 cup granola

¾ cup dried currants

3. In the bowl of a standing electric mixer, cream the butter with both sugars on medium speed until light and fluffy. Add the eggs, one at a time, beating well after each addition. Beat in the vanilla. Gradually add the dry ingredients, oatmeal, and granola, ½ cup at a time, blending until just incorporated. Stir in the currants.

4. Using a medium cookie scoop or a soup spoon, drop the dough onto the lined cookie sheets, leaving about 1½ inches between the mounds. With your fingers, flatten each cookie ½ inch thick.

5. Bake the cookies for about 16 minutes, or until the edges are golden, rotating the sheets halfway through the baking and turning them front to back, as well. Cool the cookies on the sheets, set on racks. Store in an airtight container.

MAKES ABOUT 2½ DOZEN COOKIES

Peanut Butter Domes

You achieve the domed shape of these buttery peanut butter shortbread cookies by using a small ice-cream scoop. The dough is tender and soft, and your hands won't work nearly as well as the scoop. Purchase one at a kitchenwares store, and then you will have it when the urge to make these calls, which could be often. (The scoop should be 1½ inches in diameter.) Like almost anything made with peanut butter, these are resoundingly popular.

2 cups all-purpose flour

1¼ teaspoons baking powder

½ teaspoon salt

12 tablespoons (1½ sticks) unsalted butter, at room temperature

1 cup firmly packed light brown sugar

2 cups smooth peanut butter

1 large egg

1½ teaspoons vanilla extract

I. Position the rack in the middle of the oven. Preheat the oven to 350 degrees F. Line 2 large cookie sheets with parchment paper.

2. Into a small bowl, sift the flour, baking powder, and salt.

3. In the bowl of a standing electric mixer, cream the butter and the brown sugar over medium speed until light and fluffy. Add the peanut butter and beat until incorporated. Beat in the egg and vanilla.

4. Add the dry ingredients in two batches and beat until the dough is smooth.

5. To shape the domes, use a small cookie scoop; pack the dough tightly into it and, with your finger, shave off any excess so that the dough is level. (You want the bottoms of the cookies to be flat and the tops nicely rounded like a dome.) Drop the dough, by scoopfuls, onto the lined cookie sheets, leaving 1 inch between the domes. (The cookies do not spread while baking, so you can line them close to each other.)

6. Bake the cookies for 13 to 15 minutes, or until uniformly golden, turning the sheets halfway through the baking time front to back. Cool the cookies on the sheets, set on racks. Store in an airtight container.

MAKES ABOUT 3 DOZEN COOKIES

White Chocolate Cherry Cookies

These are chocolate chip cookies, with a rich twist—white chocolate chips and dried cherries. These are splendid at teatime or for dessert.

1. Position the racks in the middle and lower third of the oven. Preheat the oven to 350 degrees F. Line 3 large cookie sheets with parchment paper.

2. Into a large bowl, sift together the flour, baking soda, and salt.

3. In the bowl of a standing electric mixer, cream the butter with both sugars on medium speed until light and fluffy. Add the whole egg and egg yolk and beat until blended. Beat in the vanilla. Gradually add the dry ingredients, and then the chips and cherries, blending until just incorporated.

4. Using a medium cookie scoop or a soup spoon, drop the dough onto the lined cookie sheets., leaving 1½ inches between the mounds. With your fingers, flatten each cookie ½ inch thick.

5. Bake the cookies for 15 minutes, or until golden, rotating the sheets halfway through the baking time and turning them front to back, as well. (If all 3 sheets will not fit in the oven at the same time, hold 1 in the refrigerator until the first batch of cookies is removed.) Cool the cookies on the sheets, set on racks. Store in an airtight container.

3 cups all-purpose flour

1½ teaspoons baking soda

¼ teaspoon salt

20 tablespoons (2½ sticks) unsalted butter, at room temperature

⅔ cup granulated sugar

⅔ cup firmly packed light brown sugar

1 large egg

1 large egg yolk

1 teaspoon vanilla extract

1½ cups white chocolate chips

1½ cups dried cherries

MAKES ABOUT 40 COOKIES

Espresso Bars

We started baking these bars in November 1996. They were an immediate hit then, and they still are. Mocha-flavored chocolate on a rich shortbread base is a great combination. The instruction in the recipe of wrapping the still-hot pan of pastry in plastic wrap is admittedly unorthodox, but necessary. When the pan is enclosed so that it is airtight, the topping steams and achieves a lovely, custardlike texture. These bars are tailor-made for entertaining and have the advantage of being made in advance on account of the pastry. We know these bars keep for 3 days, but if your household is like either of ours, you won't have them for that long.

1 recipe Basic Short Pastry Dough (recipe follows), baked

12 tablespoons (1½ sticks) unsalted butter

2 ounces semisweet chocolate

¾ cup sugar

2 large eggs

1 large egg yolk

¼ cup all-purpose flour

2½ tablespoons unsweetened cocoa powder

1½ tablespoons finely ground espresso powder, such as Medaglia D'Oro

1. Preheat the oven to 350 degrees F.

2. Cut the butter and chocolate into chunks and put them in the top of a double boiler set over simmering water. Melt the butter with the chocolate, stirring, until smooth. Remove the top of the double boiler and let the chocolate mixture cool slightly.

3. Meanwhile, in the bowl of a standing electric mixer, beat together the sugar and eggs until the mixture falls in a ribbon when the beater is lifted. Next fold in the melted chocolate. Next fold in the flour, cocoa powder, and espresso powder until well combined. Spread the topping evenly over the prebaked short pastry base.

4. Bake for 35 minutes, or until springy yet firm on top. Remove from the oven, let cool a few minutes, then carefully wrap the entire pan in plastic wrap, gently pressing the plastic against the topping. Let cool completely, allowing several hours.

5. Unwrap, run a knife around the edges, and cut into 1½ x 3-inch rectangles. To store, wrap tightly in plastic and refrigerate for up to 3 days.

MAKES 1½ DOZEN BARS

Basic Short Pastry Dough

This rich shortbread crust serves as the base for our Espresso Bars. The dough is simple to put together and even easier to handle: You roll it out between sheets of wax paper, then use the paper to transfer it to the baking pan. You need to make the dough at least 1 day in advance of finishing the bars because it needs to freeze overnight—an extra step, but a necessary one that prevents shrinking. And unlike most other pastry doughs, this one you bake while still frozen solid.

¼ cup confectioners' sugar

1½ cups all-purpose flour

Pinch of salt

8 tablespoons (1 stick) unsalted butter, at room temperature

2 large egg yolks

¼ teaspoon vanilla extract

1½ tablespoons heavy cream

If you are baking for a party or the holidays and want to avoid as much last-minute preparation as possible, you can make this dough up to 3 days ahead. See page 68 for instructions.

1. Sift the premeasured confectioners' sugar onto a sheet of wax paper; set aside. Into a large bowl, sift together the flour and salt.

2. Using a standing electric mixer or hand-held mixer, cream the butter and confectioners' sugar on medium-high speed until light and fluffy. Add the egg yolks, one at a time, beating well after each addition. Beat in the vanilla.

3. Add the dry ingredients in two batches, alternating them with the heavy cream and mixing well after each addition, until smooth and well blended.

4. Remove the dough from the bowl, shape it into a ball, and then flatten it into a disk. Wrap in plastic wrap and chill in the refrigerator for 1 hour before rolling. Have ready a 9-inch square baking pan.

5. Remove the plastic wrap from the dough and place it between 2 sheets of wax paper. Roll out the dough into a 10-inch square, ¼ inch thick. Remove the top sheet of paper. Invert the baking pan on top of the dough. Hold the edges of the wax paper over the baking pan and flip the pan, with the dough over it, right side up. Remove the wax paper and gently press the dough into the pan. Trim the edges and discard the scraps. Prick the dough all over with a fork.

6. Transfer the baking pan to the freezer and freeze the dough, uncovered, overnight.

7. The next day, when ready to bake, preheat the oven to 350 degrees F.

8. Remove the dough from the freezer and immediately place the pan in the oven. Bake the frozen dough for 20 minutes, or until evenly golden brown. Cool in the pan set on a rack. The dough is now ready for topping.

NOTE: This dough can be frozen up to 3 days in advance of baking. Complete step 6, cover the pan tightly or place it in a plastic freezer bag, and freeze. Remember not to thaw before using.

Strawberry Almond Rounds and Apricot Almond Triangles

These are beautiful party cookies and a delicious challenge for the experienced cook or cookie maker. The effort, including two different bakings, will be worth it when you see just how lovely looking (and tasting) these are when finished. Delicate hazelnut dough cutouts are topped with strawberry or apricot preserves, ringed with piped almond paste, and then drizzled with melted chocolate. You have several options for making these: You can make 6 dozen of the same cookie; make the same cookie two different ways, varying the shape and filling; or bake half the recipe, freezing the remaining dough for another time. If you are new to making elaborate, multistep cookies, the last option may be the one to begin with.

To make the full recipe, about 70 cookies, you will need 3 or 4 large baking sheets, some parchment paper, and plenty of time. A final reminder: If you are making only half the recipe, remember to halve the almond topping and filling measurements as well.

FOR THE HAZELNUT DOUGH

1¼ cups whole hazelnuts, toasted and skinned (page 57)

1 cup confectioners' sugar

3 cups all-purpose flour

¾ pound (3 sticks) cold unsalted butter

2 large egg yolks

2 tablespoons heavy cream

Parchment paper for baking the cookies

FOR THE ALMOND TOPPING

1 pound almond paste (do not use marzipan)

6 large egg whites

FOR THE FILLING

1 cup strawberry preserves, at room temperature

1 cup apricot preserves, at room temperature
(Or 2 cups fruit preserves of your choice)

FOR THE CHOCOLATE GARNISH

3 ounces semisweet chocolate

1. Make the hazelnut dough: Place the toasted and skinned hazelnuts in a food processor. Sift the confectioners' sugar into the processor. Add the flour. Pulse, using the on/off button, until the nuts are very finely ground. Add the butter and process until crumbly.

2. Combine the egg yolks and cream in a cup.

3. With the motor running, pour the egg mixture through the feed tube and process until the dough starts to come together. Do not overmix. Flatten the dough into a disk, wrap it in plastic, and chill for 1 hour.

4. Make the almond topping: In the bowl of a standing electric mixer, blend chunks of almond paste with the egg whites, adding one egg white at a time until well mixed and creamy. Continue to add almond paste and egg whites until you have the amount of topping you need and its texture is suitable for piping.

5. Prepare the filling: Place each fruit preserve in a separate bowl and whisk with a fork to lighten.

6. Position the oven racks in the middle and lower third of the oven. Preheat the oven to 325 degrees F. Line 4 large cookie sheets with parchment paper.

7. Divide the hazelnut dough into thirds, and work with only one piece at a time, keeping the remaining pieces refrigerated. On a lightly floured surface, roll out the dough ⅛ inch thick. With a 2¼-inch round cutter or a 2¼-inch triangular cutter, or both, cut out cookies and place them, 1 inch apart, on the lined cookie sheets. Slide the cookie sheets onto the racks, placing 1 sheet above and 2 on the rack below. Hold the remaining cookie sheet in the refrigerator until the first batch of cookies is removed from the oven. Bake for 15 minutes, rotating the sheets between the racks

halfway through the baking time and turning them front to back, as well. Remove from the oven, but do not remove the cookies from the cookie sheets. Bake the remaining cookies in the same manner.

8. Gather the scraps, knead them into a ball, and refrigerate until chilled before rolling again. Reroll only once, or the dough will be tough. Continue to roll out dough, one piece at a time, cut out cookies, and bake them. (You now have all the bases of the cookies, half cut into rounds, the other half into triangles, semibaked.)

9. Fill a medium pastry bag fitted with a ¼-inch tip with the almond paste. Pipe an edge all the way around the tops of the baked cookies, leaving the centers empty.

10. Spoon a dollop of preserves into the center of each cookie.

11. Bake the cookies for approximately 20 minutes, until golden. Cool on the cookie sheets, set on racks, for 10 minutes.

12. While the cookies are baking, make the chocolate garnish: In the top of a small double boiler, melt the chocolate, stirring, until smooth. Keep the chocolate warm.

13. Dip a fork into the hot melted chocolate and hold it over the cookies, letting the chocolate drip over them in streaks. Let the cookies dry a bit before you serve, or store them in airtight containers.

MAKES ABOUT 3 DOZEN STRAWBERRY ALMOND ROUNDS
AND 3 DOZEN APRICOT ALMOND TRIANGLES

The Soup Table

Every day at Mangia we offer five or six different soups at the soup table. Years of experience have taught us that it makes a marvelous lunch, either on its own or with a sandwich or panino. Soup comforts, it soothes, it is convenient, and it is eminently doable when other, more filling options are not possible, especially at midday.

We will usually have two chicken soups, a fish or shellfish combination, a vegetarian soup, and a bean offering on a daily basis. What they all have in common is a carefully prepared base, for it is the base that is a soup's largest and most important ingredient. Sometimes we start with stock that is Mangia-made; at other times, we use canned broth. In the recipes that follow, we suggest you use good-quality canned broth. If you have home-made stock, your soup will be better for it.

When it comes to serving soup at Mangia or at home, there is more to it than just ladling it into a bowl or cup and plunking it down on the table. First, decide if it is to be a main-course bowl or part of a meal. If you are serving it as a main course, be sure to select a recipe that is appropriate. Soup on its own, even a thick soup, does not a meal make unless you add to it. "Dress" a soup with good bread, a selection of crackers, a salad or cheese, or both. Place croutons, a salsa or hot sauce, or bruschetta on the table. Have some fun with the selection.

Like every recipe you will ever make, the fresher the ingredients, the better the soup. Lots of fresh herbs go into our soup pots, and we urge you to use them, too. Beyond that, remember that soups are meant to please—and this is especially true of the ones that follow. Serve them hot when they are meant to be hot; chilled when they are meant to be cold. We have included one soup that is to be served at room temperature: Yellow Tomato Soup with Roasted Peppers and Basil (page 112). It is a celebration of summer, plain and simple, and will never be better tasting than it is when just made.

SOUPS

SOUPS WITH SEAFOOD AND CHICKEN

Salmon Chowder with Fresh Corn and Bacon

Scallop and Roasted Tomato Soup

Shrimp Bisque

Chicken Soup with Mushrooms and Sun-Dried Tomatoes

Chicken and Wild Rice Soup

Chicken Soup with Chorizo, Potatoes, and Peas

Puebla Chicken Soup

Fresh Corn Soup with Smoked Chicken

Spicy Corn Soup with Poblano Chiles and Cream

SOUPS WITH VEGETABLES AND LEGUMES

Broccoli Soup with Cheddar Cheese and Jalapeño Pepper

Ginger and Honey Carrot Soup

Chilled Curried Cauliflower Soup

Chilled Cucumber Soup with Yogurt and Dill

Mexican Gazpacho

Pasta and Leek Soup with Goat Cheese

Sweet Potato Soup with Ginger and Lime

Chilled Butternut Squash Soup with Apple Cider

Tomato and Fennel Soup

Roasted Tomato and Eggplant Soup with Parmigiano

Yellow Tomato Soup with Roasted Peppers and Basil

Fresh Vegetable Soup with Orzo

Chilled Zucchini Soup with Basil Mascarpone Cream

Moroccan Lentil Soup

Black Bean Soup with Salsa

Tuscan Bean Soup with Prosciutto

SOUPS WITH SEAFOOD AND CHICKEN

Salmon Chowder with Fresh Corn and Bacon

This very American fish chowder has a rich flavor without a cream base. The small amount of cream that is added at the end is there to "finish" the soup, to enrich and smooth it. This chowder is not about cream; it's about fresh salmon, corn and potatoes, and bacon. Serve it as a warming main dish, in bowls or in cups, followed by a crisp, clean-tasting salad. The flavors are fullest if you serve right after adding the cream.

1 fillet of salmon, 1½ pounds

½ yellow onion

2 garlic cloves

4 large red potatoes (about 12 ounces)

3 ears of fresh corn

1 slice of bacon

1 tablespoon extra-virgin olive oil

1 tablespoon unsalted butter

4 cups clam juice

1 teaspoon freshly ground black pepper

½ cup heavy cream

1. Run your fingers over the salmon to make sure there are no bones. If you feel a hard point, push down with two fingers to expose the tip of the bone and pull it out with a pair of tweezers. Turn the salmon flesh side down and with a sharp paring knife, separate the skin from the flesh (the salmon can be skinned by your fishmonger). Discard the skin and cut the salmon into 1-inch cubes.

2. Peel, trim, and finely dice the onion. Peel, trim, and slice the garlic.

3. Peel the potatoes and cut them into small cubes; put the cubes in a bowl of water.

4. Shuck the corn and remove the silk on the ears. Holding each ear of corn upright on a cutting board and starting from the tip, slice off the kernels, cutting as close to the cob as possible. Gather the kernels and set aside.

5. In a heavy medium pot, sauté the bacon in the olive oil and butter over low heat until well done and crisp, but not burned. Remove the bacon and let cool, then crumble it.

6. In the oil mixture remaining in the pot, sauté the onion over medium heat, stirring, until translucent. Add the garlic and sauté it, taking care that it does not brown. Add the clam juice and bring to a boil. Drain the potatoes, add them to the soup, and cook it over low heat until the potatoes are soft, about 20 minutes.

7. Add the corn and salmon to the pot and cook over medium heat for about 10 minutes. Add the crumbled bacon and fresh pepper, and stir in the cream. Turn off the heat.

8. Before serving, stir the soup vigorously. It is best served right after you make it.

SERVES 6

Scallop and Roasted Tomato Soup

This is remarkably rich tasting and full flavored, more like a stew than a soup, thanks in large part to the generous amount of roasted tomatoes that serve as the base. You can prepare the tomatoes and make the soup base 1 day in advance. Then it is just a matter of reheating the soup and adding the scallops. The key to keeping them tender is to add them right before serving. With crusty bread and fruit and cheese, this makes a stylish light lunch or supper.

2 large shallots

1 medium carrot

½ fennel bulb

2 tablespoons extra-virgin olive oil

24 roasted plum tomato halves (see page 197)

4 cups chicken broth

2 bay leaves

1 tablespoon salt

¼ teaspoon sugar

1 pound bay scallops

3 tablespoons grated lemon zest

2 teaspoons fresh thyme leaves

1. Peel, trim, and coarsely chop the shallots. Peel, trim, and coarsely slice the carrot. Trim and coarsely chop the fennel. In a food processor, chop the shallots, carrot, and fennel medium fine.

2. In a medium skillet, sauté the vegetables in the olive oil over medium heat, stirring, for 3 minutes. Cover and sweat over low heat for 5 minutes, until tender.

3. In a blender or food processor, puree half of the tomatoes with 2 cups of the chicken broth until smooth. Pour into a heavy large pot. Puree the remaining tomatoes and 2 cups of chicken broth using the on/off button,

and stop chopping when the mix is chunky; add to the pot. Stir in the chopped-vegetable mixture. Add the bay leaves, salt, and sugar. Cover and cook over moderate heat for 30 minutes.

4. Add the scallops to the soup, stir to distribute, and cook for 5 minutes.

5. Remove the bay leaves; add the lemon zest and thyme, and stir well. Serve the soup immediately.

SERVES 6

PREPPING IN ADVANCE: The soup base can be made 1 day ahead of time through step 3. Let cool, cover the pot tightly, and refrigerate. When ready to serve, bring the base to a gentle boil and proceed with steps 4 and 5 to finish the soup.

Shrimp Bisque

When made classically, bisque is a thick, creamy, super-rich seafood soup. At one time, a cup of bisque set the stage for still richer things to come. Times have changed, though, and so have people's preferences, including our own. We kept the seafood, but cut way back on the amount of cream, with no loss to either texture or flavor. Easy to prepare and slightly retro but still very *au courant*, this stands beautifully on its own, as a main-course bowl. Or use it as a first course and pull out all the stops: Capitalize on the bisque's intriguing pink color by garnishing the bowls with snipped chives, the blossoms still attached. A roasted or grilled fish entree to follow would work just fine.

1 small white onion

2 garlic cloves

1 large baking potato

4 plum tomatoes

3 tablespoons unsalted butter

Pinch of saffron threads

½ cup dry white wine

6 cups clam juice

½ teaspoon cayenne

1½ pounds baby shrimp, peeled

½ cup heavy cream

1. Peel, trim, and finely dice the onion. Peel, trim, and slice the garlic. Peel and cut the potato into small chunks. Wash, trim, seed, and chop the tomatoes.

2. In a large, heavy pot, sauté the onion in the butter over low heat, stirring, until translucent. Add the garlic, and sauté it, stirring, for 3 to 5 minutes, taking care not to let it burn. Add the tomatoes and saffron and sauté for 5 minutes. Add the white wine and cook until the wine has evaporated.

3. Stir in the clam juice and the cayenne; then add the potatoes and cook until they are tender, about 30 minutes.

4. Add the shrimp and bring the soup to a boil. Cover the pot, turn off the heat, and let the bisque cool.

5. Puree the soup in batches in a blender or food processor. Pour the puree back into the soup pot, place it over medium heat, and simmer the bisque for about 10 minutes to meld the flavors.

6. Turn off the heat and stir in the heavy cream until incorporated. Serve immediately.

SERVES 6

PREPPING IN ADVANCE: The bisque can be made 1 day in advance of serving through step 5. Let cool, cover the pot tightly, and refrigerate. When ready to serve, bring the soup to a gentle boil, turn off the heat under the pot, and stir in the cream. Serve immediately.

Chicken Soup with Mushrooms and Sun-Dried Tomatoes

If chicken soup can be regal, then this one is. Sophisticated ingredients—sun-dried tomatoes and oyster and cremini mushrooms, plus porcini mushroom oil—make this especially flavorful. The porcini mushroom oil is a must; it lends a singular, concentrated flavor. There is no substitute. Look for it in specialty food stores and after opening, store it in the refrigerator. (Once you have a bottle, you will find other ways of using it.)

This makes a special Sunday lunch or early supper on a cool fall or winter weekend, served with a bottle of crisp white wine and Caesar Salad (page 209). It can be made in advance up to the addition of the porcini oil, which happens right before serving.

½ cup sun-dried tomatoes (not packed in oil)

1 cup hot water

6 cups chicken broth

2 whole chicken breasts, skinned and boned, 1½ to 2 pounds

4 medium shallots

2 thin medium carrots

1 pound fresh oyster mushrooms

1 pound cremini mushrooms

¼ cup extra-virgin olive oil

1 tablespoon salt

1 teaspoon crumbled dried rosemary

1 teaspoon dried thyme

1 teaspoon freshly ground black pepper

1 teaspoon porcini mushroom oil

1. Place the sun-dried tomatoes in the hot water and let them soak while you make the soup.

2. In a medium saucepan, bring the chicken broth to a boil. Add the chicken breasts and bring the broth to a boil again. Cover the pot, turn off the heat, and let stand off the heat until ready to use.

3. Peel and chop the shallots. Peel and slice the carrots. Trim and wash both kinds of mushrooms and thinly slice.

4. In a large, heavy saucepan, sauté the shallots in the olive oil over medium heat, stirring, until translucent. Add the carrots, mushrooms, and salt and sauté until the mushrooms release their juices. Reduce the heat to low, and cook until the juices have almost entirely evaporated.

5. Remove the chicken from the broth. Add the broth, rosemary, thyme, and pepper to the mushroom mixture and bring to a boil. Cook over low heat for 30 minutes.

6. Meanwhile, cut the chicken breasts into long, thin slices, removing any cartilage. Drain the sun-dried tomatoes and cut into thin strips.

7. Add the chicken and tomatoes to the soup and simmer for about 10 minutes. Stir in the porcini oil and turn off the heat. Correct the seasonings and serve immediately, with additional porcini oil, if desired.

SERVES 6

PREPPING IN ADVANCE: The soup can be prepared 1 day ahead, up to the point of adding the porcini oil in step 7. Let the soup cool, cover the pot tightly, and refrigerate. Just before serving, bring the soup to a gentle boil and stir in the porcini oil. Serve immediately.

Chicken and Wild Rice Soup

Chicken and rice soup is one thing. Chicken and wild rice soup is another. This is a wonderful winter soup—just the one for the holidays—and it can be made almost entirely in advance. All you will need to do before serving is combine the separate components, heat the soup through, and season it with fresh black pepper—a seemingly innocent final touch that lends a sizable amount of warmth.

6 cups water

1 cup wild rice

1 small yellow onion

2 garlic cloves

1 small carrot

2 celery stalks

1 medium Idaho potato

12 flat-leaf parsley sprigs

¼ cup extra-virgin olive oil

6 cups chicken broth

1 teaspoon dried thyme

1 teaspoon salt

2 whole chicken breasts, skinned and boned, 1½ to 2 pounds

1 cup heavy cream

1 teaspoon freshly ground black pepper

1. In a medium saucepan, bring the water to a boil. Stir in the wild rice and simmer, covered, for about 45 minutes, or until cooked but not mushy. Drain and reserve.

2. Peel, trim, and finely dice the onion, garlic, and carrot. Wash and trim the celery, leaving some of the greens; finely slice. Peel and dice the potato. Tie the sprigs of parsley together with a piece of kitchen twine.

3. In a large heavy pot, briefly sauté the onion, garlic, carrot, celery, and potato in the olive oil over medium heat, stirring just to coat. Cover, reduce the heat to low, and sweat the vegetables for about 10 minutes.

4. Add the chicken broth, thyme, salt, and parsley and bring the broth to a boil. Add the chicken breasts and cook, covered, over medium heat for 15 minutes.

5. Remove the chicken breasts, and while the soup continues cooking, shred the breasts with 2 forks into bite-sized pieces.

6. Remove the parsley from the soup. Stir in the cooked wild rice and shredded chicken.

7. In a small skillet, reduce the heavy cream over high heat by half.

8. Add the reduced cream to the soup and cook over medium heat until just heated through. Add the fresh pepper and serve immediately.

SERVES 6

PREPPING IN ADVANCE: The soup can be made 1 day ahead through step 5. Let the base cool, cover the pot tightly, and refrigerate. Place the shredded chicken and wild rice in separate bowls, cover each tightly, and refrigerate. When ready to serve, bring the soup to a gentle boil and proceed with steps 6 through 8 to finish the soup.

Chicken Soup with Chorizo, Potatoes, and Peas

A classic Mediterranean pairing—potatoes and chorizo—are combined here with chicken and peas to make a full-flavored, hearty bowl that can be served as a meal in itself, or as a prelude to a dinner of simply grilled or roasted fish. Chorizo, one of our favorite ingredients, should be good and garlicky—well seasoned, in other words. Look for it in butcher shops and larger supermarkets in the pork or sausage section of the meat department.

If you are making this in advance, be sure to add the roughly cut parsley right before serving so that you get the most out of its vibrant color and fresh flavor. When it comes to adding fresh herbs, Mangia's rule of thumb is the rougher the cut, the more the herb contributes.

6 cups chicken broth

1 whole chicken breast, skinned and boned, 1½ to 2 pounds

1 medium red onion

2 garlic cloves

¾ cup flat-leaf parsley sprigs

4 medium red potatoes

3 chorizo, 3 to 4 ounces each

1 tablespoon plus 1 teaspoon extra-virgin olive oil

1 tablespoon salt

1 teaspoon dried thyme

1 teaspoon freshly ground black pepper

½ teaspoon ground cumin

1 cup frozen peas

1. In a medium saucepan, bring the chicken broth to a boil, add the chicken breast, and bring the broth to a boil again. Cover the pan, turn off the heat, and let stand until ready to use.

2. Peel and slice the potatoes into ¼-inch-thick slices; place them in a bowl with water to cover and reserve. Trim, peel, and finely dice the onion. Peel, trim, and slice the garlic. Stem, then chop the parsley and reserve. Peel the casings off the chorizo and crumble the meat.

3. In a large heavy pot, sauté the onion in the olive oil over medium heat until translucent. Add the garlic and sauté, taking care not to let it brown.

4. Add the chorizo and sauté, stirring, until cooked, about 5 minutes. The chorizo will release some fat at this point; remove some of it by tilting the pot and skimming it off with a spoon. Discard the fat.

5. Remove the chicken breast from the chicken broth, and set aside.

6. Add the broth to the chorizo mixture, and then add the salt, thyme, pepper, and cumin. Cook over medium heat for 10 minutes. Drain the potatoes and add them to the soup. Cover and simmer for 20 minutes.

7. With a fork and a knife, slice the chicken breast, removing any cartilage. Add the chicken and peas to the soup and bring it to a boil. Turn off the heat, correct the seasonings, and. stir in the chopped parsley. Serve immediately.

SERVES 6

PREPPING IN ADVANCE: The soup can be made 1 day ahead through step 6. Let cool, cover the pot tightly, and refrigerate. Place the cooked chicken breast in a bowl, cover with plastic wrap, and refrigerate. When ready to serve, bring the soup to a gentle boil and proceed with step 7 to finish the soup.

Puebla Chicken Soup

A prep person in the kitchen from Puebla, Mexico, showed us this fun and very flavorful family-style recipe. The ancho chile powder adds a smoky flavor and a dried chile scent. As for the oregano, if you have access to a market with Latino products, look for Caribbean or Mexican oregano. It has a hint of mint that makes it worth the search. The touch of crème fraîche—hardly a Mexican tradition—was our addition. It resembles crema dulce, the Mexican sweet cream that you would add if you were in Puebla, and lends a note of soothing creaminess. The tortilla chips provide just the opposite: crunch. This is a south-of-the-border original, spirited and very good.

I. In a medium saucepan, bring the chicken broth to a boil. Add the chicken breast, and bring the broth to a boil again. Cover the pot, turn off the heat, and let stand until ready to use.

6 cups chicken broth

1 whole chicken breast, skinned and boned, 1½ to 2 pounds

1 medium red onion

2 garlic cloves

1 large tomato

1 large green bell pepper

12 flat-leaf parsley sprigs

¼ cup ground ancho chile powder

1 tablespoon salt

1 teaspoon ground cumin

1 teaspoon dried oregano

1 teaspoon freshly ground black pepper

¼ cup corn oil

2 cans (14 ounces each) whole hominy

½ cup chopped cilantro

1 cup crème fraîche, for serving

1 large bag unsalted tortilla chips, for serving

2. Trim, peel, and cut the red onion into large chunks. Trim, peel, and cut the garlic into chunks. Quarter the tomato. Trim and dice the green pepper. Tie the parsley sprigs together with kitchen twine.

3. In a blender, combine the onion, garlic, and tomato with the ancho chile powder, salt, cumin, oregano, and black pepper and blend to make a paste. (Add a little water if the paste needs thinning.)

4. In a large, heavy pot, sauté the diced green pepper in the corn oil over low heat, stirring, until soft. Add the spice paste and cook until somewhat dry, about 5 minutes. (It may splatter some.)

5. Remove the chicken breast from the broth. Add the broth to the paste mixture, stirring well to combine. Add the parsley and simmer for 30 minutes.

6. On a cutting board, shred the chicken with 2 forks into thin strands.

7. Drain and rinse the hominy well in a colander under cold water. Add the hominy and chicken to the soup and bring it to a boil. Correct the seasonings and remove the parsley.

8. Sprinkle the cilantro over the soup. Serve immediately in bowls with a dollop of crème fraîche and corn chips on the side.

SERVES 6

PREPPING IN ADVANCE: The soup can be made 1 day ahead through step 5. Let the base cool, cover the pot, and refrigerate. Place the cooked chicken in a bowl, cover with plastic wrap, and refrigerate. When ready to serve, bring the soup to a gentle boil and proceed with steps 6 through 8 to finish the soup.

Fresh Corn Soup
with Smoked Chicken

This is one of those easy-to-put-together recipes that is at its very best served the same day it is made. Use local corn in the summer and frozen kernels in the winter (they make it still easier to prepare). Smoked chicken breast adds a unique, rich flavor. Fortunately, smoked chicken is becoming more and more available; look for it in specialty markets and some supermarkets, as well. A salad and crusty rolls are just the right accompaniments.

1. If using fresh corn, shuck and remove the silk. Holding each ear of corn upright on a cutting board and starting from the tip, slice off the kernels, cutting as close to the cob as possible. Gather the kernels and reserve.

2. Peel, trim, and finely dice the onion. Peel, trim, and thinly slice the garlic. Wash the celery, discard the leaves, and thinly slice the stalks. Stem the parsley, then finely chop the leaves.

6 ears of fresh corn or
3½ cups frozen corn kernels

1 medium yellow onion

2 garlic cloves

3 stalks celery

12 flat-leaf parsley sprigs

3 tablespoons extra-virgin olive oil

6 cups chicken broth

1 teaspoon dried thyme

1 teaspoon freshly ground
black pepper

2 smoked chicken breasts,
12 ounces each

2 tablespoons cornmeal

1 tablespoon salt

SERVE WITH: Cucumber, Avocado, Scallion, and Lime Salad (page 214) or another crisp green salad of choice.

3. In a large, heavy pot, sauté the onion in the olive oil over medium heat until translucent. Add the garlic and sauté it for 5 minutes, taking care not to let it brown. Add the celery and sauté it for 5 minutes. Add the chicken broth, parsley, thyme, and pepper and stir to combine. Bring the broth to a boil, cover the pot, and reduce the heat to low. Simmer the soup for 30 minutes.

4. Remove the skin from the chicken breasts and discard. Cut the chicken into thin strips. Add the chicken and corn to the soup, stirring to combine well, and bring the soup to a boil over medium heat. Slowly sprinkle in the cornmeal, stirring all the while. Cook, stirring occasionally, for 5 minutes. Add the salt, and serve immediately.

SERVES 6

Spicy Corn Soup with Poblano Chiles and Cream

Poblano chiles vary in heat. Be sure your guests are game for adventure before making this, because the recipe title says it all: It's spicy. The pomegranate seeds, used at the end for garnish, give the soup a great look and add a hint of sourness. If pomegranates are not in season, use cilantro leaves, which are pretty, too, but don't create the same "buzz" that the seeds do.

This soup can, and should, be made year-round, with local fresh corn in the summer and frozen kernels at other times. Ideally, buy corn that has been picked the same day and start the soup when you get home from the farmstand or farmer's market. Which is to say, if the only "fresh" corn available to you is shucked and prewrapped, think twice about buying it.

6 ears of fresh corn
or 3½ cups frozen corn kernels

2 large poblano chile peppers

1 medium red onion

2 garlic cloves

12 cilantro sprigs

3 tablespoons corn oil

6 cups chicken broth

1 teaspoon ground cumin

1 teaspoon dried oregano

1 teaspoon salt

¾ cup heavy cream

Seeds of 1 pomegranate
(if in season), for garnish

1. If using fresh corn, shuck and remove the silk. Holding each ear of corn upright on a cutting board and starting from the tip, slice off the kernels, cutting as close to the cob as possible with a small sharp knife. Gather the kernels and reserve.

2. Wash, halve, and seed the poblano chiles. Discard the stems and chop the chiles into small pieces. Peel, trim, and finely dice the onion. Peel, trim, and slice the garlic. Tie the cilantro sprigs together with kitchen string.

3. In a heavy medium pot, sauté the chopped chiles and onion in the corn oil over medium heat, stirring, until the onion is translucent. Add the garlic and sauté, taking care not to let it brown. Add the chicken broth, cumin, oregano, salt, and cilantro. Bring the mixture to a boil and simmer for about 30 minutes.

4. Add the corn kernels and cook for 5 minutes. Turn off the heat, remove the cilantro and discard it, and let the soup cool.

5. In a blender or food processor, puree the soup in small batches. Return the puree to the pot.

6. When ready to serve, gently bring the soup to a boil. Taste and correct the seasonings. Turn off the heat and stir in the heavy cream, mixing well. If you are using a pomegranate, carefully cut it in half (the juice makes a nasty stain). Remove some of the seeds and sprinkle a few on top of each serving.

SERVES 6

PREPPING IN ADVANCE: The soup can be made 2 days ahead through step 5. Place the puree in a large bowl, cover tightly, and refrigerate. When ready to serve, transfer the puree to a saucepan, bring to a gentle boil, stirring, and proceed with step 6 to finish the soup.

Broccoli Soup with Cheddar Cheese and Jalapeño Pepper

Broccoli and Cheddar cheese have been paired together successfully in all kinds of different ways. Here is another example of the winning combination in a rich, smooth soup that comforts and warms. On a cold day, it makes the perfect bowl, with a panini or sandwich, or a simple fresh roll. If you are looking for different ways to have that all-important intake of a cruciferous green, this is a tasty one, and the soup is easy to assemble: The base can be made up to 2 days ahead.

2 large heads of broccoli, about 2½ pounds

½ red onion

1 garlic clove

1 jalapeño pepper

1 teaspoon salt, or to taste

2 tablespoons extra-virgin olive oil

6 cups water

4 ounces mild Cheddar cheese

½ cup heavy cream, for serving

Parsley sprigs, for garnish

1. Cut the ends of the stems off the broccoli. Peel the stems and remove any leaves. Coarsely chop the broccoli.

2. Peel, trim, and cut the onion into chunks. Peel the garlic. Seed the jalapeño and chop it into a few pieces. Put the onion, garlic, and jalapeño in a food processor or blender and puree, adding just enough water to make a thick mixture; add the salt.

3. In a medium pot, heat the olive oil over moderate heat. Add the onion and jalapeño puree and sauté it, stirring, for 3 minutes. Reduce the heat, add the 6 cups of water and broccoli, and cook until the broccoli is tender, about 45 minutes. Turn off the heat and let the mixture cool.

4. When cool, puree the broccoli mixture in batches in a food processor or blender. Return the puree to the pot.

5. Close to serving time, bring the puree to a gentle boil, stirring occasionally. While the soup heats, grate the Cheddar. (You will have 1 cup grated.) When the soup boils, turn the heat off under the pot and add the Cheddar, stirring until melted. Serve immediately with a bit of heavy cream and a sprig of parsley in each bowl.

SERVES 6

PREPPING IN ADVANCE: The soup can be made 2 days ahead through step 4. Place the pureed base in a bowl, cover tightly with plastic wrap, and refrigerate. When ready to serve, transfer the puree to a large saucepan and bring it to a gentle boil, stirring occasionally. Proceed with step 5 to finish the soup.

Ginger and Honey Carrot Soup

Nothing masks the flavor of sweet carrots in this popular soup: no cream or egg enrichment. No broth even. Basic ingredients—carrots, fresh ginger, honey, and water—are responsible for this soup's magnificent color and flavor.

In addition to being easy to make, this can be served hot or chilled—an advantage for the busy cook. If you're serving it cold, add a splash of fresh orange juice for a fresh citrus taste. You can spice it up a bit, too, depending upon how well your refrigerator is stocked with what we call "accents": Stir in a teaspoon of harissa, the Tunisian (not Moroccan, although it is used there, too) hot chili sauce, just before serving. Failing that, you can add a spoonful of chipotle chile salsa (see page 287), something we have on tap frequently. If you don't have either of those and you like a touch of heat, add hot salsa from the jar.

12 medium carrots

1 yellow onion

2 garlic cloves

2 tablespoons unsalted butter

2 tablespoons extra-virgin olive oil

4 cups water

2 teaspoons grated fresh ginger

Salt

3 tablespoons honey

1. Trim, peel, and cut the carrots into 1-inch lengths. Trim, peel, and chop the onion and garlic.

2. In a heavy pot or Dutch oven, sauté the onion in the butter and olive oil over medium heat, stirring, until translucent. Add the garlic and sauté it for a few minutes, taking care not to let it brown.

3. Add the water, carrots, ginger, and salt and cook until the carrots are very tender, about 45 minutes. Turn off the heat and let the soup cool.

4. When the soup has cooled, puree it in batches in a food processor or blender. Return the puree to the pot and place it over medium-high heat. Bring the puree to a boil and reduce it to the desired thickness. Add the honey, stirring until dissolved. Taste, adjust the seasonings, if necessary, and serve immdiately.

5. To serve cold, remove the pan from the heat and let the soup cool completely. Cover the pot and refrigerate. When ready to serve, stir vigorously and ladle into chilled bowls, if desired.

SERVES 6

PREPPING IN ADVANCE: The soup can be completed 1 day ahead. Let cool, cover tightly, and refrigerate. If serving cold, just stir well and ladle into bowls. To serve hot, bring the soup gently to a boil.

Chilled Curried Cauliflower Soup

Your whole house will turn into a
Middle Eastern spice bazaar when you
toast all the seeds for this soup. What you
are doing, of course, is making your own
curry powder—something that is not
only intensely aromatic but also instruc-
tive in that it enables you to customize
the blend to your own taste. This soup,
with its golden color, looks great served
in white bowls. Clear mugs work very
nicely, too.

1 tablespoon coriander seeds

1 tablespoon cumin seeds

1 teaspoon cardamom seeds

1 teaspoon ground cinnamon

1 teaspoon ground turmeric

½ teaspoon freshly ground
black pepper

½ teaspoon cayenne

1 large head of cauliflower,
1½ to 2 pounds

1 medium Idaho potato

1 teaspoon chopped fresh ginger

6 cups chicken broth

½ cup heavy cream

I. Toast the coriander seeds, cumin
seeds, and cardamom seeds in a
small dry skillet over low heat, stirring continuously, until fragrant.
Transfer to a spice grinder and
grind them as finely as you can. (Or place the seeds between double sheets
of aluminum foil and pound them with a hammer.) Place the ground seeds
in a small bowl and add the cinnamon, turmeric, black pepper, and cayenne.

2. Wash and trim the cauliflower; cut it into small florets. Peel and cube the
potato.

3. In a large, heavy pot, combine the cauliflower, potato, ginger, chicken
broth, and spice blend, and cook, covered, over medium heat for about 30
minutes. Turn off the heat and let the soup cool to room temperature.

4. Puree the soup in batches in a blender, strain through a sieve, and pour it into a large bowl. Cover the bowl tightly and chill the puree for 2 hours.

5. Add the heavy cream and stir to combine. Serve in chilled bowls, if desired.

SERVES 6

PREPPING IN ADVANCE: The soup can be made 1 day ahead through step 4. When ready to serve, proceed with step 5 to finish the soup.

Chilled Cucumber Soup with Yogurt and Dill

Many chilled soups, including some of today's "politically correct," scaled-down chilled soups, are often made with some cream. Here, though, is one without a drop, with no fat to speak of at all, in fact. Cucumber and yogurt star here, and when combined and chilled until icy, they make for a wonderfully refreshing main bowl or starter with just the right crunch and flavor for the dog days, whenever they occur. And while chilled soups, in general, are easy on the cook, this one should not be prepared way in advance of serving. It will become watery. Cucumbers are about 95 percent water, and there is water in the soup as well. In short, make, chill as directed, serve, and enjoy.

6 large cucumbers

1 small garlic clove

5 whole scallions

3 lemons

2 cups water

1 tablespoon salt

1 teaspoon freshly ground black pepper

½ teaspoon chili powder

2 cups low-fat or nonfat plain yogurt

½ cup chopped dill

1. Peel the cucumbers, quarter them lengthwise, and with a paring knife, cut out the seeds on each spear. Chop 4 spears into small dice; reserve for garnish. Cut the remaining spears into large chunks.

2. Peel the garlic. Trim and slice the scallions, both green and white parts.

3. Cut 1 lemon crosswise into 6 thin slices; reserve for garnish. Juice the remaining 2 lemons. (It will be easier to do if you first roll the lemons with the palm of your hand on a hard surface, softening them for squeezing. This works for juicing oranges and grapefruit, too.)

4. In a blender or food processor, puree the large chunks of cucumber with the water, lemon juice, scallions, garlic, salt, pepper, and chili powder. Transfer the puree to a medium bowl, stir in the yogurt, and continue stirring until combined. Taste for seasoning. Cover and chill for 2 hours.

5. To serve, ladle the chilled soup into chilled bowls, float a slice of lemon on each serving, and sprinkle with the remaining diced cucumber and the dill.

SERVES 6

Mexican Gazpacho

We call this soup Mexican as a salute to some of the ingredients, but we doubt that there is a Mexican household that has this recipe in its treasured old recipe file. This is a glorious summer soup. Anticipate serving it, and be sure to have ripe avocados on hand.

1 small onion

3 limes

2 garlic cloves

12 cilantro sprigs

12 flat-leaf parsley sprigs

1 poblano chile pepper

4 medium leaves of romaine lettuce

3 ripe Hass avocados

3 cups water

1 tablespoon salt

1 large red beefsteak tomato

1. Peel, trim, and cut the onion into small dice. Put the onion in a small bowl and squeeze in the juice of 1 lime; toss well and let stand. Juice the 2 remaining limes and set the juice aside.

2. Peel and trim the garlic.

3. Wash and pat dry the cilantro and parsley and chop each very fine. Wash, trim, and seed the poblano chile and cut it in chunks. Wash and pat dry the lettuce leaves and chop coarse.

4. Peel the avocados and spoon the flesh into a blender or food processor. Add the lime juice, garlic, poblano chile, lettuce, water, and salt and process to a thick puree, adding more water if necessary. (The soup should be quite thick.) Do this in 2 batches, if desired.

5. Transfer the puree to a bowl and add the chopped cilantro and parsley, stirring well. Cover and chill for 2 hours.

6. Trim and slice the beefsteak tomato. To serve, spoon the gazpacho into chilled bowls and float a tomato slice on each serving. It is best served on the day it is made.

SERVES 6

Pasta and Leek Soup with Goat Cheese

The goat cheese called for in this recipe is not the one most people are accustomed to: the creamy, snowy-white fresh cheese that comes in the shape of a log or pyramid. Here you want aged goat cheese. Seldom as hard as Parmigiano, it should crumble between your fingers. In taste it is more assertive and pungent than the fresh. Look for aged goat cheese in specialty food shops.

This soup comforts. Even though it is hearty, it sets the stage beautifully as a first course to be followed by grilled or roasted meat or poultry, and a green salad. Or make a meal of it with good bread.

4 ounces small pasta shells

4 fat leeks

4 thin medium carrots

2 garlic cloves

4 tablespoons extra-virgin olive oil

2 tablespoons unsalted butter

1 cup crumbled aged goat cheese, such as imported Kasseri

6 cups chicken broth

1 tablespoon salt

1 teaspoon dried thyme

1 teaspoon freshly ground black pepper

1. In a medium saucepan of boiling salted water, cook the pasta shells for about 10 minutes, until al dente (firm to the bite). Drain and set aside.

2. Trim each leek of most of its green part, the outer layer of leaves, and the root end. Cut the trimmed leeks in half lengthwise, place them cut side down, and slice them crosswise into semicircles about ¼ inch thick. Transfer the leeks to a large colander and wash under plenty of running water until clean of all dirt and sand. Let drip dry in the colander.

3. Peel, trim, and slice the carrots into ½-inch rounds. Peel, trim, and slice the garlic cloves.

4. In a large heavy pot, sauté the leeks in the olive oil and butter over low heat until wilted. Add the garlic and sauté it, taking care that it does not brown. Add the carrots, cover the pot, and sweat the vegetables for about 5 minutes.

5. Stir in the goat cheese, chicken broth, salt, thyme, and black pepper. Simmer the soup, covered, for about 30 minutes.

6. Before serving, stir in the cooked pasta shells. Reheat the soup until it returns to a boil, and boil it for 1 minute. Serve in pasta or soup bowls. It is best served on the day it is made.

SERVES 6

PREPPING IN ADVANCE: You can make this soup ahead of time as long as you make it in stages: Delay cooking the pasta shells in step 1 until shortly before serving. (You want to avoid waterlogging them by letting them stand in liquid.)

Make the soup through step 4. Let cool, cover, and refrigerate. When ready to serve, cook the shells as directed while you gently reheat the soup base over medium heat. Add the drained shells to the soup and serve.

Sweet Potato Soup with Ginger and Lime

There is a Caribbean beat to this sweet potato soup, which you can make as thick and bisquelike as you wish. Consistency here is determined by the amount of milk you add. Use more or less, to your taste. The finishing touch of grated lime zest brings a burst of flavor to the soup—more than its delicate appearance suggests. At Mangia, citrus, both juice and zest, is used as a powerful flavoring agent.

8 medium sweet potatoes

2 garlic cloves

1 tablespoon grated fresh ginger

1 tablespoon plus 1 teaspoon unsalted butter

8 cups water

2 tablespoons dark brown sugar

1 stick cinnamon, 3 inches long

2 cups whole milk, or less if desired

2 tablespoons grated lime zest, for garnish

1. Preheat the oven to 350 degrees F.

2. Bake the sweet potatoes in the oven for about 1½ hours, or until soft. Remove and let cool. When cool enough to handle, peel them. The skin will come off easily with your fingers. Set the pulp aside.

3. Peel, trim, and chop the garlic.

4. In a large heavy pot, sauté the garlic and ginger in the butter over very low heat (so that the butter will not burn). Pour in the water and bring it to a boil. Add the brown sugar and cinnamon stick and boil over medium heat for about 15 minutes. Discard the cinnamon. Let the mixture cool.

5. In a food processor, puree the baked sweet potato pulp with the water and ginger mixture. Add the milk gradually, adjusting the thickness to taste. Adjust the seasonings.

6. Transfer the puree back to the soup pot and reheat just to the boiling point. Serve the soup in bowls and garnish with a sprinkling of lime zest.

SERVES 6

PREPPING IN ADVANCE: The soup can be completed 1 day ahead. Reheat gently. (If it has thickened while standing, stir in a little water to thin it to the desired consistency.) Serve as directed.

Chilled Butternut Squash Soup with Apple Cider

Here is the perfect soup for a warm fall evening, after a day of apple picking or a visit to a country farmstand. You can garnish this silken soup with finely shredded smoked ham, if you like. With a vegetable or green salad and toasted walnut bread, you have an easy menu for a Sunday night supper that asks almost nothing of the cook at the last minute. There is a lot to be said for the simplicity of serving chilled soup.

2 medium butternut squash (2½ pounds)

6 cups fresh apple cider

1 tablespoon chopped fresh ginger

1 tablespoon salt

1 teaspoon dried thyme

1 teaspoon freshly ground black pepper

½ teaspoon ground nutmeg

4 ounces crème fraîche, for serving

1. Preheat the oven to 350 degrees F.

2. Cut the butternut squash in half lengthwise; scoop out the seeds. Wrap the squash in aluminum foil, place on a baking sheet, and bake for 1 hour. Remove and let cool.

3. In a large saucepan, bring the apple cider to a boil with the ginger, salt, thyme, pepper, and nutmeg and simmer it for 20 minutes. Let cool, then strain.

4. When the butternut squash is cool enough to handle, scoop out the flesh carefully. Place the squash, in batches, in a blender or food processor with the apple cider mixture and puree. (The puree should be thick but easy to ladle.) Transfer to a large bowl, cover tightly, and refrigerate for 2 hours.

5. Close to serving time, bring the crème fraîche to room temperature; whisk briskly with a fork until smooth. Remove the soup from the refrigerator and stir to make uniform. If it has thickened while standing, thin it with apple cider to the desired consistency.

6. To serve, spoon some crème fraîche into each bowl and ladle the chilled soup around it. You can also serve the crème fraîche separately, in a bowl, for passing.

SERVES 6

PREPPING IN ADVANCE: The soup can be made 1 day ahead through step 4. When ready to serve, proceed with steps 5 and 6 to finish and serve.

Tomato and Fennel Soup

his is a marvelous soup—a chunky, thick, rich reduction of tomatoes, lightened with a big splash of heavy cream just at serving. Use local or homegrown tomatoes in the summer and well-drained canned San Marzano tomatoes when really good tomatoes are no longer available. A bowl of this with country-style bread, and you have a treat in store.

12 large ripe tomatoes

1 large fennel bulb

1 medium red onion

2 garlic cloves

12 flat-leaf parsley sprigs

12 basil sprigs

¼ cup extra-virgin olive oil

1 teaspoon salt

5 cups chicken broth

1 teaspoon freshly ground black pepper

¾ cup heavy cream, for serving

1. Wash, core, and cut the tomatoes into chunks, chopping some of them fine, some of them medium, and leaving some of them in large chunks.

2. Wash and trim the fennel bulb, discarding the stems. Slice the bulb lengthwise as finely as you can; then cut the slices lengthwise. (The goal is to have uneven strips of fennel.)

3. Peel, trim, and slice the onion into rings. Peel, trim, and thinly slice the garlic. Tie the parsley and basil sprigs together with a piece of kitchen twine.

4. In a large heavy pot, sauté the sliced onion and fennel in the olive oil over low heat until the onion is limp and translucent. Add the garlic and sauté it for 5 minutes, taking care not to let it brown.

5. Add the tomatoes and salt and cook, covered, for about 30 minutes. (Salt will make the tomatoes release their water, so that by the end of the cooking time, you should have a stewed tomato mixture.)

6. Add the chicken broth, parsley and basil bouquet, and pepper. Cook, covered, over low heat, stirring every now and then, for about 1 hour. When done, the soup should be chunky, shiny, and thick. Discard the herb bouquet.

7. Correct the seasonings and serve immediately, with a generous splash of heavy cream added to each bowl.

SERVES 6

PREPPING IN ADVANCE: The soup can be made 1 day ahead through step 6. Let cool, cover, and refrigerate. Reheat over medium heat and proceed with step 7 to serve.

Roasted Tomato and Eggplant Soup with Parmigiano

This rich soup is a Mangia classic, a mainstay on our winter menu. When we take it off in the summer months, customers clamor for its return. We have a number of versions, depending upon the chef at each of our locations. This is the canned tomato version, preferably made with San Marzano tomatoes. If you have roasted the eggplant ahead of time, putting this together is a very simple matter. In fact, it can be made almost entirely a day in advance of serving.

1. Peel, trim, and dice the onion, garlic, and carrot. Thinly slice the celery.

2. In a large heavy pot, heat the olive oil over medium heat and sauté the onion, carrot, and celery, stirring, for about 5 minutes. Add the garlic and sauté it, taking care not to let it brown. Stir in the tomatoes with their

1 yellow onion

2 garlic cloves

1 carrot

1 celery stalk

1 tablespoon extra-virgin olive oil

3 pounds canned Italian plum tomatoes, undrained

1 cup water

1 teaspoon salt

1 teaspoon chopped marjoram

1 teaspoon chopped oregano

1 teaspoon dried thyme

½ teaspoon light brown sugar

6 roasted eggplant slices (see page 195)

6 tablespoons freshly grated Parmigiano-Reggiano cheese

SERVE WITH: Prosciutto, Green Olive Paste, and Arugula on Peasant Bread (page 180) or another panino of choice, as long as it does not have either tomato or eggplant in it.

juice, water, salt, marjoram, oregano, thyme, and brown sugar. Cook over low heat until the vegetables are soft, about 20 minutes.

3. In a food processor, puree the soup in batches. Return the soup to the pot. Reheat and adjust the seasonings to taste.

4. Meanwhile, chop the roasted eggplant slices, add to the soup, and cook just until the eggplant pieces are heated through. Ladle the soup into bowls and sprinkle a little Parmigiano over each serving. Serve immediately.

SERVES 6

PREPPING IN ADVANCE: The soup can be made 1 day ahead through step 3. Let cool, cover tightly, and refrigerate. When ready to serve, bring to a gentle boil and proceed with step 4 to finish the soup.

Yellow Tomato Soup with Roasted Peppers and Basil

If soup with both extraordinary color and flavor sounds intriguing, then make this, but when you do, use only ripe yellow tomatoes. Anything less, and you will be disappointed. Of course, you can also make this with red tomatoes, but you'll miss out on the color, which is part of the pleasure.

With the exception of roasting the peppers, which can be done ahead of time, no other cooking is required here. Raw tomatoes and garlic are blended together until smooth, crushed tomatoes are added for texture, and that is basically it. Serve just as is, no chilling required, as a luncheon entree on a summer afternoon with toasted slices of country bread topped with mashed anchovies and a few capers.

2 yellow bell peppers, roasted, skinned, seeded, and cored (see page 193)

12 ripe yellow tomatoes

2 garlic cloves

1 cup tender basil leaves, for serving

½ cup water, as needed

1 tablespoon salt

1 tablespoon freshly ground black pepper

3 tablespoons extra-virgin olive oil, plus additional, for serving

1 cup heavy cream, for serving

1. Cut the roasted peppers into strips; reserve for serving.

2. Wash, trim, and quarter the tomatoes. Peel and trim the garlic. Wash and pick off the most tender leaves of basil; reserve.

3. In a food processor or a blender, puree one-quarter of the tomatoes and the garlic, adding water only if necessary for pureeing. Transfer to a large bowl.

4. In batches, using the on/off button, process the remaining tomatoes to a chunky, thick consistency. Add to the puree, then add the salt and pepper, and stir to combine well.

5. To serve, ladle soup into each bowl. In the center of each serving, drop a few basil leaves; then make a nest with some of the roasted pepper strips. Drizzle with olive oil and add a splash of heavy cream. (Do not stir the cream into the soup, because that might disturb the presentation.) Serve immediately, with additional heavy cream and olive oil on the table.

SERVES 6

NOTE: Because this soup is fresh and contains raw ingredients, it should be served on the day it is made.

Fresh Vegetable Soup with Orzo

You will be raiding your vegetable garden (or the farmstand or produce department) when you make this soup! And it is the shopping that takes the time. The soup itself is a breeze to put together. If you have homemade chicken broth, by all means use it. Otherwise, choose a good-quality canned broth, not too salty, so that the flavor of each of the many vegetables shines. And while we would like to suggest reserving this for the next day—it is vegetable soup, after all—we don't recommend it. The orzo becomes waterlogged, and the vegetables are no longer al dente, either.

1 cup orzo or pastina

1 medium yellow onion

2 garlic cloves

2 thin medium carrots

2 medium turnips

2 medium zucchini, cut into rounds

1 cup cremini mushrooms

¼ cup extra-virgin olive oil

10 cups chicken broth

1 teaspoon dried thyme

1 teaspoon salt

1 teaspoon freshly ground black pepper

1 cup broccoli florets

1 cup fresh peas

2 large tomatoes, chopped

½ cup chopped flat-leaf parsley

SERVE WITH: Parmigiano Croutons (page 316).

1. In a medium saucepan, cook the orzo in plenty of boiling salted water for about 5 minutes. Drain and reserve. (If you are using pastina, cook it according to the directions on the package.)

2. Peel, trim, and finely dice the onion. Peel, trim, and thinly slice the garlic. Peel, trim, and dice the carrots into cubes. Peel the turnips, cut into thin slices, and cut the slices in half. Wash, trim, and slice the zucchini into thin rounds. Wash, trim, and quarter the mushrooms.

3. In a large heavy pot, sauté the onion in the olive oil over moderate heat, stirring, until translucent. Add the garlic and sauté it, taking care that it does not brown. Add the carrots, turnips, zucchini, and mushrooms, and sauté for 1 minute. Cover the pan, reduce the heat to low, and sweat the vegetables for 10 minutes.

4. Add the broth, thyme, salt, and pepper and simmer the soup for 30 minutes.

5. Add the broccoli to the soup and cook for 5 minutes. Add the peas and cook for 2 minutes more. Taste and correct the seasonings.

6. Stir in the reserved orzo and bring the soup to a boil. Add the chopped tomatoes and parsley, stir to combine well, and serve immediately.

SERVES 6 TO 8

NOTE: The soup is best served on the day it is made.

Chilled Zucchini Soup with Basil Mascarpone Cream

If you grow zucchini in your garden and are looking for ways to use up the proverbial bumper crop, this recipe is an excellent place to start. It is elegant and easy to prepare on a hot summer's day. The basil mascarpone cream lends a luxurious note. For maximum flavor, be sure to bring the cheese to room temperature before adding the herb to it.

When you are entertaining, Wild Rice and Roasted Corn Salad (page 279) makes a fine accompaniment and looks especially appealing with this soup.

10 medium zucchini

1 small yellow onion

2 garlic cloves

10 basil leaves

1 tablespoon extra-virgin olive oil

4 cups chicken broth

1 teaspoon dried thyme

1 teaspoon dried oregano

1 teaspoon salt

¾ cup mascarpone cheese

1. Wash and trim the zucchini and slice it into 1-inch rounds.

2. Peel, trim, and dice the onion fine. Peel, trim, and slice the garlic. Wash the basil leaves and chop fine.

3. In a large heavy pot, sauté the onion in the olive oil over medium heat, stirring, until translucent. Add the garlic and sauté for 3 to 5 minutes, taking care not to let it brown. Add the chicken broth and bring to a boil. Add the zucchini, thyme, oregano, and salt. Cook, covered, for 30 minutes. Turn the heat off under the soup and let cool.

4. In the meantime, place the mascarpone in a bowl and whisk vigorously; add the chopped basil. Let the mascarpone cream stand at room temperature until serving.

5. Puree the soup in batches in a blender or food processor. Transfer to a bowl, cover, and chill for 1 hour. When ready to serve, spoon a dollop of the basil mascarpone cream on top of each serving.

SERVES 6

PREPPING IN ADVANCE: The soup can be made 1 day ahead through step 3. Let cool, cover tightly, and refrigerate. One hour before serving, proceed with steps 4 and 5 to finish and serve.

Moroccan Lentil Soup

We call this lentil soup "Moroccan" simply because we added some traditional Moroccan spices, to supply flavor that is usually provided by either meat broth or the addition of a ham hock in the best made of lentil soups. And while harissa is Tunisia's renowned very hot chili sauce, it is frequently used in Moroccan cooking and even thought by some to be Moroccan in origin. (Perhaps we should be calling this North African Lentil Soup!) In any event, and recipe title aside, this soup is exotically flavored and satisfying; it is not overly spicy, even with the full complement of harissa.

1. Rinse the lentils.

2. Peel, trim, and cut the onion into large chunks. Peel and trim the garlic. Wash and cut the tomato into large chunks. Peel, trim, and dice the carrots into small cubes. Tie the parsley and cilantro sprigs together with kitchen twine.

2 cups brown lentils

1 small onion

2 garlic cloves

1 medium-large tomato

2 thin medium carrots

12 flat-leaf parsley sprigs

12 cilantro sprigs

¼ cup extra-virgin olive oil

8 cups chicken broth

½ teaspoon chopped fresh ginger

1 tablespoon ground cumin

2 teaspoons harissa

1 teaspoon salt

½ teaspoon freshly ground black pepper

½ teaspoon ground turmeric

¼ teaspoon saffron threads

SERVE WITH: Mixed green salad with House Mustard Dressing (page 356)

3. In a blender or food processor, puree the onion, garlic, and tomato.

4. In a large, heavy pot, heat the olive oil over medium heat, add the puree, and sauté it until fragrant. Add the carrots and cook about 5 minutes, until the mixture is somewhat reduced—enough to see the bottom of the pot when you stir.

5. Add the lentils, chicken broth, chopped ginger, cumin, harissa, salt, pepper, turmeric, saffron, and the fresh herb bouquet. Reduce the heat to low, and cook, covered, for about 45 minutes. Taste the lentils for doneness, and continue cooking, if necessary, until soft. Correct the seasonings, discard the herb bundle, and serve.

SERVES 6

PREPPING IN ADVANCE: The soup can be completed 1 day ahead. Let cool completely, cover tightly, and refrigerate. When ready to serve, bring the soup to a gentle boil. If the soup has thickened while standing, thin it to the desired consistency with a little water. Serve hot.

Black Bean Soup with Salsa

Mangia's black bean soup is thick and luscious. The fresh salsa lends zip and beautiful color. We make it with 2 serrano chiles, seeded, which lend just enough heat. If mild salsa is more to your liking, use 1 serrano, or go with one small jalapeño pepper, which tends to be less hot.

1. Put the black beans in a large, heavy pot.

2. Trim and peel the yellow onion and garlic cloves. Add the onion, garlic, water, cumin, oregano, and bay leaves to a large pot. Slowly bring the water to a boil over very low heat. Cook the beans for 2 to 3 hours, depending on how old and dry they are. If necessary, add more *hot* water to keep the beans covered as they cook. Taste for doneness. The beans should be firm, with no hard core. Add the salt and boil, still over low heat, for 15 minutes more.

3. While the soup is cooking, make the salsa: Trim the onion and tomato and dice each very fine.

2 cups dried black beans, picked over

1 medium yellow onion

3 garlic cloves

6 cups cold water

2 teaspoons ground cumin

1 teaspoon dried oregano

2 bay leaves

1 tablespoon salt

FOR THE SALSA

½ red onion

1 large tomato

2 serrano chile peppers

12 cilantro sprigs

½ teaspoon salt

Sour cream, for serving (optional)

4. Seed the serrano chiles and chop very fine. Rinse the cilantro, pat dry, and chop very fine.

5. Place all the salsa ingredients in a bowl, add the salt, and stir well to combine. Let stand at room temperature while finishing the soup.

6. Remove about ¾ cup of the cooked beans with some of the broth from the soup pot and puree them in a blender or food processor. Return the puree to the pot. You should now have a rather thick soup. Correct the seasonings, discard the bay leaves, and serve. If you serve the soup in a tureen, leave the onion in; it is a delicacy for some onion lovers. Remove it if you are serving the soup in bowls. Serve the salsa on the side. If desired, place a bowl of sour cream on the table.

SERVES 6

PREPPING IN ADVANCE: You can make this soup ahead if you do it in stages. Delay making the fresh salsa until the day you plan to serve it. Remember that it is best served at room temperature. Prepare the soup (steps 1, 2, and 6) as directed 1 day ahead. Let cool, cover tightly, and refrigerate.

Before serving, heat the soup over very low heat, stirring now and then. Be careful to stir up from the bottom of the pan because beans scorch easily. The soup may have thickened with standing. Add a little water to thin it to the desired consistency, if necessary. Taste the soup and correct the seasonings once more before serving hot, with the salsa as garnish.

Tuscan Bean Soup with Prosciutto

Beans, vegetables, and water are the basic components of many of northern Italy's world-renowned soups. A long, gentle cooking time guarantees the melding of textures and flavors. Here we've used chicken broth as the liquid and added thin slices of prosciutto as a sophisticated accent just before serving. Make a pot of this on a cold winter's day, enjoy the aroma that will fill your house, then eat. See for yourself how satisfying a bowlful of bean soup can be. A loaf of crusty bread, a piece of Asiago cheese, and good olive oil on the table are all you need as accompaniments.

2 cups dried great Northern or cannellini beans, picked over

1 small yellow onion

2 garlic cloves

3 celery stalks

½ fennel bulb

¼ head white cabbage

12 flat-leaf parsley sprigs

¼ cup extra-virgin olive oil

6 cups chicken broth

½ teaspoon dried rosemary

1 tablespoon salt

1 teaspoon freshly ground black pepper

¼ pound thinly sliced prosciutto (see Note)

1. Soak the beans overnight in plenty of water.

2. Peel, trim, and chop the onion into large chunks. Peel, trim, and thinly slice the garlic. Wash and trim the celery, including some of the greens, then finely chop. Dice the fennel and shred the cabbage. Tie the parsley bunch together with kitchen twine.

3. In a large heavy pot, sauté the onion in the olive oil over low heat, stirring, until translucent. Add the garlic, fennel, cabbage, and celery and sauté for a few more minutes, taking care that the garlic does not brown.

4. Drain the beans, and add them to the pot. Then add the chicken broth, rosemary, and parsley. Bring to a boil, cover, and reduce the heat to low; simmer the soup for about 1½ hours. Taste the beans—they should be tender. If not, since beans absorb liquid, add some hot water. Add the salt and pepper and cook for 15 minutes more. Discard the parsley.

5. While the soup cooks, slice the prosciutto into narrow strips. Add them to the soup, and stir to combine well. Correct the seasonings, and serve.

SERVES 6

NOTE: If you have either hot or sweet Italian sausage on hand, you can use it in place of the prosciutto: Slice 2 sausages and sauté them separately in a medium skillet; add the slices to the soup with the salt and pepper in step 4.

PREPPING IN ADVANCE: The bean soup can be completed 1 day ahead through step 4. Let cool, cover, and refrigerate. Reheat over very low heat, being careful not to let the beans burn, and stirring every now and then, until heated through. The soup may thicken with standing. Add a little water when reheating to thin it to the desired consistency. Meanwhile, slice the prosciutto and proceed with step 5 to finish the soup.

The Sandwich Table

SANDWICHES

PANINI

We sell a tremendous number of sandwiches at Mangia. Whether it is a simple sandwich, a sophisticated sandwich, or a special of the day, it starts with the same question: What can be put together to make this taste good? Sandwiches are generally considered to be casual, informal fare, but a good sandwich is not accidental.

Everything counts in a sandwich and, we believe, the bread most of all. We go to extraordinary lengths at Mangia to find the very best breads we can. To that end, we are blessed: The metropolitan area of New York City is now the world capital for artisanal bread making. Is the bread fresh? How is the crust? What is the flavor? Is it sweet, like brioche, or tangy, like sourdough? The flavor of the crumb as well as its texture play a large part in what we put between the slices.

Which brings us directly to the filling. "Juicy" is the word Sasha likes to use to describe a successful filling. Our sandwiches are intentionally overstuffed and generous, with a layering of components around one main, or starring, ingredient. Everything else in the filling then works as supporting cast, right down to the texture of the lettuce.

The combinations don't always have to be one-of-a-kind exceptional, like Soft-Shell Crab with Bacon, Tomato, and Garlic Aïoli on a Brioche Bun (page 149) or Pecan-Crusted Chicken with Red Onion Jam on Pullman Bread (page 156). Those are events, perfect for special occasions—company sandwiches, if you will. No, some of the simpler, most traditional sandwiches are the most pleasing: We make mountains of tuna salad and can barely keep up with the demand. White Tuna Salad on Sourdough Bread (page 148) is a hit and has been for years. Egg Salad with Salmon Roe on Focaccia (page 134), while a little more edgy, runs a close second.

When you are making sandwiches, the same guiding principles we use apply. First and foremost, the overall taste of the combination. Choose the best and freshest ingredients you can. If you cannot find the specific bread we suggest in a recipe, like Pullman loaf, use the best you can find—in this case, a quality white bread. It is that simple. But keep your eye out for specialty breads and rolls where you shop, and try them. Remember, too, that the spread in a sandwich is a powerful flavor tool. Go to The Accents Table (page 351) and see what we suggest by way of mayonnaises, pestos, condiments, and dips. The merest layer of Tapenade (page 364) or Hummus (page 378) or aïoli (garlic mayonnaise), can transform a sandwich.

The second part of this chapter offers recipes for something we also sell a lot of: panini, or small sandwiches. They are not the juicy concoctions discussed above, but light bites, good for lunch when a big dinner is planned the same evening or after the theater, when you want a little something that won't weigh you down. A selection of them, three or four different ones, cut into smaller pieces for serving, makes a lovely platter of hors d'oeuvres with cocktails. The thinking behind a good panino is the same as for our sandwiches: good taste.

SANDWICHES

Black Bean Hummus with
  Red Onions, Farmer's Cheese,
  and Ancho Chile Sauce in
  Pita Bread

Chèvre with Grilled Radicchio
  and Roasted Red Peppers
  on Olive Bread

Egg Salad with Salmon Roe
  on Focaccia

Washed Feta, Yellow Tomatoes,
  Red Onion Rings, and
  Tapenade on Semolina Bread

Parmigiano-Baked Portobellos
  with Roasted Red Peppers
  on Country Bread

Smoked Mozzarella with
  Baby Spinach and Roasted
  Tomatoes on Country Bread

Fried Tilapia Fillet with
  Red Onions and Olive Tartar
  Sauce on Pane Rustico

Grilled Tuna Club with Bacon,
  Tomato, Arugula, and Herb
  Mayonnaise on Focaccia

Roasted Tuna Niçoise on
  French Baguette

Pan Bagna

White Tuna Salad on
  Sourdough Bread

Soft-Shell Crab with Bacon,
  Tomato, and Garlic Aïoli
  on a Brioche Bun

Ham with Avocado, Red Onion,
  Tomato, Bibb Lettuce, and
  Crème Fraîche on Pullman
  Bread

French Ham, Vermont Cheddar,
  Green Apples, and Walnut
  Aïoli on Country Bread

Chorizo Stewed with Onion
  and Red and Yellow Peppers
  on Semolina Bread

Pecan-Crusted Chicken
  with Red Onion Jam
  on Pullman Bread

Chicken Salad with Hazelnut
  Sauce on Ciabatta Bread

Mustard Meat Loaf with Sautéed
  Mushrooms on Brioche Bread

Barbecued Pork Loin with
  Coleslaw on Baguette Bread

Roasted Shell Steak with
  Caper Sauce on Italian
  Country Bread

Black Bean Hummus with Red Onions, Farmer's Cheese, and Ancho Chile Sauce in Pita Bread

The Middle Eastern dish hummus, made of pureed chickpeas and tahini (sesame seed sauce), is justly renowned not only for its rich flavor but also for its remarkable versatility. It can be used as a dip, spread, or sandwich filling. It also lends itself to any number of variations—the addition of roasted garlic, for example, or hot spices. Given its appeal, we were wondering one day what it might be like if it were made with another bean and different spices. We experimented with black beans and discovered that black bean hummus, with Southwestern overtones, is also a winner.

The ancho chile sauce on these sandwiches serves as a strong accent. It can be made well in advance and is good to have in the refrigerator to spice up any number of dishes. If you make both the hummus and sauce in advance, then it is just a matter of filling the pita pockets, which makes for a quick lunch or light supper with a bowl of soup. Remember the

FOR THE HUMMUS

1½ cups dried black beans, picked over

1 tablespoon sweet paprika

1 tablespoon salt

½ cup extra-virgin olive oil

FOR THE CHILE SAUCE

4 dried ancho chile peppers

2 cups water

½ onion

2 garlic cloves

4 plum tomatoes

3 tablespoons extra-virgin olive oil

½ tablespoon ground cumin

½ tablespoon dried oregano

1 tablespoon salt

2 tablespoons sugar

1 tablespoon white vinegar

FOR THE SANDWICHES

1 red onion

12 ounces farmer's cheese or feta cheese

1 medium cucumber

6 pita breads

hummus when you want an easy appetizer, and serve it with triangles of pita bread. Use the sauce as you do here, as an accent.

1. Make the black bean hummus: In a saucepan, combine the black beans with water to cover. Bring the water to a boil over high heat, skim off the foam on the surface, and reduce the heat to medium-low. Cover and cook the beans for about 45 minutes, until tender. Drain, reserving about ½ cup of the cooking liquid. Let the beans cool.

2. Puree the beans in a blender or food processor, adding some of the reserved cooking liquid to loosen the mixture. Add the paprika and salt. Pour in the olive oil and blend until combined. (The hummus should be thick.) Spoon the hummus into a bowl, and hold it at room temperature while making the remaining components of the sandwich.

3. Make the ancho chile sauce: Place the ancho chiles in a small saucepan, cover with the water, and bring to a boil. Remove from the heat and let stand for 1 hour. When the chiles are fat, soft, and pliable, remove them from the pan, reserving the soaking liquid. Seed the peppers over the sink under a trickle of water. Discard the stems.

4. Finely dice the onion. Peel, trim, and mince the garlic. Trim and cut the tomatoes into small chunks.

5. Put the tomatoes and chiles in a food processor with about ⅓ cup of the soaking liquid and puree. The consistency should be like a a loose sauce. (If needed, add more liquid.)

6. In a medium saucepan, sauté the onion and garlic in the olive oil over medium heat. Stir in the pureed tomato mixture, cumin, oregano, and salt. Cook for about 30 minutes, or until thickened. Turn off the heat, stir in

the sugar and vinegar, and let the sauce cool to room temperature. For a smoother sauce, strain through a sieve, pressing on the solids with a wooden spoon.

7. Assemble the sandwiches: Preheat the oven to 350 degrees F. Peel, trim, and thinly slice the onion. Peel and thinly slice the cucumber. Slice the farmer's cheese.

8. Warm the pita breads for about 5 minutes. Cut each pita in half to create 2 half circles with pockets that are easy to handle. Stuff each with some of the hummus, red onion slices, cucumber, and farmer's cheese, and spoon 1 or 2 tablespoons of the ancho chile sauce over all. Serve 2 pockets per person.

SERVES 6

PREPPING IN ADVANCE: The hummus can be completed 2 days in advance; store, well covered, in the refrigerator.

The ancho chile sauce can be completed 1 week in advance; store in a well-sealed glass jar in the refrigerator.

This sandwich will be best—crisp in texture and filled with flavor—if assembled just before serving.

Chèvre with Grilled Radicchio and Roasted Red Peppers on Olive Bread

A relative of lettuce, radicchio is shaped like a small cabbage and has a similar crunchy texture and reddish-purple color. Its slightly bitter flavor isn't very interesting raw, but when grilled or roasted, it makes a strong statement. Grill the radicchio for this sandwich when you are using your grill to cook something else; then refrigerate it until ready to use. Covered, it will keep 1 day. You can also roast radicchio in the oven, with similar results.

2 heads of radicchio, about 6 ounces each

¼ cup extra-virgin olive oil

1 tablespoon salt

6 red bell peppers, roasted, skinned, seeded, and cored (see page 193)

12 ounces fresh goat cheese, such as Montrachet

6 individual small olive loaves OR 12 slices olive bread

You can roast the peppers and the radicchio together in advance on the same baking sheet. Just be sure to keep an eye on the radicchio to prevent it from overcooking. Done that way, this sandwich is an absolute breeze to put together, and the combination of ingredients tastes a lot more complex than it really is. When you come right down to it, there are just four main ingredients here. The key is that they are *good* ingredients.

1. Separate the leaves of each radicchio from the core, working as if it were a head of cabbage. Discard the cores. Toss the leaves in a bowl with the olive oil and salt until well covered with oil.

2. To Grill: Preheat your charcoal grill. With long-handled kitchen tongs, place the radicchio, leaf by leaf, on the grill, preferably around the edges of the fire, for better control of the cooking time. When you finish arranging them in a circle,

start turning the radicchio, proceeding all the way around. Check for doneness. The leaves should be limp, with the characteristic black markings of the grill.

To Roast: Position a rack near the top of the oven. Preheat the oven to 400 degrees F. Place the oiled and salted radicchio leaves on a baking sheet and roast for 15 minutes.

3. When ready to make sandwiches, set out all the ingredients in front of you, as in an assembly line. Slice the roasted peppers into strips.

4. Cut open the loaves or arrange the bread slices in a row. Cover the bottoms of the loaves with radicchio, spreading the leaves to the edges, and top with 2 full tablespoons of goat cheese, then slices of roasted pepper. Cover with the remaining bread, cut the sandwiches in half, and serve.

SERVES 6

Variation

This sandwich makes a wonderful appetizer. If you want to serve it as a "little something" before dinner with wine or cocktails, use sliced bread instead of individual loaves, and cut the sandwiches into smaller pieces.

Egg Salad with Salmon Roe on Focaccia

You can make this simple sandwich on other breads as well, in addition to focaccia, as long as you choose a soft bread, with no major flavoring. You don't want to intrude upon the flavor and fragrance of the salmon roe. This is an excellent example of a very ordinary sandwich that is transformed by a spoonful of something special.

1 dozen large eggs

1 cup mayonnaise

¼ cup chopped dill

1 tablespoon salt

6 focaccia rolls
or 12 slices of a mild-flavored
soft bread

1 jar (10 ounces) salmon roe

1. Hard-boil the eggs in a large pot with a lid: Place the eggs in the pot and add enough cold water to cover them by about 2 inches. Cover the pot and bring the water to a boil over medium heat. When the water boils, turn off the heat and let the eggs cool in the water. By not boiling the eggs vigorously, you avoid the blue ring you frequently see around hard-cooked yolks.

2. Peel the cooled eggs, chop them coarsely in a bowl, and add the mayonnaise, dill, and salt; mix thoroughly.

3. When ready to make sandwiches, cut open the buns or arrange the bread slices on the counter. Spoon the egg salad on the bottom halves of the rolls or on top of 6 of the bread slices; spoon a generous dollop of salmon roe on top. Finish making the sandwiches with the roll halves or remaining bread slices, pressing them down slightly. Cut in half, and serve.

SERVES 6

PREPPING IN ADVANCE: You can get a headstart on this sandwich by cooking the eggs 1 day in advance of making the egg salad. Hard-boil and cool as directed in step 1. Then peel them and place in a covered container in the refrigerator overnight.

Make the egg salad and assemble the sandwiches just before serving.

Washed Feta, Yellow Tomatoes, Red Onion Rings, and Tapenade on Semolina Bread

This is a delicious vegetarian sandwich that is light and just right for a summer lunch on a hot afternoon. The reason for the extra step of "washing" the feta cheese the night before is to remove some of its saltiness. It is a simple procedure, requiring nothing more than changing the water once or twice, and it makes a difference in the way the feta tastes.

1 chunk imported feta cheese, 2 pounds

2 ripe yellow tomatoes

1 large red onion

6 individual semolina heroes or 12 slices of semolina bread

¾ cup Tapenade (page 364)

We have tapenade on hand as a matter of course. If you don't, use store-bought black or green olive paste here. Both are readily available in jars at most supermarkets and are useful to have on hand for additional bursts of flavor on sandwiches or even stirred into pasta. But make our tapenade when you have the time. It stores beautifully.

1. The night before you make the sandwiches, place the feta cheese in a bowl and cover it with water. Store in the refrigerator, changing the water once or twice before using the cheese.

2. Wash, trim, and thinly slice the tomatoes. Peel, trim, and slice the red onion as thin as possible.

3. Rinse the feta, pat it dry, and then slice: If you handle the cheese carefully, you can cut ½-inch slices. In any case, slice the cheese as best you can, making sure you have enough for 6 sandwiches.

4. When ready to make sandwiches, set out all the ingredients in front of you, in an assembly line. Cut the heroes in half horizontally. Smear the 6 bottom halves or 6 of the bread slices generously with tapenade, spreading it to the edges. Arrange the sliced feta on top, then add a layer of tomatoes, and finally a layer of onion rings. Top the sandwiches with the bun halves or remaining bread, pressing down hard on them. Cut the sandwiches in half, and serve.

SERVES 6

PREPPING IN ADVANCE: You will need to start soaking the feta the night before you plan to use it.

Tapenade, on the other hand, can be kept in the refrigerator for up to 1 month— which is to say you can make it way in advance.

Parmigiano-Baked Portobellos with Roasted Red Peppers on Country Bread

Even those who cannot go a day without meat will be happy with this satisfying sandwich. And while at first glance this may seem like a summer sandwich, it is wonderful year-round, especially in the fall or winter, when it makes the perfect complement to a bowl of hearty soup. The parts can be made beforehand: the peppers, well in advance, and the mushrooms, several hours ahead.

18 arugula leaves

6 Parmigiano-Baked Portobello Mushrooms with Oregano Crust (page 218)

3 red bell peppers, roasted, skinned, seeded, and cored (see page 193)

12 slices of country bread

1. Wash the arugula, remove the stems, and pat the leaves dry.

2. Slice the baked portobello mushrooms on the diagonal. Halve the roasted peppers.

3. When ready to make sandwiches, arrange 6 slices of bread on the counter in front of you. Arrange 3 arugula leaves on each of the slices. Fan slices of the portobello mushrooms on top. Arrange a roasted pepper half over the mushrooms on each of the bread slices and cover with a slice of the remaining bread. Cut the sandwiches in half and serve.

SERVES 6

PREPPING IN ADVANCE: You can roast the peppers up to 1 week in advance; store, covered, in the refrigerator.

As for prebaking the mushrooms, we suggest you do that up to several hours in advance. Let them remain on the baking pan at room temperature until ready to slice. Assemble the sandwiches before serving.

Smoked Mozzarella with Baby Spinach and Roasted Tomatoes on Country Bread

Smoked mozzarella serves as the perfect counterpoint to the juiciness of roasted tomatoes here. Warming these sandwiches in the oven so that the cheese has barely melted makes this combination totally unforgettable. Good country bread is a must.

Smoked mozzarella is becoming more widely available, but if you can't find it, fresh mozzarella can be substituted. It won't be the same sandwich, but it will still be very good.

1½ pounds smoked mozzarella

6 tablespoons mayonnaise

12 slices of country bread

8 ounces baby spinach or very tender spinach leaves, stemmed

24 roasted plum tomato halves (see page 197)

1. Preheat the oven to 350 degrees F.

2. Slice the mozzarella.

3. Arrange the ingredients in front of you on the counter. Spread mayonnaise on 6 of the bread slices. On the remaining 6 slices, place a layer of spinach, covering the slice completely; top with 4 roasted tomato halves, and cover them with slices of the smoked mozzarella.

4. Place all 12 slices of bread, mozzarella and mayonnaise sides up, on a baking sheet and bake for 10 minutes. Remove from the oven, assemble the sandwiches, cut in half, and serve.

SERVES 6

PREPPING IN ADVANCE: You can roast the plum tomatoes up to 1 week ahead of time; store, covered, in the refrigerator.

Fried Tilapia Fillet with Red Onions and Olive Tartar Sauce on Pane Rustico

There are everyday sandwiches and then there are heavenly combinations like this one—the sweet, white flesh of tilapia crisply fried and sauced with olive-flecked tartar sauce. This is a sandwich for company, room temperature food of exactly the right kind—full of flavor, sophisticated, but easy to make. Accompany it with a bottle of good chilled white wine; then while away a summer afternoon.

For very practical reasons, we suggest you fry the fillets in advance. In that way, any smell of fish, which deters some people from cooking fish at home, should have disappeared from your house by the time you are ready to eat. To keep things really easy, make the tartar sauce ahead of time, too. Which brings us to the bread:

2 red onions

Juice of 3 limes

FOR THE TARTAR SAUCE

¼ cup pitted kalamata olives

2 tablespoons pitted green olives

¾ cup mayonnaise

¼ cup chopped flat-leaf parsley

1 tablespoon sherry vinegar

1 tablespoon grainy mustard

1 cup all-purpose flour

1 teaspoon salt

½ teaspoon freshly ground black pepper

6 tilapia fillets, about 6 ounces each

½ cup extra-virgin olive oil

12 slices *pane rustico*

Pane rustico, a variation of country bread, is crusty and not too flavorful. It is the contrast of textures—crustiness on the outside, softness within—that makes it so appealing. You will have to assemble the sandwiches before serving, but even so, when it comes to dishes that are good for entertaining, these tasty sandwiches figure near the top of the easy-to-prepare list.

1. Peel, trim, and slice the onions. Put the onion slices in a bowl and pour the lime juice over them, turning and separating the rings slightly. Let stand for at least 1 hour.

2. Make the kalamata tartar sauce: Chop the kalamata and green olives fine. In a bowl, fold the olives into the mayonnaise and add the parsley, vinegar, and mustard.

3. Season the flour with the salt and pepper and spread it out on a platter. Roll each tilapia fillet in the flour and shake off the excess.

4. In a large skillet, heat the olive oil over medium heat until hot. Add the fish fillets, in batches, and fry them for 3 minutes on each side, transferring them as they are done to paper towels to drain.

5. Put 1 fried fillet each on 6 of the bread slices. Spoon plenty of olive tartar sauce over each fillet, and top with a few onion rings. Cover with a slice of the remaining bread, cut each sandwich in half, and serve.

SERVES 6

PREPPING IN ADVANCE: The olive tartar sauce can be completed 1 day in advance of serving; cover the bowl tightly and refrigerate it.

The tilapia fillets can be fried and drained 2 hours in advance of serving. Hold at room temperature until you are ready to assemble the sandwiches, which should be done just before you eat.

Grilled Tuna Club with Bacon, Tomato, Arugula, and Herb Mayonnaise on Focaccia

This is a showy, marvelous combination. It takes time to prepare, but as everyone knows who loves club sandwiches, it is worth every minute of cooking and cutting. The truth is that none of it is difficult, and most of it is fun. We selected focaccia, a flat bread originally from Genoa, as the vehicle of choice here. Sliced horizontally through the middle, it is sturdy enough to hold a whole lot of ingredients and absorb juices and sauces without falling apart. It also has a chewiness that is superb.

This recipe calls for grilled tuna. If you are not planning to use your grill, cook your tuna under the broiler. You can also pan-sear it if your kitchen has good ventilation. Either way, it is a matter of quickly searing the tuna, using intense heat to create a crust while the inside remains rare—as you would do with a charbroiled beefsteak.

18 slices of bacon, cooked until crisp (see Note)

1 tuna steak, about 2 pounds

2 tablespoons olive oil

6 cups loosely packed arugula

2 tablespoons chopped scallions

2 tablespoons minced oregano

1 tablespoon minced thyme

6 flat-leaf parsley sprigs

1 garlic clove, minced

¾ cup mayonnaise

2 tablespoons fresh lemon juice

2 ripe tomatoes

6 servings of focaccia, about 6 x 4 inches each

1. Set the rack as close to the fire as possible on a charcoal grill, then preheat the grill until the coals are hot. Alternatively, preheat the broiler or a grill pan on the stove top.

2. Brush both sides of the tuna with the olive oil. To grill the tuna, place the tuna on the grill, and grill about 2 minutes per side for rare, and 3 minutes per side for medium-rare. Transfer the tuna to a plate and let cool. To broil the tuna, arrange it on the broiler pan and broil 4 inches from the heat. To pan-sear the tuna on the stove top, heat the grill pan over medium-high heat until smoking. Arrange the tuna steak on the pan and cook. The timing for broiling and pan-searing is the same as for grilling.

3. Wash the arugula well, pat dry with paper towels, and stems. Put the scallions, oregano, thyme, parsley, and garlic in a large bowl, add the mayonnaise and lemon juice, and stir well.

4. Slice the charred tuna into slices about ½ inch thick. (You should have 12 slices—2 per sandwich.) Slice the pieces of focaccia horizontally through the center. Slice the tomatoes.

5. Spread the herbed mayonnaise thickly on the cut side of 6 slices of the *focaccia*. Arrange the tuna on top, and on it 3 slices of bacon, 2 slices of tomato, 3 or 4 arugula leaves, and top with another piece of focaccia. Cut each sandwich in half and serve.

SERVES 6

NOTE: For crisp, evenly cooked bacon, place the strips in an unheated large skillet over medium heat. This will render the fat slowly, allowing the bacon to cook evenly. Turn the strips as needed, cooking the bacon for 5 to 8 minutes. As the strips are done, transfer them to paper towels to drain. Depending upon the size of your skillet, you will need to cook 18 strips in 3 or 4 batches.

PREPPING IN ADVANCE: Make the herbed mayonnaise either the night before serving or the morning of; cover the bowl with plastic wrap and refrigerate until ready to use.

You can grill the tuna up to 1 hour before using; hold at room temperature.

Roasted Tuna Niçoise on French Baguette

This sandwich makes us feel as if we're in Nice, France. We close our eyes, and we're walking down a sidewalk there, munching on this sunny, glorious combination. It makes a wonderful lunch and is perfect for summer entertaining. To enjoy your own party, follow our suggestions at the end of the recipe for making some of the components in advance.

1. Preheat the broiler.

2. Brush the tuna on both sides with the olive oil and season with the salt and pepper. Place on a baking sheet and roast as close to the heat as possible for 2 minutes. Turn and roast for another 2 minutes. The tuna will be cooked medium-rare at this point. Remove and reserve at room temperature.

1 tuna steak, 1 pound (1½ inches thick)

1 tablespoon extra-virgin olive oil

1 teaspoon salt

1 teaspoon freshly ground black pepper

3 large eggs

1 large potato, peeled

1 small red onion

½ cup pitted kalamata olives

1 red bell pepper

6 romaine lettuce leaves

1 can (14 ounces) artichoke hearts packed in brine

1 cup loosely packed basil leaves

FOR THE DRESSING

2 anchovy fillets packed in oil

1 teaspoon minced garlic

½ cup extra-virgin olive oil

3 tablespoons red wine vinegar

1 teaspoon dried thyme

1 tablespoon freshly ground black pepper

1 teaspoon salt

2 large French baguettes

3. Place the eggs in cold water to cover by 1 inch. Cover the pan and bring the water to a boil over low heat. Turn off the heat and let the eggs cool to room temperature in the water.

4. Cook the potato in simmering salted water to cover until soft when pricked with a fork, about 15 minutes. Remove from the heat, cut in half lengthwise, and, cut side down, thinly slice. Reserve.

5. Prepare the remaining ingredients: Peel, trim, and thinly slice the onion; break it into rings and reserve. Coarsely chop the olives. Trim, seed, and cut the red pepper into julienne strips. Wash the lettuce, pat dry, and cut into 2-inch chunks. Drain the artichokes in a colander and rinse well with cold water; drain again and squeeze as much water as you can out of them. Wash the basil leaves and pat dry.

6. Peel the hard-boiled eggs and thinly slice. Thinly slice the tuna.

7. Make the dressing: In a small bowl or mortar, mash the anchovies. Add the garlic and mix well. Stir in the olive oil. Add the vinegar, thyme, black pepper, and salt and whisk until creamy.

8. In a bowl, combine the tuna, lettuce, artichokes, onion, potato, pepper strips, olives, and basil leaves. Add the dressing and toss gently.

9. To make sandwiches, first make sure that the baguettes are nice and crisp. (If they are limp, preheat the oven to 350 degrees F and recrisp the baguettes for 5 minutes before cutting them.) Cut each baguette into 3 pieces. Cut each portion horizontally through the center without cutting all the way through. Press the halves, cut side down, on the counter to open them. Place a generous amount of tuna salad in the middle of each hinged sandwich. Arrange 2 or 3 slices of hard-boiled egg on top of the salad. Partially close the sandwich and cut in half.

SERVES 6

PREPPING IN ADVANCE: You can hard-boil the eggs 1 day in advance of using. Let them cool in the water as directed in step 3; then peel them and place in an airtight container in the refrigerator overnight.

The dressing can also be made 1 day in advance; cover the bowl tightly and refrigerate it.

The olives, peppers, artichoke hearts, and romaine can all be prepared the night before using them. Place each in a separate bowl, cover tightly, and refrigerate.

Boil the potatoes 1 hour before using; and hold at room temperature.

The tuna can be roasted up to 1 hour in advance of using; hold at room temperature. That said, we urge you to assemble these sandwiches as close to serving time as possible. Otherwise, you will be forced to refrigerate the roasted tuna. Refrigeration will alter its texture and flavor, and not for the better.

Pan Bagna

This classic niçoise sandwich is the essence of summer. *Pan bagna* means "bathed bread" and refers to the oil that is generously spooned on thick slices of country bread, which, in turn, are topped with juicy tomato, red onion, and anchovy fillets. These three ingredients comprise the main components of a *pan bagna*, but hard-boiled egg, olives, and green peppers can also be added. If you love sandwiches in which the bread becomes soppy and a little soft, add this to your list of favorites.

This sandwich is simplicity itself to make, perfect for a quick snack for last-minute guests, and can be fully prepared in advance. Serve with plenty of napkins, as these are delicious but messy.

3 ripe beefsteak tomatoes, 8 ounces each

1 large red onion

2 small garlic cloves

2 medium green peppers, 8 ounces each (optional)

¾ cup extra-virgin olive oil

6 unseeded kaiser rolls or 12 slices dense country bread, cut ½ inch thick

12 anchovy fillets packed in oil

3 tablespoons coarsely chopped basil leaves

Salt

Freshly ground black pepper

3 large hard-boiled eggs, cooled, peeled, and quartered (optional)

12 pitted kalamata olives (optional)

1. Wash and dry the tomatoes, then slice ¼ inch thick. Peel and slice the red onion into ⅛-inch-thick slices and separate the rings.

2. Peel, trim, and mince the garlic. If using, cut off the tops of the green peppers, remove the seeds and ribs, and slice into ¼-inch-thick rings.

3. In a bowl, stir together the oil and garlic. Slice the rolls in half horizontally.

4. Assemble the sandwiches: Generously spoon some of the garlic oil onto both the bottoms and tops of all the rolls. Lay 2 slices of tomato on each bottom half. Top with 2 anchovy fillets, then 3 onion rings. Sprinkle with some of the chopped basil and salt and pepper. If using eggs, place 2 quarters on each sandwich and top with 2 pitted olives and slices of green pepper, if desired. Cover each sandwich with its remaining top half. Press down on the sandwiches to release the juices, cut in half, and serve.

SERVES 6

PREPPING IN ADVANCE: The sandwiches can be fully assembled up to 1 hour in advance of serving. Hold at room temperature.

White Tuna Salad on Sourdough Bread

This tuna salad was on the menu the very first day Mangia opened. Right from the beginning, it was one of our bestsellers, and it still is. People just don't get tired of it.

You can add lettuce, watercress, sliced onions, sliced tomatoes, cornichons (they are particularly good), crisp bacon, olives—or just about anything you like. And, if you place all (or some) of these ingredients separately on the table and let your guests fix their own sandwiches, they may create tuna salad sandwiches that are memorable.

2 cans (12 ounces each)
white albacore tuna packed in water

2 thin medium carrots

½ cup plus 2 tablespoons
mayonnaise, or more to taste

2 tablespoons chopped dill

12 slices sourdough bread

1. Drain the tuna, put it in a medium bowl, and flake it with 2 forks.

2. Trim and peel the carrots, cut them into chunks, and chop them fine in a food processor. Add to the tuna, and then add the mayonnaise and dill; mix well. If you need more mayonnaise, add it 1 tablespoon at a time until you get the consistency you like.

3. Spread the tuna salad thickly on 6 slices of the sourdough, mounding it. Cover with the remaining sourdough slices, cut the sandwiches in half, and serve.

SERVES 6

PREPPING IN ADVANCE: The tuna salad can be completed 1 day in advance of using; cover tightly and store in the refrigerator.

Soft-Shell Crab with Bacon, Tomato, and Garlic Aïoli on a Brioche Bun

Tradition has it that you should buy soft-shell crabs live and dress them right before you cook them. In reality, it is more convenient to have your fishmonger do it for you. If you decide to do it yourself, however, hold each one down firmly with one hand; then with a pair of scissors in the other, cut about half an inch off their "face," where the eyes and the gills are. That is all there is to dressing a crab.

Soft-shell crab lovers, and there are legions of them, anticipate soft-shell crab season as a very special time of year. If you count yourself among them, plan a gathering of like-minded connoisseurs in spring or early summer; then make a feast of this superb seasonal sandwich. Pile the platter high. Don't even think about trying to make these ahead of time, though. They are "make-and-serve."

6 large soft-shell crabs, dressed

1 cup all-purpose flour

1 teaspoon salt

1 teaspoon freshly ground black pepper

1 teaspoon sweet paprika

1 cup corn oil

1 teaspoon minced garlic

¾ cup mayonnaise

6 brioche buns
or 12 slices brioche loaf

12 strips of bacon, cooked until crisp and drained (see Note, page 142)

2 ripe tomatoes, cored and sliced thin

6 to 8 leaves of Boston lettuce

I. In a shallow bowl, combine the flour with salt, pepper, and paprika. One by one, dredge the crabs in the seasoned flour and set aside.

2. In a large frying pan, heat the corn oil over medium heat until hot. (The oil is hot when a pinch of flour dropped into it sizzles on contact.) Carefully add the crabs, a few at a time, and fry them for about 1 to 2 minutes on each side, until brown. As they are done, transfer them to paper towels to drain.

3. In a bowl, stir together the garlic and mayonnaise until combined.

4. When you are ready to assemble sandwiches, cut the brioche buns in half. Spread 6 of the halves with the garlic mayonnaise. Place a whole crab on each one, and top it with tomato slices, 2 strips of bacon, and a leaf or two of lettuce. Cover with the remaining bun half.

SERVES 6

Ham with Avocado, Red Onion, Tomato, Bibb Lettuce, and Crème Fraîche on Pullman Bread

Mangia is always looking for interesting breads for its sandwiches. Pullman bread may or may not be available where you live, but it is worth keeping an eye out for it. Also known as *pain de mie*, it has little or no crust. It is baked in long rectangular loaf pans with lids, which produce a dense crumb that is ideal for slicing. Which brings us to its name: The shape of the baking pans is reminiscent of the Pullman railroad car. If you can't find Pullman bread, simply use another good-quality white bread, which should be readily obtainable.

Select a good baked country ham, and have it sliced a touch thicker than normal; you want to be able to bite into it. To maximize the overall effect of this lovely, simple combination be sure to use ripe avocados. Plan ahead and ripen hard avocados at home by placing them in a paper bag and holding them at room temperature for 3 or 4 days. Lastly, crème fraîche always tastes better if you take it out of the refrigerator 2 hours before using.

1 cup crème fraîche

1 large red onion

2 ripe beefsteak tomatoes

2 heads Bibb lettuce

3 ripe Hass avocados

12 slices white Pullman bread

1½ pounds sliced baked country ham

1. Remove the crème fraîche from the refrigerator 2 hours before using it.

2. Peel, trim, and thinly slice the red onion. Wash, trim, and thinly slice the tomatoes. Wash and dry the lettuce; separate the leaves, pressing each one with the palm of your hand to flatten it. Whip the crème fraîche with a fork. Cut the avocados in half and remove the pits; scoop the flesh into a bowl.

3. Arrange the ingredients in a row in front of you on the counter. On each of 6 slices of the bread, layer ham, sliced tomatoes, avocado, sliced onions, and lettuce. Spoon a dollop of crème fraîche on top. Cover with a remaining bread slice. Cut each sandwich in quarters, slicing from one corner to the opposite to form triangles, and serve.

SERVES 6

French Ham, Vermont Cheddar, Green Apples, and Walnut Aïoli on Country Bread

One day we decided to add walnuts to aïoli, Provence's fabulous garlic mayonnaise, and it worked! When you are in the mood for something other than plain mayo, good as it is, remember our moment of inspiration and make aïoli—walnut or plain. And when you do, plan to make it ahead, which will allow it to mellow in flavor. Great on sandwiches like this one—it *makes* this sandwich, in fact—it is also wonderful used as a dip, with steamed vegetables, for example.

FOR THE WALNUT AÏOLI

1 cup walnut pieces

1 teaspoon Roasted Garlic (page 374)

1 cup mayonnaise

2 tablespoons sherry vinegar

1 tablespoon water

2 Granny Smith apples, or other firm green apple

6 ounces Vermont Cheddar cheese

12 slices dense country bread

1 pound sliced French ham or Black Forest Ham

1. Preheat the oven to 350 degrees F.

2. Make the walnut aïoli: Spread the walnuts on a baking sheet and toast them for 5 minutes until golden brown. Remove from the oven and let cool. Put the toasted walnuts in a food processor, add the roasted garlic, and process to a paste. Add the mayonnaise, sherry vinegar, and water (the water helps keep the mayonnaise from separating), and blend until just combined.

3. Do not peel the apples. Cut them in half, core them, and thinly slice. (If you are not using the apples right away, sprinkle them with lemon juice.) Slice the Cheddar.

4. When you are ready to make sandwiches, arrange the ingredients on the counter in front of you. Spread 6 slices of the bread with walnut aïoli to the edges. Top with slices of the ham and Cheddar, and finish with slices of apple. Cover with the remaining bread, cut the sandwiches in half, and serve. If you like, serve a little extra walnut aïoli at the table.

SERVES 6

PREPPING IN ADVANCE: The aïoli can be completed 1 day in advance of using through step 2. Transfer it to a bowl or jar, cover tightly, and refrigerate. For the fullest flavor, bring to room temperature before using.

Chorizo Stewed with Onion and Red and Yellow Peppers on Semolina Bread

Chorizo is an air-dried pork sausage. It is spicy, with robust flavor. An essential ingredient in Spanish, Portuguese, and Mexican cookery, most of the time it is used as a condiment; but in this case, for these sandwiches, it stars.

There are many types of chorizo, as well as many brands. Really good chorizo is available at specialty markets.

12 small chorizo, 3 to 4 ounces each,
or 6 large, 6 to 8 ounces each

1 red onion

2 red bell peppers

2 yellow bell peppers

1 large ripe tomato

2 tablespoons extra-virgin olive oil

½ cup dry red wine

¼ cup water, if needed

6 semolina heroes

¼ cup plus 2 tablespoons sour cream

1. Remove the casings from the chorizo.

2. Peel, trim, and slice the red onion. Trim, seed, and slice the red and yellow peppers into thin strips. Wash, trim, and dice the tomato.

3. In a large skillet, sauté the chorizo and onion in the olive oil over medium heat, stirring often, for 5 minutes. Add the red wine and cook until it has evaporated. Add the tomato and peppers and sauté, stirring, for 1 minute. Cover the pan, reduce the heat to very low, and cook for about 30 minutes. If the mixture becomes too dry, stir in the water. Set aside to cool.

4. To assemble the sandwiches, slice the semolina rolls in half, without cutting all the way through. Spoon the chorizo and pepper mixture over the bottom half of the bread and top with a spoonful of the sour cream.

PREPPING IN ADVANCE: The chorizo and pepper mixture can be made 1 day in advance of serving. Transfer the cooled mixture to a container, cover tightly, and refrigerate. Remove from the refrigerator 2 hours before using to allow it to reach full flavor.

Assemble the sandwiches as directed in step 4.

Pecan-Crusted Chicken with Red Onion Jam on Pullman Bread

A pecan coating makes these chicken breasts very appealing, and two different condiments—red onion jam and mustard mayonnaise—contribute mightily to the delicious whole. Improvise here, if you like. Serve the chicken, without bread, with lovely little pots of the spreads on the side. Then make a salad of the lettuce and tomatoes. One of our vinaigrettes (pages 355–357) would work just fine. In other words, serve these chicken breasts as a sandwich or an entrée, for lunch or for supper, or build a buffet around a platter of them. You can't go wrong. Everyone loves this dish, and, as if that weren't enough, it is simple to prepare ahead of time.

2 large eggs

2 cups milk

½ cup fresh bread crumbs

½ cup finely crushed pecans, ground in a food processor

1 teaspoon salt

6 chicken breast halves, skinned and boned, about 8 ounces each without the skin

2 tablespoons unsalted butter

2 tablespoons extra-virgin olive oil

1 head curly red leaf lettuce

2 beefsteak tomatoes

6 tablespoons mayonnaise

1 tablespoon grainy mustard

Red Onion Jam (page 372)

12 slices of white Pullman bread

1. Preheat the oven to 375 degrees F.

2. In a bowl, beat the eggs with the milk, just until blended.

3. In a bowl, mix the bread crumbs with the pecans and salt; spread out on a platter.

4. Trim the chicken breasts of all cartilage and fat. Swirl each chicken breast in the milk mixture; then dredge in the crumb mixture, patting the crumbs on well to make sure both sides are uniformly covered.

5. Melt the butter with the olive oil over low heat in a small pan. Brush a baking sheet with the mixture; then arrange the breasts in a layer on the sheet. Drizzle the remaining butter mixture over them. Bake for 20 minutes. Remove the breasts from the oven, transfer them to a plate, and let stand for 30 minutes.

6. Separate the leaves of red leaf lettuce; then wash and pat dry. Slice the tomatoes very thin. Combine the mayonnaise with the mustard.

7. Place the chicken breasts on a cutting board. Holding a sharp knife at an angle, cut each breast on the bias into 1-inch-thick slices.

8. To assemble the sandwiches, place 1 sliced chicken breast half on each of 6 slices of the bread and top with 2 slices of tomato; add a generous soup spoonful of the onion jam, then a leaf of lettuce. Smear a little mustard mayonnaise on the remaining 6 slices of bread, cover the sandwiches with them, and cut each in half.

SERVES 6

PREPPING IN ADVANCE: There are very simple ways to make the assembly of this sandwich easy. To begin with, the onion jam can be made well in advance and stored in the refrigerator.

All the remaining components—the chicken, the mustard mayonnaise, and the prepping of the vegetables—can be done 2 hours in advance of serving. You can keep the chicken at room temperature, but be sure to store the flavored mayonnaise in the refrigerator.

Assemble the sandwiches just before serving to allow all the different textures to shine.

Chicken Salad with Hazelnut Sauce on Ciabatta Bread

We tasted a salad like this, with chicken and a splendid nut sauce, in Turkey one summer. When we got home, we decided to try it with hazelnuts. It is elegant company fare, thanks in large part to the hazelnuts. Ciabatta loaves, made from flour, yeast, and water, are shaped like old and much-used slippers—hence the name, which is Italian for "old slipper." If they are not available where you live, use baguettes, which should be easy to find.

While many people think of sandwiches only at lunchtime, this one makes a swell supper served alongside a simple green salad.

1. Preheat the oven to 350 degrees F.

2. Wash the chicken outside and inside, and pat it dry with paper towels. Rub the outside of the chicken well with the butter, sprinkle with the salt, and place in a roasting pan. Roast for 1 hour, or until the leg joints move easily and the juices run clear when the flesh is tested with a fork. Remove the pan from the oven and let the chicken cool to room temperature.

1 roasting chicken, 3 to 4 pounds

2 tablespoons unsalted butter

1 tablespoon salt

FOR THE HAZELNUT SAUCE

1 tablespoon coriander seeds

1 tablespoon fennel seeds

2 garlic cloves

4 slices white bread, crusts removed

2 cups chicken broth

1 teaspoon salt

½ teaspoon cayenne

½ cup heavy cream

1 cup hazelnuts, toasted and skinned (see page 57)

2 beefsteak tomatoes

6 individual ciabatta loaves

3. To make the hazelnut sauce: In a small skillet, toast the coriander and fennel seeds over medium heat, shaking the pan continually, until they become fragrant.

4. Peel and trim the garlic cloves. Soak the bread in the chicken broth.

5. In a blender or food processor, puree the toasted seeds, garlic, salt, and cayenne with the cream. In small amounts, add the hazelnuts and broth with the bread to the processor, blending after each addition. When you are done, you should have a sauce somewhat thinner than mayonnaise. Taste for salt, and add if necessary.

6. Remove the skin from the chicken. With your fingers, pull off the meat in bite-size strips and put in a large bowl. Be careful to avoid all cartilage, dark veins, or gristle. Add the hazelnut sauce to the chicken and toss to combine.

7. When you are ready to assemble sandwiches, thinly slice the tomatoes. Cut each ciabatta lengthwise, horizontally, without cutting all the way through. The breads should remain hinged on one side. Fill each bread with some of the chicken salad, top the salad with 2 or 3 tomato slices, cover with the top crusts, and cut the sandwich in half.

SERVES 6

PREPPING IN ADVANCE: The chicken can be roasted 1 day in advance of using; let cool as directed, then cover and store in the refrigerator.

Similarly, prepare the sauce 1 day ahead of time; store in a covered container in the refrigerator.

This sandwich is best when assembled just before serving.

Mustard Meat Loaf with Sautéed Mushrooms on Brioche Bread

For some of us, meat loaf sandwiches, spread with ketchup or mayonnaise, summon up fond memories. They were the treat, the "special of the day," in the lunch box we took to school. Nothing rivaled a mother's meat loaf sandwich. We've gone beyond the ketchup and mayonnaise here. We've placed the meat loaf, topped with sautéed cremini mushrooms, on brioche bread. Call it a grown-up meat loaf sandwich, if you like. It is a little different, but it still comforts right down to your toes.

Make the meat loaf 1 day ahead if you like. Then it is just a matter of quickly sautéing the mushrooms and assembling the sandwiches. All in all, not much to ask for all you get in return.

1. Preheat the oven to 350 degrees F.

2. To make the meat loaf: Beat the eggs. Peel, trim, and finely dice the onion. Peel, trim, and mince the garlic.

FOR THE MEAT LOAF

2 large eggs

1 onion

2 garlic cloves

2 tablespoons olive oil

1½ pounds lean ground beef, preferably sirloin

½ cup dried unseasoned bread crumbs

½ cup coarsely chopped flat-leaf parsley

6 tablespoons grainy mustard

2 tablespoons Worcestershire sauce

1 teaspoon salt

1 teaspoon freshly ground black pepper

¼ teaspoon ground cinnamon

FOR THE MUSHROOMS

12 ounces fresh cremini mushrooms

4 shallots, chopped

1 garlic clove, minced

3 tablespoons extra-virgin olive oil

½ cup dry white wine

1 teaspoon salt

½ teaspoon freshly ground black pepper

12 slices of brioche bread

3. In a small skillet, sauté the onion in the olive oil, over medium heat, stirring, until translucent. Add the garlic and sauté it, stirring, until cooked but not brown.

4. Put the onion and garlic in a large bowl, and add all the remaining meat loaf ingredients, mixing well with your fingers. Place in a 9-inch loaf pan, cover with aluminum foil, and bake for 45 minutes. Remove the foil and bake for 15 minutes longer to brown. Remove from the oven and cool to room temperature. Refrigerate, if desired.

5. Make the sautéed mushrooms: Rinse the mushrooms, cut off the stem ends, and thinly slice, top to bottom.

6. In a large skillet, sauté the shallots and garlic in the olive oil over medium heat, stirring, until the shallots are translucent. Add the wine and let it cook until almost evaporated. Add the mushrooms and salt and pepper, and sauté about 10 minutes, or until softened but not dry. Remove the pan from the heat and let cool.

7. In the meantime, unmold the meat loaf and cut into 12 slices.

8. To make sandwiches: Place 2 slices of meat loaf on each of 6 of the brioche slices. Spoon some of the sautéed mushrooms over the meat loaf, cover with a remaining slice of bread, and cut each sandwich in half.

SERVES 6

PREPPING IN ADVANCE: You can make the meat loaf 1 day in advance. Let it cool as directed in step 4; then cover and refrigerate. Let it come to room temperature before assembling the sandwiches.

The mushrooms can also be prepared 1 day ahead of time. When cool, cover and refrigerate. Bring to room temperature before using in the sandwiches.

Barbecued Pork Loin with Coleslaw on Baguette Bread

At Mangia, we have a somewhat less formal name for this: Barbecue on a Bun. This is very similar to pulled pork, if you have ever had that great southern favorite. The meat, cooked slowly and for a long time, should almost fall apart when poked with a fork. There is nothing better to serve with pork made like this than fresh coleslaw. While the barbecued meat can be made in advance, the coleslaw should not be. It will become watery and "off tasting." Make it close to serving time so that it is creamy and rich, tart and sweet, and let it serve as the perfect foil to the delicious, saucy pork.

3 pounds pork tenderloins

2 cups Nancy's BBQ Sauce (page 366)

FOR THE COLE SLAW

½ medium head of white cabbage, about 1½ pounds

1 carrot, peeled

1 small red pepper

¾ cup mayonnaise

½ cup cider vinegar

2 tablespoons sugar

1 tablespoon grainy mustard

1 teaspoon salt

1 teaspoon freshly ground black pepper

2 large baguettes

1. Preheat the oven to 350 degrees F.

2. Place the pork tenderloins in a roasting pan and baste them with the BBQ sauce. Roast basting frequently with the sauce (reserve some of it for serving), for about 1 hour, or until a meat thermometer registers 150 degrees F. Remove from the oven and cool to room temperature in the pan.

3. Make the coleslaw: With a sharp knife, slice the cabbage, cut side down, into thin shreds, being sure to cut around the hard core; discard the core. Place the cabbage in a large bowl. Grate the carrot on the largest holes of

a box grater. Seed and trim the red pepper and slice it very thin. Add the carrot and pepper to the cabbage and then add the remaining ingredients, stirring to combine well. Cover and store in the refrigerator for 2 hours, stirring occasionally.

4. When ready to assemble the sandwiches, cut the pork tenderloins into ½-inch-thick slices. Cut the baguettes into 3 pieces each, then slice each piece lengthwise in half, but do not cut all the way through. On the cutting board, open up each piece of hinged bread and flatten it by pressing down on it, cut sides down, with your hands. Fill with 3 slices of pork, a generous amount of coleslaw, and a couple of tablespoons of BBQ sauce on top.

SERVES 6

PREPPING IN ADVANCE: You can make the BBQ sauce well ahead of time. Store it covered in the refrigerator.

The day before you plan to serve the sandwiches, barbecue the pork. Let cool, cover, and refrigerate. Be sure to remove it from the refrigerator 1 hour in advance to let it come to full flavor before assembling the sandwiches.

Make the coleslaw on the day you plan to serve it, no more than 2 to 3 hours in advance; cover and refrigerate. There is no need to bring it to room temperature before making the sandwiches; use it straight from the fridge.

Roasted Shell Steak with Caper Sauce on Italian Country Bread

This is a great sandwich. Steak sandwiches should be, after all. And it is really easy to prepare because both the steak and sauce can be made in advance. Shell steak is as much sought after as filet, but it is not as expensive. Its robust flavor is complemented here by the emphatic taste of capers. If you want to allow your guests to assemble their own sandwiches, place the steak on a platter, the sauce in a bowl, and the bread in a napkin. Then watch as it all disappears. A lush, big green salad is always a good accompaniment.

1. Preheat the oven to 400 degrees F. Place the roasting pan in the upper third of the oven to preheat, as well.

2. Roast the steak: Season the steak on both sides with salt and pepper. Carefully place on the preheated roasting pan. Roast for 8 minutes. Turn the steak with a spatula and roast for 8 minutes more. (It will be medium.) Remove from the oven and let cool to room temperature.

For the steak

1 shell steak, 3 pounds

Salt

Freshly ground black pepper

For the caper sauce

1 small white onion

2 garlic cloves

2 celery stalks

3 large ripe tomatoes

3 tablespoons extra-virgin olive oil

1 cup dry white wine

1 teaspoon salt

1 teaspoon freshly ground black pepper

3 tablespoons drained capers

½ cup finely chopped flat-leaf parsley

12 slices of peasant bread

3. Make the caper sauce: Peel, trim, and thinly slice the onion and garlic. Trim and dice the celery stalks, including some of the leaves. Wash, trim, and cut the tomatoes into small chunks.

4. In a medium skillet, sauté the onion, garlic, and celery in the olive oil over medium heat, stirring, until the onion is limp. Add the wine and cook until it evaporates. Add the tomatoes and salt and pepper. Reduce the heat to low, cover, and cook for 10 minutes more. Stir in the capers, cover, and cook for 10 minutes more. Remove the pan from the heat and let the sauce cool. Add the parsley and stir until well combined.

5. Holding a carving knife at an angle, cut the steak into thin slices on the bias on a cutting board.

6. To assemble the sandwiches, arrange 6 of the bread slices on the counter in front of you. Top them with slices of the steak, and then a generous amount of the caper sauce. Cover each one with a slice of the remaining bread and cut in half.

SERVES 6

PREPPING IN ADVANCE: The steak can be roasted 2 hours in advance of serving. Let rest at room temperature and slice right before you plan to make the sandwiches.

The caper sauce, on the other hand, can be made 1 day in advance, up to the point of stirring in the parsley in step 4. Transfer it to a bowl, cover tightly, and refrigerate. Remove the sauce 1 hour before using to allow it to come to room temperature. Then stir in the parsley.

PANINI

Fresh Mozzarella, Tomato,
and Cracked Black Pepper
on Focaccia

Asparagus and Sautéed Onions
on Walnut Bread

Artichoke Hearts, Roasted
Tomatoes, and Sautéed
Greens on Baguette

Sauteed Broccoli Rabe with
Golden Raisins, Pine Nuts,
and Pecorino Romano on
Ciabatta Bread

Roasted Eggplant, Tomatoes,
and Peppers with Gorgonzola
Cream on Country Bread

Spanish Tortilla with Poached
Tomatoes on Ciabatta Bread

Roasted Tomato and
Potato Frittata

Prosciutto, Green Olive Paste,
and Arugula on Peasant Bread

Roasted Turkey Breast with
Parsley Pesto with Capers
on Pane Rustico

Poached Chicken Breast with
Mock Cajun Sauce and
Sliced Red Onions on
Whole-Wheat Bread

Jumbo Shrimp with Chorizo
Salsa on Olive Rolls

Fresh Mozzarella, Tomato, and Cracked Black Pepper on Focaccia

These panini are so simple to prepare and so delicious, that they should become a summer staple when tomato season is in swing. Use only fresh mozzarella and luscious, juicy tomatoes. If you can't find focaccia, try country bread—just toast the slices in the oven at 350 degrees F for 5 minutes. (If the slices are too big, cut the 6 slices in half before toasting. These are best bite size.) When the ingredients here are at peak, all in top form, these are true works of art.

1 pound fresh mozzarella

2 ripe beefsteak tomatoes

6 focaccia rolls
or a slab of focaccia bread (about 12 x 12 inches), cut into 6 equal pieces

3 tablespoons extra-virgin olive oil

1 tablespoon salt

2 tablespoons freshly cracked black pepper (see Note)

1. Slice the mozzarella as thin as possible.

2. Wash, then slice the tomatoes as thin as possible.

3. To assemble panini, slice the focaccia rolls in half. On each bottom half, alternate 1 slice of mozzarella and 1 slice of tomato until the bread is covered. Drizzle with olive oil, sprinkle with salt and a generous amount of cracked black pepper, and cover with the top of the roll. Slice in half and serve.

SERVES 6

NOTE: To crack peppercorns: First make an envelope out of a piece of aluminum foil; place the peppercorns inside, and pound them with a hammer until coarsely cracked. Do not hammer them too fine.

Asparagus and Sautéed Onions on Walnut Bread

At first glance, these may appear ambitious for sandwiches. But wait: The asparagus can be grilled or parboiled, if you'd rather not fire up the grill, and it can be done ahead of time. The sautéing of the onions takes all of 10 minutes. Which leaves the walnut bread. Now that's what you should use your time looking for here.

24 spears asparagus

2 tablespoons extra-virgin olive oil

2 small white onions

6 slices of walnut bread

Freshly ground black pepper to taste

1. If you are grilling the asparagus: Begin by preheating the grill. While it heats, trim the asparagus. Hold each stalk by the end and bend the stalk. The thick white end will snap off about one-third of the way from the end. Discard it. Brush the tips with olive oil and place them up on the grill across the bars. Grill for 2 minutes and turn with long kitchen tongs. Grill for another 2 minutes and remove.

    If you want to parboil the asparagus: Snap the thick stem ends off the asparagus as directed above. In a large skillet, bring about 1 inch of water to boil. Add 1 teaspoon of salt—this will maintain the asparagus's bright green. Add the asparagus, cook for 3 minutes, or until tender, and drain.

2. Peel, then cut the onions in half lengthwise. Place each half, cut side down, on a cutting board and thinly slice.

3. In a medium skillet, sauté the onions in the olive oil over medium heat, stirring, until translucent.

4. Preheat the oven to 350 degrees F.

5. Toast the bread lightly on a baking sheet for about 5 minutes. It should be firm, but not dry. Cut each slice in half.

6. To assemble the panini, arrange the 12 pieces of bread in front of you on the counter. Top each one with 2 asparagus spears and 1 tablespoon of sautéed onions. Season with a few twists of your pepper mill.

SERVES 6

PREPPING IN ADVANCE: The asparagus can be grilled or boiled 1 day in advance of serving. Let cool, cover tightly with plastic wrap, and refrigerate. Remove and let stand 1 hour at room temperature before making the panini.

Variation

Roasted rounds of butternut squash lend great color and an interesting sweetness to this vegetable combination. Roast the rounds ahead of time (see page 200). When you assemble the panini, place a round of the squash on each piece of bread, then proceed with making the sandwiches as directed.

Artichoke Hearts, Roasted Tomatoes, and Sautéed Greens on Baguette

Lots of vegetables with wonderful colors and different flavors fill the lightly toasted crust of a French baguette. These panini, a summer special, should be enjoyable to make. Roast the tomatoes well in advance; wash, dry, and trim the greens and store them in a plastic bag in the refrigerator; drain the artichokes. In short, leave yourself just the sautéing of the greens to do shortly before serving. You fill the skillet with mounds of leafy greens and in seconds, like magic, they cook down to almost nothing!

3 cans (14 ounces each) artichoke hearts in brine

8 ounces baby spinach

8 ounces arugula

2 garlic cloves

5 tablespoons extra-virgin olive oil

1 teaspoon salt

1 tablespoon freshly ground black pepper

3 tablespoons freshly grated Parmigiano-Reggiano cheese

3 tablespoons grated Pecorino Romano cheese

1 large baguette

12 roasted plum tomato halves (see page 197)

1. Drain the artichoke hearts, put them in a colander, and rinse with cold water. With your hand, squeeze out as much water as you can; let them drain over the sink. Rinse, pat dry, and cut off the stems on the spinach and arugula. Peel, trim, and finely mince the garlic.

2. In a large skillet, cook the garlic in 2 tablespoons of the olive oil over low heat. When it looks translucent, add the spinach and arugula and sprinkle with the salt. Swirl the leaves around a little to start cooking; then cover the pan and turn off the heat. Reserve.

3. Put the artichoke hearts in a bowl, add the remaining 3 tablespoons olive oil and the black pepper, and toss well. Add both cheeses and toss again.

4. Preheat the oven to 350 degrees F.

5. Cut the baguette into 3 equal pieces. Slice each piece horizontally through the middle and cut each piece in half. (You will have 12 pieces.) Remove as much of the soft crumb on the inside of each piece as possible, leaving 12 crusty boats. Bake on a baking sheet for about 5 minutes.

6. Drain the sautéed greens of all extra liquid and spread a few of the pieces in each crust of bread. Top each crust with 2 artichoke hearts and 1 roasted tomato half, mashing them together slightly.

SERVES 6

Sautéed Broccoli Rabe with Golden Raisins, Pine Nuts, and Pecorino Romano on Ciabatta Bread

There are big, bold flavors in this tasty combination. The ingredients here have a natural affinity for one another and come together without a hitch. Make this easy for yourself by preparing the broccoli rabe sauté in advance. As for the bread, we always recommend toasting it for panini—reason being that you don't want it to be chewy. If ciabatta is unavailable, simply use a baguette, and toast it as well.

A note on Pecorino Romano: It can be tricky to slice. For optimum results, have the cheese at room temperature and slice it with a cheese slicer or a sharp knife. Shards taste just as good if you can't get thin even slices.

3 ciabatta loaves, each about 8 inches long

1½ pounds broccoli rabe

2 garlic cloves, thinly sliced

3 tablespoons extra-virgin olive oil

3 tablespoons golden raisins

1 teaspoon salt

¼ cup pine nuts (pignoli)

12 thin slices of Pecorino Romano cheese

1. Preheat the oven to 350 degrees F.

2. Cut each ciabatta bread crosswise for a total of 6 halves. Then cut each half horizontally to make 12 pieces. Place the bread on a baking sheet and toast for 5 minutes.

3. Wash the broccoli rabe and cut off and discard the thicker stems. On a cutting board, chop the broccoli rabe into 2-inch pieces.

4. In a skillet, sauté the garlic in the olive oil over medium heat, taking care not to let it brown. Add the broccoli rabe, raisins, and salt. Sauté briefly, cover, and reduce the heat to very low; cook for 10 minutes. Uncover and cook until the juices have evaporated. Remove from the heat.

5. In a small dry skillet, toast the pine nuts over medium heat, stirring constantly, until fragrant. Transfer to a dish.

6. Place a slice of Pecorino on each piece of bread to cover it. Pat dry any excess liquid around the broccoli rabe; then stir in the toasted pine nuts. Place a heaping tablespoon of the mixture over the cheese on the panini and serve.

SERVES 6

PREPPING IN ADVANCE: The broccoli rabe sauté can be completed through step 4 several hours in advance of serving; hold at room temperature.

The pine nuts can be toasted 1 day in advance. Store in a covered container at room temperature.

Roasted Eggplant, Tomatoes, and Peppers with Gorgonzola Cream on Country Bread

Roasted vegetables, wonderful bread, and cheese. It sounds straightforward, and it is, in a way. How the parts intermarry, though, is what makes these panini so very good. If you haven't roasted the vegetables ahead of time, roast them all at once, on the same baking sheet. Be sure to keep on eye on them, though, and remove each one as it is done.

6 thick slices country bread, cut from the center of the loaf

4 ounces gorgonzola cheese, at room temperature

6 tablespoons crème fraîche, at room temperature

3 red bell peppers, roasted, skinned, seeded, and cored (see page 193)

12 roasted eggplant slices (see page 196)

12 roasted plum tomato halves (see page 197)

1. Preheat the oven to 350 degrees F.

2. Cut each slice of bread in half and toast for 5 minutes.

3. Remove the gorgonzola's rind. In a small bowl, using 2 forks, cream the gorgonzola and the crème fraîche, mashing the cheeses together.

4. Slice the roasted peppers lengthwise into thin strips.

5. To assemble the panini, place 1 slice of roasted eggplant on each piece of bread. Take 2 or 3 strips of roasted pepper and form a nest in the center of the eggplant. In the nest, place a roasted tomato half, cut side up. Drop a dollop of the gorgonzola cream on top, part on the tomato, part on the pepper, and finally on the eggplant.

SERVES 6

PREPPING IN ADVANCE: Each of the roasted vegetables can be prepared well in advance; store in the refrigerator. Remove 1 hour before serving to let come to room temperature.

Spanish Tortilla with Poached Tomatoes on Ciabatta Bread

We picked up the habit of tortilla in Barcelona, then worked on it in New York. The open-faced omelet, which is what *tortilla* means in Spain, can be served either at room temperature, as we do at Mangia, or hot, which you can do at home. Just bring the skillet straight from the broiler to the table, with the ciabatta in a basket alongside. And if ciabatta is not available, substitute a large baguette.

8 plum tomatoes

½ cup chicken broth

1 teaspoon salt

2 tablespoons unsalted butter

3 medium red potatoes

3 individual ciabatta loaves

1 small red onion

1 garlic clove

9 extra-large eggs

½ cup minced flat-leaf parsley

¼ cup extra-virgin olive oil

1 tablespoon sweet paprika

1 teaspoon freshly ground black pepper

I. Wash the tomatoes and coarsely chop them. In a small saucepan, combine the tomatoes, chicken broth, and salt. Cover the pan and bring to a boil. Reduce the heat to low and poach the tomatoes for 10 minutes. Swirl in the butter, cover the pan again, and reserve.

2. Peel the potatoes and slice them ¼ inch thick. Drop the slices into a pan of salted boiling water and cook for 10 minutes, or until tender. Be careful not to overcook. Drain and let cool.

3. Preheat the oven to 350 degrees F.

4. Cut each ciabatta bread crosswise for a total of 6 halves. Then cut each half horizontally to make 12 pieces. Remove as much of the soft crumb inside as possible, leaving 12 crusty boats. Toast the shells of bread on a baking sheet for 5 minutes.

5. Reset the oven to preheat the broiler.

6. Trim, peel, and dice the onion. Trim, peel, and mince the garlic.

7. Break the eggs into a bowl and add the minced parsley. Whisk with 2 forks for a couple of minutes, until well combined.

8. In a large (12-inch) ovenproof skillet, preferably cast-iron, sauté the onion in the olive oil over low heat, stirring, until translucent. Add the garlic and sauté it, taking care not to let it brown. Add the potatoes and paprika and sauté about 5 minutes. With a spoon, distribute the potatoes to cover the bottom of the pan.

9. Spoon the poached tomatoes over the potatoes, covering as much of them as possible. Add the eggs and, with the tip of the spoon, lift up the edges of some potatoes and let the eggs run underneath (try not to disturb the potatoes too much) to cover the bottom of the pan. Cook the eggs gently until bubbles begin to appear on top. Sprinkle with the black pepper.

10. Place the skillet under the broiler, about 4 inches from the heat, for about 2 minutes, or until the top of the omelet is evenly browned. Watch closely because it can burn very easily.

II. Serve hot or at room temperature, To serve, cut the tortilla into 12 wedges. Lift each one with a spatula and set it on top of a piece of the toasted ciabatta.

SERVES 6

PREPPING IN ADVANCE: You can complete the tortilla 3 hours ahead of serving. Let cool, cover with plastic wrap, and let stand at room temperature.

Roasted Tomato and Potato Frittata

Given how successful a Spanish tortilla is served as a panino (see page 175), we thought we'd try it with another open-faced omelet: the Italian frittata. No surprises here—it works beautifully, too. In fact, when it comes to the perfect example of room temperature food, there may be no better example than the frittata. Serve it as suggested below or in larger pieces for a superb brunch, late-morning breakfast, or late-evening snack.

3 large redskin potatoes

2 tablespoons extra-virgin olive oil

Salt

Freshly ground black pepper

2 ounces pancetta (Italian bacon)

12 roasted plum tomato halves (see page 197)

1 dozen large eggs

¼ cup milk

Ciabatta or a baguette for serving

A preparation note: While there are few ways to use leftover roasted potatoes that we can recommend, this recipe happens to be an exception. They work deliciously here.

1. Preheat the oven to 400 degrees F.

2. Scrub the potatoes, and cut them into ½-inch cubes. Coat with the olive oil and season with salt and pepper. Spread the potatoes on a baking sheet and roast until golden brown, about 30 minutes. Remove and let cool. Leave the oven set at 400 degrees F.

3. Cut the pancetta into ¼-inch dice. Saute it in a 10-inch nonstick oven-proof skillet over medium heat, stirring, until the fat has rendered and the pancetta is golden brown. Transfer to paper towels to drain.

4. Remove all but 2 tablespoons of the fat in the skillet. Add the roasted tomatoes and potatoes and the pancetta to the pan and spread in an even layer to cover the bottom.

5. In a large bowl, beat the eggs together with the milk. Pour the egg mixture over the vegetables in the skillet. Place the skillet in the oven and bake until the omelet is set, 15 to 20 minutes. Let cool.

6. Loosen the edges of the frittata with a knife. Cover the skillet with a serving platter, turn the skillet upside down, and unmold the frittata onto the platter. Cut the frittata into wedges. Serve on slices of the ciabatta or baguette.

SERVES 6

PREPPING IN ADVANCE: The frittata can be completed 3 hours ahead of serving. Let cool, cover with plastic wrap, and store at room temperature.

Prosciutto, Green Olive Paste, and Arugula on Peasant Bread

Prosciutto is now available almost everywhere, as is green olive paste, to say nothing of really good arugula, which means this could be one of the easiest-to-make combinations in this book. If you want to add a little something here, these are lovely served with pieces of sweet melon or pear.

6 slices country bread

2 cups stemmed loosely packed arugula

6 tablespoons commercially prepared green olive paste

12 ounces thinly sliced prosciutto

There is a way you can make these even more interesting. Use smoked prosciutto in place of the regular. Known as *speck*, it originated in northern Italy, where there weren't always enough sunny or dry days to cure the pork legs. Someone resourceful did the next best thing: moved the legs inside the chimney to dry. Smoked prosciutto has a deep rosy color and exquisite flavor. While it is still not widely available, it is becoming easier to find and is definitely worth the search.

1. Preheat the oven to 350 degrees F.

2. Cut the slices of bread in half and toast them for 5 minutes.

3. Wash and pat dry the arugula.

4. To assemble the panini, spread some of the olive paste thickly on each slice of toasted bread. Arrange 2 arugula leaves on each toast, pressing down a little to make them adhere to the paste. "Swirl" 1 or 2 slices of the prosciutto on top of each.

SERVES 6

Roasted Turkey Breast with Parsley Pesto with Capers on Pane Rustico

Once you have a roasted turkey breast on hand, you will be astonished at the number of ways you will find to use it. This is just one very simple example.

6 slices of *pane rustico*

Roasted Breast of Turkey (page 310)

Parsley Pesto with Capers (page 363)

The capers in the pesto make a sizable contribution. If you don't have parsley pesto, stir capers into a flavored mayonnaise. Or use olive paste or plain pesto. The point is to use the spread, whatever it might be, to provide a burst of big flavor for the turkey and bread. *Pane rustico* is a crusty rustic bread traditionally baked in a wood-fired oven. Look for it in specialty markets.

1. Preheat the oven to 350 degrees F.

2. Toast the bread for 5 minutes. Remove and cut the slices in half.

3. Trim the turkey breast of all gristle and discard the skin. Cut the meat into ½-inch-thick slices, cutting on the diagonal.

4. To assemble the panini, spread 1 tablespoon of the pesto on each piece of bread. Arrange 1 or 2 slices of turkey on top, and then a dollop more of the pesto.

SERVES 6

PREPPING IN ADVANCE: Both the turkey and pesto can be made 1 day ahead and stored, covered, in the refrigerator. Remove both from the refrigerator to stand at room temperature for 1 hour before using.

Poached Chicken Breast with Mock Cajun Sauce and Sliced Red Onions on Whole-Wheat Bread

Poaching chicken is simple and making the sauce is, too, because it is nothing more than mayonnaise, with all kinds of different Cajun spices added. We've even used whole-wheat sandwich bread!

1. Make the Cajun sauce: In a bowl, mix together all the ingredients, stirring until well blended.

2. Preheat the oven to 350 degrees F.

3. Toast the bread on a baking sheet for 5 to 10 minutes. It should be toasted, but not dry. Cut each slice in half.

4. Peel and trim the onion, then slice very thin. In a small bowl, separate the onion rings and pour the lemon juice over them, turning them often.

5. Cut the chicken breasts on the diagonal into ½-inch-thick slices.

6 poached chicken breast halves (see Basil-Parmesan Chicken Salad, page 333)

FOR THE CAJUN SAUCE

1 cup mayonnaise

2 tablespoons chopped flat-leaf parsley

1 garlic clove, finely minced

1 tablespoon drained capers

½ tablespoon grainy mustard

½ teaspoon sweet paprika

½ teaspoon ground cumin

¼ teaspoon freshly ground black pepper

¼ teaspoon ground allspice

¼ teaspoon cayenne

6 slices whole-wheat bread

1 large red onion

Juice of 2 lemons

6. To assemble the panini, arrange sliced chicken on each piece of bread to cover it. Top with a generous dollop of Cajun sauce, and then press 2 or 3 onion rings into it.

SERVES 6

PREPPING IN ADVANCE: The chicken can be poached 2 hours ahead of serving. Let cool, cover with plastic wrap, and hold at room temperature.

Similarly, combine the Cajun sauce 1 day ahead, cover tightly, and store in the refrigerator. Let come to room temperature before using.

Jumbo Shrimp with Chorizo Salsa on Olive Rolls

In our book, any dish made with jumbo shrimp is special. Top jumbo shrimp with a one-of-a-kind garlicky sausage salsa, and the result is worthy of a celebration. That's why we're recommending you serve these with champagne or port.

Should you have any of the chorizo salsa left over, add it to scrambled eggs the next day. Come to think of it, buy twice as much chorizo, and make an extra batch of the salsa for just that reason.

6 cups water

Juice of 1 lemon plus the peel

3 garlic cloves

2 bay leaves

1 teaspoon dried oregano

1 teaspoon salt

12 jumbo shrimp, peeled and deveined

2 medium tomatoes

½ small onion

2 small chorizo, 3 to 4 ounces each

3 tablespoons extra-virgin olive oil

6 olive rolls or 12 slices of olive bread

1. Fill a medium pot with water, add the lemon juice, lemon peel, 2 of the garlic cloves, the bay leaves, oregano, and salt; bring to a boil and continue boiling for 10 minutes. Add the shrimp, return to a boil, cut the heat, and cover the pot. Let the shrimp cool to room temperature undisturbed in the water.

2. Wash, trim, and chop the tomatoes.

3. Peel, trim, and thinly slice the remaining 1 clove of garlic. Peel, trim, and dice the onion.

4. Peel the casing off each chorizo sausage and crumble the meat.

5. In a small skillet, sauté the onion in 2 tablespoons of the olive oil over medium heat, stirring, until translucent. Add the garlic and chorizo and sauté for 3 to 5 minutes more. Add the tomatoes and stir well. Cover the pan and cook over low heat for about 20 minutes. Remove the pan from the heat and let cool to room temperature. The salsa should be chunky and thick.

6. Drain the shrimp and pat dry with a paper towel. Slice each olive roll in half or, if you are using slices of olive bread from a loaf, cut each slice in half.

7. To assemble the panini, place a shrimp on each piece of bread and brush the shrimp with some of the remaining 1 tablespoon of olive oil. Drop a spoonful of the chorizo salsa in the middle of each shrimp.

SERVES 6

PREPPING IN ADVANCE: You can poach the shrimp as directed 1 hour ahead of time through Step 1. Let stand in the cooking water until ready to proceed with the recipe.

The chorizo salsa can be made 1 day in advance. Cover the bowl tightly with plastic wrap and store in the refrigerator. Remove 30 minutes before using to allow it to come to full flavor.

As for the extra salsa we think you should make to have with eggs, keep that covered in the refrigerator, too. It will keep for 1 day.

The Salad Table

VEGETABLES

PASTA

GRAINS AND BEANS

This chapter offers recipes from our antipasto table: the selection of roasted vegetables, pastas, grains, beans, salad greens, and composed salads that appear on our ice tables at lunchtime. It is an astonishing array, tempting, beautiful, and bold. Loyal customers know exactly where to go to find what they like and want. New customers stand a little dumbstruck. There is a lot to choose from, and deciding takes practice. It is not a matter of how to start, but where.

Many of our customers start with our vegetable salads, and for that reason we decided to begin this chapter with them, as well. We buy an enormous number of vegetables at Mangia. Our preferred method of cooking them is to roast them. On any given day, there will be a platter of our Roasted Tomatoes and Peppers (page 198), still as popular as it was when we opened in 1982. We love what roasting does to the flavor, look, and texture of almost any vegetable and from the way roasted vegetables sell, our customers do, too. Then there are all the other colorful vegetable combinations: fresh Green Bean Salad (page 217), Corn and Oven-Burst Cherry Tomatoes and Cilantro-Lime Dressing (page 213), Orange and Arugula Salad (page 220), Grilled Whole Baby Zucchini with Fresh Tomato and Herb Salsa (page 236), to name just a few. If there is truth to the statement that people eat with their eyes, then our vegetable salads are a feast to behold.

Turn around, and you have arrived at our pasta salads, which require a word or two of explanation. While the name of our store is Mangia, we sell pasta in a very non-Italian way. We need to serve it at room temperature, something Italians find unacceptable. But this is New York City, not Italy, and we don't claim authenticity. We do, however, boast that our pastas are delicious and are made as all the wonderful authentic cooking of Italy is, with the freshest ingredients possible.

Which bring us to a selection of salads with grains. Choose among white rice or wild rice combinations. Try Wheat Berries with Roasted Beets and Sage (page 275) or our version of tabbouleh, made with bulgur, of course, and pickled ginger and cilantro as well (page 273). When you want a change of pace from a pasta salad, a grain or bean salad is just the thing. And it may be more healthful, too.

When you are selecting recipes to make on the pages that follow, we would urge you to do as our customers do at lunchtime. Pick out recipes that appeal and try them. Match them with complementary flavors and textures, or serve them in glorious contrast to something else. Serve them in small amounts, as a tasting, or in bigger servings, as entrees, if you prefer. Use the freshest ingredients you can, and serve the finished salads in the simplest platters or bowls possible. Like the best antipasto platters, in Italy, the most appealing tapas selections in Spain, and the mezze in Greece, these dishes will speak for themselves. Beyond that, there are no rules.

A THOUGHT OR TWO ON STORING SALADS FOR RE-SERVING

The best-tasting salad, be it vegetable, pasta, or bean or grain, is the one made as close to serving time as possible. In general, we do not recommend trying to store leftover salad for re-serving. There are several main reasons why:

- If the salad contains raw ingredients, like cucumbers or tomatoes, with time, the raw ingredients will break down, becoming limp, old tasting, and unappealing. They will also start to leach water into the salad.

- If the salad has cream in the dressing, it will separate and alter the character of both the salad and the dressing.

Remember, too, that certain green vegetables—green beans and broccoli, among them—turn a dull brownish green when left to stand in vinaigrette. For that reason alone, which is primarily aesthetic, but important, we do not suggest serving them a second time.

VEGETABLES

ROASTING VEGETABLES

Bell Peppers

Eggplant

Tomatoes

Potatoes

Butternut Squash

Zucchini

VEGETABLE SALADS

Roasted Baby Artichokes with
Garlic and Parmigiano Shavings

Steamed Asparagus with
Aromatic Herb Dressing

Whole Roasted Beet Salad with
Orange Moroccan Dressing

Roasted Brussels Sprouts
with Red Onion and Thyme

Pan-Seared Cauliflower
with Pecan Bread Crumbs

Caesar Salad

Corn and Roasted Potatoes
with Poblano Chile

Corn and Oven-Burst Cherry Tomatoes
and Cilantro-Lime Dressing

Cucumber, Avocado, Scallion,
and Lime Salad

Grilled Fennel, Black Olive,
and Golden Raisin Salad

Roasted Fennel with Parmigiano

Green Bean Salad

Parmigiano-Baked Portobello
Mushrooms with Oregano Crust

Grilled Portobello Mushrooms
with Parsley Pesto

Orange and Arugula Salad

Charred Red Bell Peppers Stuffed with
Mozzarella, Prosciutto, and Olives

Potato Salad with Roasted Prosciutto,
String Beans, and Olives

Roasted Potatoes and Eggplant
with Sun-Dried Tomato Salsina

Grilled Radicchio with Parmigiano
Shavings and Anchovy Croutons

Roasted Butternut Squash with
Mint and Brown Sugar Sauce

Fresh Tomato Salad with Mint Pesto

Tomato Salad

Cherry Tomato, Sautéed Leek,
and Pine Nut Salad

Yam and Fennel Salad

Roasted Yams with Curried Apples

Grilled Whole Baby Zucchini with
Fresh Tomato and Herb Salsa

ROASTING VEGETABLES

We do a tremendous amount of roasting at Mangia: fish, meat, poultry, and especially vegetables—all kinds, including delicate lettuces. The reason we do so much roasting is straightforward, like the method itself: Roasting concentrates the flavor, maintains the integrity of the item, and sometimes—not always, we admit—it enhances appearance. There is very little that can compare with the elegance of a platter of burnished roasted red, yellow, and orange bell peppers brushed with a little olive oil on a simple white platter. Those peppers say summer, sweetness, Italy. They say Mangia.

Almost any vegetable can be roasted. When roasting vegetables at home, you will want the very best you can find, be it a bell pepper, shallot, or tomato. Use good-quality extra-virgin olive oil, salt, and fresh pepper. That is all. It is simplicity itself.

BELL PEPPERS

At Mangia, we roast bell peppers three different ways—whole, in quarters, and in strips. How we plan to use the roasted pepper determines whether we cut it or not. When roasted, the quarters take on a subtle charred flavor. Thin strips that are roasted have more charred flavor still and more texture, and can therefore be used as a powerful accent.

To Roast Whole Bell Peppers

To char whole red bell peppers on the stove top: Put the pepper directly on the gas burner, in the flame. Keep turning the pepper with tongs until the outside is charred—actually blackened, all over. The flame chars the skin only and does not overcook the flesh. Carefully place the blackened pepper in a brown paper bag or plastic bag, close it, and let steam until cool enough to handle.

To char bell peppers on the grill: Position the rack as close to the coals as possible and preheat the coals until they are ashy. Place the peppers on the rack and cook them, turning frequently, until blackened. Transfer them to a bag as directed above to steam.

To skin, seed, and core whole roasted bell peppers: With the dull side of a paring knife, scrape the blackened skin off the flesh of the pepper. (Some of it will remain, and that is good because a few flecks here and there lend flavor.) Halve the pepper, and remove the seeds and core. Use as directed. Store in the refrigerator in a covered container for up to 1 week.

The skin can also be removed with your fingertips under a trickle of cool water. Simply hold the pepper under the tap and pull off the blackened skin with your fingertips. Seed, core, and store as directed above.

To Roast Bell Pepper Quarters or Strips

Whereas it is very important to turn whole bell peppers while they char so that they roast evenly, no turning is necessary when the peppers are cut into pieces.

6 to 8 medium red bell peppers

2 garlic cloves

¼ cup extra-virgin olive oil

2 tablespoons coarsely chopped fresh rosemary

Salt

Freshly ground black pepper

1. Preheat the oven to 400 degrees F.

2. Cut the bell peppers into quarters, and remove the seeds, cores, and ribs. Or cut the quarters into ½-inch-wide strips. Peel, trim, and thinly slice the garlic.

3. In a bowl, combine the pepper quarters or strips, olive oil, sliced garlic, rosemary, and salt and pepper to taste; toss to coat well. Arrange the pieces in a single layer on a large baking sheet and roast about 40 minutes, until charred around the edges. Let cool on the baking sheet. Store in a covered container in the refrigerator for 1 week.

EGGPLANT

Eggplant takes on a superb caramel flavor when roasted. Sautéing and frying impart different flavors and textures, but neither gives that sweetness characteristic of roasting. Like bell peppers, we roast eggplant cut into two different sizes—cubes and slices—for two different results. The cubes are best added to salads or soups, whereas the slices are nice on an antipasto platter or in sandwiches or panini. They also make a wonderful topping for pizza or as a snack on a piece of baguette.

A practical consideration when you are roasting eggplant slices, especially if you are going to be serving them as part of an antipasto platter or on top of a pizza when appearance counts: When roasted, eggplant softens, and slices of it can easily collapse. Because the appearance of food and its presentation both play such a large part in how that food is received—it has been said that people eat with their eyes—we like to present it as naturally as possible. One way of doing that is to maintain the integrity of the original shape. Lining the baking sheet with parchment paper prevents the slices from sticking and makes removing them whole a lot easier. They may not be tastier, but they are infinitely more appealing to the eye.

To Roast Eggplant Cubes and Slices

1. Preheat the oven to 400 degrees F.

2. *To roast eggplant cubes:* Stem the eggplants. Cut each lengthwise into 4 pieces. Cut each quarter crosswise into pieces about 1½ to 2 inches thick. In a bowl, combine the eggplant cubes with the olive oil, balsamic vinegar, and salt and pepper to taste and toss well to coat. Place in a single layer on a large baking sheet and roast 20 minutes, until the pieces are golden brown. Remove and let cool on the baking sheet. Store in a covered container in the refrigerator for up to 24 hours.

To roast eggplant slices: Stem the eggplants, then cut them crosswise into ½-inch-thick slices. Mix the olive oil, vinegar, salt, and pepper in a small bowl. Line a large baking sheet with parchment paper. Brush the paper with some of the seasoned oil, then arrange the slices on it in one layer; brush the slices with the remaining seasoned oil. Roast for 20 minutes. (There is no need to turn the slices.) Let cool on a rack. Store as directed for roasted eggplant cubes.

2 eggplants, 1 pound each

½ cup extra-virgin olive oil

1 tablespoon balsamic vinegar

1 teaspoon salt, or to taste

1 teaspoon freshly ground black pepper, or to taste

Parchment paper for lining the baking sheet (for slices only)

TOMATOES

Roasting concentrates the flavor of tomatoes as it softens their texture. We specifically like to roast plum tomatoes because they retain their shape when roasted, making them better suited for our sandwiches. That is just one of the ways we use them, though. At Mangia, roasted tomatoes find their way into dishes in almost as many ways as roasted peppers do: soups, sandwiches, salads, pasta sauces.

We also roast cherry tomatoes. We call them "oven-burst," because that is just what happens to them. They are tasty, too.

To Roast Plum Tomatoes

1. Preheat the oven to 400 degrees F.

2. Wash the tomatoes and halve them lengthwise, from top to bottom.

3. In a large bowl, combine the tomato halves, olive oil, salt and pepper to taste and toss to coat the tomatoes. Place the tomatoes, cut side up, in one layer on a large baking sheet and roast until the edges start to caramelize, about 35 minutes. Let cool on the baking sheet. Store in a covered container in the refrigerator for 1 week.

20 red or yellow plum tomatoes

3 tablespoons extra-virgin olive oil

1 teaspoon salt, or to taste

1 teaspoon freshly ground black pepper, or to taste

To Roast Cherry Tomatoes

Toss 2 pints of cherry tomatoes in the seasoned oil, but do *not* halve them. Roast them on a baking sheet in a 400-degree F oven until they swell and the skin starts to burst, about 20 minutes. Let cool on the baking sheet. Store in a covered container in the refrigerator for 1 week.

Roasted Tomatoes and Peppers

Now that you know how to roast both tomatoes and peppers, assemble one of our most commented-on and sought-out platters, which is just as much a still life as a salad. Serve as is, or with pesto or fresh mozzarella, if desired.

12 roasted plum tomato halves, 6 red and 6 yellow (see page 197)

10 roasted yellow cherry tomatoes (see page 197)

8 yellow bell pepper quarters (2 peppers), roasted (see page 193)

10 mini red bell peppers, oiled, then roasted whole for 25 minutes (seeding is not necessary; see page 193)

To serve, arrange the tomatoes in rows to cover half of a white serving platter, if you have one, or another simple platter, preferably without a pattern. Arrange the peppers by type in rows to cover the remaining half of the platter.

POTATOES

For some people, ourselves included, roasted potatoes are at the top of the list of favorite vegetables. Hot out of the oven, slightly crispy and brown on the bottom, and sprinkled with sea salt or a little bit of fresh oregano or parsley, they are superb. Served just as is, turned into salads, spooned next to sausages or eggs, added to frittatas or our Spanish Tortilla (page 175), roasted whole potatoes are perfect packages, mines of flavor and texture.

We like small (meaning new) red or white potatoes for roasting. If you feel compelled to flavor them, add chopped rosemary, sage, or thyme to the seasoned oil. You don't have to. A simply roasted plain potato can stand entirely on its own.

To Roast Whole New Potatoes

1. Preheat the oven to 400 degrees F.

2. Scrub the potatoes and pat dry completely before using. Peel, trim, and mince the garlic.

3. In a medium bowl, combine all the ingredients. Arrange the potatoes on a baking sheet and roast for 40 minutes, or until tender and golden brown. Let cool on the baking sheet.

1½ pounds new white or red potatoes, about 1 inch in diameter

3 garlic cloves

¼ cup extra-virgin olive oil

1½ teaspoons salt

1 teaspoon freshly ground black pepper

SERVES 6 AS A SIDE DISH

BUTTERNUT SQUASH

Roasted butternut squash has a sweet caramelized flavor and lovely soft texture that adds something unexpected to salads and sandwiches and panini, in particular.

When selecting a butternut squash for roasting, pick one with a long neck. Our reasons for suggesting this are not entirely aesthetic. Slices from the neck are generally uniform in size. Just as important, there are no seeds in the neck, which means that all you have to do to prep the slices is to skin them. The bottom of the squash, also cut into slices, can be roasted as well, of course. You will have to contend with slices that have hollow middles, which require seeding before you can roast them. That said, do not let size or the configuration of a slice, wherever it has come from on the squash, deter you.

To Roast Butternut Squash Slices

1. Preheat the oven to 350 degrees F.

2. With a vegetable peeler, remove the skin on the squash. Cut the neck off and slice it crosswise into ½-inch-thick slices. If desired, halve the squash "bowl," seed and remove the strings, and cut it crosswise into slices, too. Place the slices on a baking sheet, brush with the olive oil, and season with salt and pepper to taste. Roast for 45 minutes, or until the slices begin to caramelize around the edges. Let cool on the baking sheet. Store in a covered container in the refrigerator for 1 week.

1 butternut squash, about 2 pounds

Extra-virgin olive oil for brushing the slices

Salt

Freshly ground black pepper

SERVES 6 AS A SIDE DISH

ZUCCHINI

Roasting zucchini gives it flavor, plain and simple, and great color. We like to roast it with seasoned olive oil that has reduced balsamic vinegar added. The balsamic reduction adds sweetness and deeper color. Do not, of course, use your most expensive bottle of aged balsamic vinegar to do this. An everyday brand will work just fine.

To Roast Zucchini Slices

1. Preheat the oven to 400 degrees F.

2. In a small saucepan, bring the balsamic vinegar to a boil and boil it rapidly over high heat until reduced to a syrupy consistency, about 5 minutes. Let cool.

½ cup balsamic vinegar

1½ pounds medium zucchini

3 tablespoons extra-virgin olive oil

Salt

Freshly ground black pepper

3. Wash and dry the zucchini. Trim the ends, then slice on the diagonal into ⅜-inch-thick ovals. Put the slices in a bowl and add the olive oil, reduced balsamic vinegar, and salt and pepper to taste. Toss the zucchini to coat.

4. Arrange the zucchini slices in a single layer on a large baking sheet and roast until the edges start to brown, about 20 to 25 minutes. Let cool on the baking sheet. Store in a covered container in the refrigerator for up to 2 days.

SERVES 6

Roasted Baby Artichokes with Garlic and Parmigiano Shavings

Make these in the spring, when new-crop baby artichokes are available. Look for ones that are no longer than 1½ inches. Their sweet flavor takes on a nutty edge when roasted. Good alone, these chokes are also nice with pork or chicken. Leftovers can be added to pasta or white beans.

1½ to 2 pounds whole baby artichokes

2 tablespoons fresh lemon juice

2 or 3 garlic cloves

¼ cup extra-virgin olive oil

Salt

Freshly ground black pepper

½ cup Parmigiano-Reggiano cheese shavings

½ cup coarsely chopped flat-leaf parsley

1. Trim the artichokes by removing the tough outer leaves to expose the more tender pale green leaves underneath. With a paring knife, trim around the stems and cut off the ends of the stems and the tops of the leaves. Put in a bowl of water with 1 tablespoon of the lemon juice.

2. Bring a pot of lightly salted water to a boil. Preheat the oven to 375 degrees F. Meanwhile, mince the garlic.

3. Drop the trimmed artichokes into the boiling water and cook about 5 minutes to soften. Drain. When cool enough to handle, cut each artichoke in half through the core. In a large bowl, combine the artichokes with the minced garlic, olive oil, and salt and pepper to taste.

4. Place the artichokes on a baking pan and roast until they are crisp and brown on the outside and cooked through, about 15 minutes.

5. Let the artichokes cool; then toss them with the Parmigiano shavings, remaining 1 tablespoon of lemon juice, and the chopped parsley.

SERVES 6

PREPPING IN ADVANCE: The artichokes can be cooked early on the day of serving. Toss with olive oil just to coat, cover, and refrigerate. Remove 1 hour before serving and add the cheese, lemon juice, and parsley.

Steamed Asparagus with Aromatic Herb Dressing

The herb of choice here is fresh tarragon, and it goes beautifully with the mustard and cream in the dressing. When you want an elegant accompaniment to roasted meat or fish, something without vinaigrette, serve this. It is especially nice at Easter, with lamb.

1 to 1½ pounds medium-thick asparagus spears

FOR THE DRESSING

2 tablespoons tarragon leaves

2 tablespoons flat-leaf parsley leaves

3 tablespoons minced chives

2 tablespoons Dijon mustard

2 tablespoons champagne vinegar

¼ cup heavy cream

1. Wash the asparagus and trim off any woody stems. Place the asparagus in a steamer basket set over a pot of boiling water. Cover the pot, reduce the heat to a simmer, and steam until the asparagus is tender, about 5 minutes.

2. While the asparagus is cooking, make the dressing: On a cutting board, combine the tarragon and parsley and finely chop them together. Place in a bowl, add the chives, mustard, vinegar, and cream, and whisk until well combined. (The dressing will be thick.)

3. To serve, arrange the asparagus spears on a serving platter and spoon the dressing over them.

SERVES 6

PREPPING IN ADVANCE: The asparagus can be steamed early on the day of serving. Let cool, cover, and refrigerate. Remove 30 minutes before serving to come to room temperature. Then make the dressing and serve.

NOTE: We don't recommend trying to store this to serve a second time because the asparagus discolors, turning a muddy shade of green, on account of the vinegar in the dressing. If you think you may have more asparagus than you need, dress some, not all of it. You can always add to the platter, if need be.

Whole Roasted Beet Salad with Orange Moroccan Dressing

The flavor of the beets in this salad is measurably better when you roast them whole; then cut them up. The dressing is only a little sparky, even with the harissa—Tunisian hot chili sauce, available in specialty markets. (It is also good on roasted yams or fennel.) When it comes to looking great on a buffet table, few other vegetables beat out beets.

1½ pounds beets

FOR THE DRESSING

½ cup orange juice

3 tablespoons extra-virgin olive oil

½ teaspoon harissa

¼ teaspoon ground cumin

¼ teaspoon sweet paprika

⅛ teaspoon ground cinnamon

⅛ teaspoon ground allspice

1 teaspoon salt

1 teaspoon freshly ground black pepper

1. Preheat the oven to 350 degrees F.

2. Trim off the greens and stems on the beets; then wash the beets well. If they are small, place 2 or 3 on a square of aluminum foil and wrap; larger beets should be wrapped individually. Place the packets on a baking sheet and roast until tender, about 45 minutes. Remove from the oven and let cool in the foil.

3. Make the dressing: Pour the orange juice in a medium bowl, and stir in the remaining dressing ingredients, and continue stirring until well combined.

4. Peel the beets and dice into bite-sized pieces. Put in a serving bowl, pour the dressing over them, and toss gently to combine.

SERVES 6

PREPPING IN ADVANCE: The beets can be roasted 24 hours ahead. Let cool and store, still in the foil, in the refrigerator. The next day, peel and dice them.

Roasted Brussels Sprouts with Red Onion and Thyme

If you have never roasted Brussels sprouts, try this recipe—a good one any time in the fall, and especially for Thanksgiving.

3 pounds Brussels sprouts

3 tablespoons extra-virgin olive oil

2 tablespoons white wine

1 teaspoon dried thyme

Salt

Freshly ground black pepper

2 medium red onions

1. Preheat the oven to 375 degrees F. Bring a large pot of salted water to a boil.

2. Trim the stems on the Brussels sprouts. Add the sprouts to the boiling water, and blanch for 5 minutes. Drain.

3. In a medium bowl, toss the sprouts with some of the olive oil, just to coat, white wine, thyme and salt and pepper to taste. Place the sprouts on a baking sheet.

4. Peel the red onions and slice them into ¼-inch-thick rounds. Toss with the remaining olive oil and salt and pepper. Place the onions in a single layer on another baking sheet.

5. Roast the sprouts until tender and browned, about 20 minutes; roast the onion slices until browned and tender, too, about 30 minutes.

6. When ready to eat, put the sprouts in a serving bowl, add the roasted onions, and toss to combine.

SERVES 6

PREPPING IN ADVANCE: You can roast the sprouts and red onions several hours ahead of serving. Let cool, combine in a large bowl, and hold at room temperature.

Pan-Seared Cauliflower with Pecan Bread Crumbs

The topping here is loosely based on the French butter sauce, polonaise, except that olive oil substitutes for butter. What lies behind the addition of the pecans? Serendipity—another culinary tradition.

Plan on making this no more than 1 hour before serving. You don't want the crumbs, a large part of the pleasure when fresh, to become soggy. For how to get a jumpstart on prepping the ingredients, go to the end of the recipe.

1 cup pecan pieces

1 large head of cauliflower, about 1½ to 2 pounds

1 cup dried unseasoned bread crumbs

3 tablespoons extra-virgin olive oil

1. Preheat the oven to 350 degrees F.

2. Spread the pecans on a small baking sheet and toast them, stirring once, for 10 minutes, or until fragrant. Let cool.

3. Meanwhile, bring a large pot of salted water to a boil. Drop the cauliflower florets into the boiling water and blanch several minutes until crisp-tender; drain.

4. In a food processor, process the pecans and bread crumbs until the mixture is ground medium-fine.

5. Heat the olive oil in a large skillet over medium heat. When the oil is hot and starting to sizzle, add the cauliflower. Cook, stirring, for several minutes, until the cauliflower turns a golden brown.

6. Add the pecan and bread crumb mixture and stir to combine; cook 1 minute. Transfer the crumbed cauliflower to a serving bowl.

SERVES 6

PREPPING IN ADVANCE: Toast the pecans 1 day ahead. Let cool and store in an airtight container at room temperature.

Break the cauliflower into florets in advance and store them in a covered container in the refrigerator until cooking time.

Assemble the dish no more than 1 hour in advance.

Variation

Pan-Seared Cauliflower with Pancetta and Black Olive Sauce

For an entirely different combination of flavors and colors, blanch and pan-sear the florets as above (steps 3 and 5). Omit the pecan crumbs and top with Pancetta and Black Olive Sauce (page 365).

Caesar Salad

Caesar salad makes a very serviceable main course, first course, or small serving alongside other salads. It is marvelously flavorful (even without anchovies in the dressing, which we have included here, by the way) and filled with toothsome textures. Needless to say, it is incredibly popular and is always inviting on a buffet table. There are several considerations for making it successfully:

- Use the tender inner leaves, the hearts, of the romaine. The outer leaves are tough and unsuitable. Be sure that the leaves are well dried after a careful rinsing.

- Good Parmigiano-Reggiano is a must. It is a large flavor component. Just as important is when to add it: at the end, just before the croutons, so that it does not have a chance to absorb a lot of dressing before the salad is served.

- Classic Caesar dressing contains raw egg. Raw ingredients should not be left to stand at room temperature for any length of time. In short, once assembled, the salad should be served and enjoyed.

This recipe, in particular, is ideal for a large party or gathering. The yield is generous, and each of the components—the lettuce, dressing, and croutons—can be prepared in advance.

12 cups loosely packed 2-inch pieces of tender romaine lettuce leaves (about 3 heads)

FOR THE DRESSING

1 large egg

1 garlic clove

4 anchovy fillets packed in oil

2 tablespoons Worcestershire sauce

½ teaspoon dry mustard

½ teaspoon salt

1 teaspoon freshly ground black pepper

¾ cup extra-virgin olive oil

⅓ cup fresh lemon juice

¾ cup freshly grated Parmigiano-Reggiano

1 cup Croutons (page 361)

1. Have ready a large salad bowl, preferably a wooden one, with tongs.

2. Make the dressing: Place the egg, still in its shell, in a cup and cover it with warm water.

3. Peel, trim, and finely dice the garlic.

4. In the salad bowl, using a fork, crush the anchovies together with the Worcestershire sauce to start a paste. Add the garlic and mustard and stir to combine. Add the salt and pepper and mash to incorporate.

5. Break the slightly warmed egg into a small bowl. Using a wire whisk, add the egg to the anchovy mixture, whisking until thoroughly blended. Continue whisking, and add the olive oil in a slow stream. Whisk until it is incorporated. Whisk in the lemon juice in the same manner. (You will have 1½ cups dressing.)

6. Assemble the salad: Add the lettuce to the salad bowl and, using tongs, toss it, turning the leaves over from the bottom of the bowl to the top to coat them with dressing. Sprinkle with the Parmigiano and then the croutons. Serve at once.

SERVES 6 GENEROUSLY

PREPPING IN ADVANCE: The lettuce can be washed, dried, and cut into pieces 1 day ahead of time. Be sure that it is dry before storing it in plastic bags in the refrigerator.

The dressing can be made in a bowl, tightly covered, and stored in the refrigerator for 2 to 3 days.

As long as the croutons are stored in an airtight container, they can be made up to 1 week in advance of using.

That said, it is best to assemble this salad just before serving and to serve it immediately.

Corn and Roasted Potatoes with Poblano Chile

This combines two of our favorite vegetables with a mildly spicy fresh chile pepper and crème fraîche. Each of the components can be prepared ahead, but wait to combine them until just before serving for the very best in both flavor and texture. This dish is not a keeper, which gives some of us more incentive than we need to overindulge! Simple and unadulterated, it doesn't get better than this.

3 ears fresh corn

2 tablespoons extra-virgin olive oil, plus additional for roasting

½ teaspoon salt, plus extra for seasoning

Freshly ground black pepper

1 large poblano chile pepper

1¼ pounds white new or Yukon gold potatoes

2 tablespoons chopped cilantro

½ cup crème fraîche

1. Shuck the corn and remove the silk. Holding each ear of corn upright on a cutting board and starting from the tip, slice off the kernels, cutting as close to the cob as possible.

2. In a saucepan, sauté the corn kernels in the 2 tablespoons of olive oil over medium heat for 2 minutes. Season with the salt and a few grinds of pepper. Set aside.

3. Char the skin on the poblano pepper over a gas burner, on a medium-hot grill, or under the broiler about 3 inches from the heat, turning frequently, until blackened all over. Transfer the pepper to a plate and let cool. When cool enough to handle, with your hands or the dull side of a knife, remove the charred skin. (It is okay to leave some of the charred bits intact—they add flavor.) Seed and cut into ½-inch squares. Reserve.

4. Preheat the oven to 400 degrees F.

5. Scrub the potatoes and cut them into ½-inch-thick wedges. Put in a bowl, add enough olive oil to coat, and season with salt and pepper to taste. Spread the potatoes in a single layer on a baking sheet and roast for 30 minutes. Let cool for 5 minutes on the baking sheet.

6. To serve, transfer the potatoes to a serving bowl and add the corn, diced charred poblano, cilantro, and crème fraîche, and toss to combine. Serve within the hour.

SERVES 6

PREPPING IN ADVANCE: Store the corn kernels, uncooked, in a plastic bag in the refrigerator up to 1 day before using.

Scrub and cut the potatoes into wedges, place them in a pan of water to cover, and store in the refrigerator 1 day in advance as well. Be sure to pat the potatoes dry with paper towels before oiling and seasoning them for roasting.

Char, seed, and dice the poblano chile the night before using. Cover and store in the refrigerator.

Corn and Oven-Burst Cherry Tomatoes and Cilantro-Lime Dressing

This is a true summer salad, best made with just-picked corn and tomatoes.

1. Preheat the oven to 400 degrees F.

2. Shuck the corn and remove the silk. Holding each ear of corn upright on a cutting board and starting from the tip, slice off the kernels, cutting as close to the cob as possible. Place the corn in a large bowl and toss with a little olive oil (just enough to coat), and salt and pepper to taste. Spread the corn on a baking sheet and roast until the kernels just start to brown, approximately 15 minutes. Let cool on the baking sheet.

3. Oil, season, and place the cherry tomatoes on a separate baking sheet in the same manner as the corn; roast for 15 minutes, until the skins burst and the tomatoes start to collapse. Let cool on the baking sheet.

4. Peel, trim, and dice the red onion and place it in a large serving bowl. Add the roasted corn and tomatoes, cilantro, the ¼ cup of olive oil, the lime juice, and salt and pepper to taste, and toss gently to combine.

6 large ears fresh corn

¼ cup extra-virgin olive oil, plus extra for roasting the vegetables

Salt

Freshly ground black pepper

1 pint cherry tomatoes

1 medium red onion

2 tablespoons coarsely chopped cilantro

Juice of 2 limes

SERVES 6

PREPPING IN ADVANCE: The corn and tomatoes can be roasted the morning of serving. Let cool, cover with plastic wrap, and hold at room temperature.

Assemble the salad as directed in step 4 just before serving.

Cucumber, Avocado, Scallion, and Lime Salad

Crisp cucumbers, smooth avocados, and the bite of fresh lime make a wonderful combination. This is simple to prepare and best made at the last minute. It goes beautifully with simply grilled or roasted fish and is exquisite with the Mexican-inspired red snapper we suggest below.

1. Peel the cucumbers, slice each lengthwise, and halve the slices. Cut out the seeds on each slice; then cut the cucumber crosswise into half-moons. Put in a ceramic or glass serving bowl.

2. Cut each avocado in half, remove the pit, and with a small spoon, scoop out the flesh, and place in the bowl with the cucumbers.

3. Add the scallions, lime juice, and olive oil, toss to combine, and season with salt and cracked pepper. Serve immediately.

SERVES 6

3 cucumbers

3 ripe Hass avocados

¼ cup chopped scallions (white and green parts)

Juice of 2 limes

¼ cup extra-virgin olive oil

Salt

Freshly cracked black pepper (see Note, page 167)

SERVE WITH: Pan-Fried Ancho Chile–Rubbed Red Snapper (page 309).

Grilled Fennel, Black Olive, and Golden Raisin Salad

This is a fabulous salad, with all kinds of different textures, flavors, and colors. It warrants pointing out that it goes beautifully with the orange-marinated salmon we suggest below. From a purely practical point of view, if you do decide to pair them, you can use the grill to cook both. Add another dish, a grain or bean salad, and you have a very appealing menu for an al fresco dinner for family or friends.

3 medium fennel bulbs, about 12 ounces each

1 teaspoon extra-virgin olive oil

Salt

Freshly cracked black pepper (see Note, page 167)

1 cup pitted kalamata olives

¾ cup golden raisins

Juice of ½ lemon

SERVE WITH: Grilled Orange-Marinated Salmon (page 310).

1. Preheat the grill or broiler.

2. Trim each fennel bulb: Cut off the fronds and pare the ends. Cut into a "fan" by slicing it top to bottom into ¼-inch-thick slices, being careful to keep the bulb attached at the stem end.

3. Brush the fennel all over with the olive oil and season with salt and cracked pepper. To grill: Place the fennel on the grill and grill until crisp-tender, turning when needed, about 3 minutes on each side. To broil: Place the fennel on a broiler pan and broil, 6 inches from the heat, for 5 minutes without turning.

4. Transfer the fennel to a serving bowl and add the olives, raisins, and lemon juice. Toss gently to combine.

SERVES 6

PREPPING IN ADVANCE: The salad can be completed up to 4 hours ahead. Cover and hold at room temperature until serving time.

Roasted Fennel with Parmigiano

Fennel is crisp when raw and tastes of licorice. When roasted, it mellows in flavor, but maintains a nice firmness, which is complemented here with just a simple dusting of Parmigiano. The key to preventing Parimigiano from drying out in the refrigerator? Don't buy too large a piece: The smaller the chunk, the faster it is used, the fresher it stays.

3 medium fennel bulbs, about 1 pound each

2 tablespoons extra-virgin olive oil

1 teaspoon salt

1 teaspoon freshly ground black pepper

½ cup coarsely grated Parmigiano-Reggiano cheese

1. Preheat the oven to 400 degrees F.

2. Trim the fennel bulbs, cutting off the fronds, and cut the bulbs in half; then cut into ¼-inch-thick slices from top to bottom. Place in a bowl and toss with the olive oil, salt, and pepper. Spread the fennel in a single layer on a baking pan and roast 15 minutes.

3. Sprinkle the Parmigiano over the fennel and roast 10 to15 minutes longer, until the fennel starts to brown. Remove and serve at room temperature.

SERVES 6

PREPPING IN ADVANCE: The fennel may be completed several hours in advance of serving. Let cool, cover, and hold at room temperature.

If you are really pressed for time, trim and slice the fennel the day before and store it, covered, in the refrigerator overnight. Follow the directions for roasting it in steps 2 and 3.

Green Bean Salad

At Mangia, we frequently serve this salad on a platter and top it with the stuffed chicken breasts we suggest below. That presentation, in particular, makes a very handsome centerpiece for a summer buffet. Add sliced tomatoes, wine, good bread, and enjoy!.

3 shallots

1 lemon

1½ pounds green beans

6 cups water

1 teaspoon salt

3 tablespoons extra-virgin olive oil

1 tablespoon sherry vinegar

2 tablespoons chopped flat-leaf parsley

SERVE WITH: Roasted Herb-Stuffed Chicken Breasts (page 335).

1. Peel, trim, and mince the shallots. Place in a small bowl and juice the lemon over them. Toss and set aside while cooking the beans.

2. Wash and trim the beans; cut off the stem ends only.

3. Bring the water with the salt to a boil in a medium saucepan over medium-high heat. Reduce the heat to medium, add the beans, and blanch for about 3 minutes. Drain and run under cold water to stop the cooking and set the color. Drain well.

4. Squeeze the shallots of all lemon juice. Put in a serving bowl with the olive oil, vinegar, and parsley; stir to combine.

5. About 1 hour before you plan to serve the beans, add them to the dressing and toss to combine.

SERVES 6

PREPPING IN ADVANCE: Cook the beans several hours ahead of time. Cover and store in the refrigerator.

Make the dressing and add the beans about 1 hour before serving.

Parmigiano-Baked Portobello Mushrooms with Oregano Crust

These are good right out of the oven, or make them several hours ahead for serving at a buffet. They also make a great sandwich filling.

2 garlic cloves

½ cup extra-virgin olive oil

¼ cup finely chopped oregano

Salt

Freshly ground black pepper

6 large portobello mushroom caps, 4 inches in diameter

1 cup coarsely grated Parmigiano-Reggiano cheese (grated on the largest holes of a box grater)

1. Preheat the oven to 400 degrees F.

2. Peel, trim, and mince the garlic.

3. In a bowl, combine the olive oil, garlic, oregano, and salt and pepper to taste. Lay the mushroom caps, stem side up, on a baking sheet and brush with the oregano oil. Bake for approximately 15 minutes.

4. Sprinkle the caps with the grated Parmigiano and bake 5 minutes, until the cheese is melted and golden.

SERVES 6

PREPPING IN ADVANCE: The mushrooms can be completed up to 2 hours ahead. Let stand at room temperature until serving time.

Grilled Portobello Mushrooms with Parsley Pesto

Portobello mushrooms are so meaty in texture that they are often thought of as the vegetarian answer to steak. In other words, serve this as main course or side dish. Easy as is, this can be made easier still: Substitute classic pesto, made with basil, from the jar.

6 large portobello mushroom caps, 3 inches each in diameter

2 tablespoons extra-virgin olive oil

Salt

Freshly ground black pepper

Parsley Pesto (page 363)

If you do have time, there is a way to enhance this already lovely combination. Add a dozen or so roasted shallots (see page 373) to the platter.

1. Preheat the grill or broiler.

2. Brush the portobellos with the olive oil and season with salt and pepper to taste. Place the mushrooms, stem side up, on a medium-hot grill or under the broiler, about 5 inches from the heat, and grill or broil about 5 minutes. Turn and cook 3 minutes more. Set aside to cool.

3. Arrange the grilled portobellos on a serving platter and serve the pesto in a bowl alongside.

SERVES 6

PREPPING IN ADVANCE: The pesto can be made up to 1 week in advance. Cover and store in the refrigerator. Let stand at room temperature 1 hour before serving.

The mushrooms can be grilled several hours ahead. Let cool, cover, and hold at room temperature.

Orange and Arugula Salad

This salad is as refreshing as it is pretty and goes with any number of different types of foods—fish, meat, poultry—especially rich ones. We are particularly partial to it when served with the swordfish we suggest below.

1 pound arugula

4 navel oranges

½ red onion

6 tablespoons extra-virgin olive oil

2 tablespoons fresh lemon juice

Salt

Freshly cracked black pepper (see Note, page 167)

SERVE WITH: Pan-Fried Cajun Swordfish (page 313).

1. Trim the stems off the arugula. Wash the leaves in several changes of cold water and pat dry.

2. With a sharp knife, cut the top and bottom off each orange. Starting at the top and continuing down to the bottom, following the contour of the fruit, cut off the peel and pith (the white membranes). Cut the oranges crosswise into ¼-inch-thick slices.

3. Cut the red onion into ⅛-inch-thick slices. Separate the slices into rings.

4. Just before serving, combine the arugula and the orange and onion slices in a large serving bowl. Drizzle with the olive oil and lemon juice, and season with salt and cracked pepper to taste.

SERVES 6

PREPPING IN ADVANCE: As long as the arugula is well dried, it can be stored in a plastic bag in the refrigerator 1 day ahead of time.

The oranges can also be peeled and sliced 1 day ahead. Store in a tightly covered container in the refrigerator. They will give off juice. Use some of it to sprinkle over the salad.

Charred Red Bell Peppers Stuffed with Mozzarella, Prosciutto, and Olives

Try to find fresh mozzarella for this recipe. Its creamy, supple quality melds beautifully with the caramel-sweet peppers and salty prosciutto. Leftovers make tasty sandwiches. In fact, these peppers should be served with wonderful crusty bread.

6 large red bell peppers, roasted and cooled (see page 193)

¾ to 1 pound mozzarella

6 thin slices prosciutto

12 pitted kalamata olives, cut in half

1. When the whole peppers are cool enough to handle, with your fingers or the dull side of a knife, remove the blackened skin on each. Cut off the tops of the peppers and remove the seeds. (The peppers will be very soft.) Leave them whole.

2. Preheat the oven to 400 degrees F. Oil a baking pan lightly.

3. Slice the mozzarella into approximately ⅜-inch-thick slices. Place 1 slice of the mozzarella inside each pepper. Drape a slice of prosciutto on top of the mozzarella and top with 4 olive halves.

4. Place the stuffed peppers in the baking pan and heat them just until the cheese softens, about 5 minutes. Serve immediately or at room temperature.

SERVES 6

PREPPING IN ADVANCE: The peppers can be roasted and seeded the morning of the day they are to be served. Let cool, cover, and store in the refrigerator. Remove 1 hour before stuffing and finishing.

Potato Salad with Roasted Prosciutto, String Beans, and Olives

By roasting prosciutto, you end up with a salty crisp strip, like bacon. It crumbles nicely and adds to this European-style rendition of the great summer standby.

1½ pounds red-skinned potatoes (about 4 large)

FOR THE VINAIGRETTE

¼ cup plus 2 tablespoons extra-virgin olive oil

2 tablespoons red wine vinegar

1 tablespoon minced shallot

½ teaspoon minced garlic

1 tablespoon Dijon mustard

2 ounces prosciutto, thinly sliced

4 ounces slender string beans

¼ cup pitted kalamata olives

¼ cup coarsely chopped flat-leaf parsley

1. Wash the potatoes and cut them into ¼-inch-thick slices. Cook the sliced potatoes in boiling salted water until tender but not falling apart, about 10 minutes.

2. While the potatoes are cooking, make the vinaigrette: In a large bowl, combine all the ingredients.

3. Drain the potatoes in a colander. While they are still warm, add them to the vinaigrette, tossing gently to coat. Set aside to cool.

4. Preheat the oven to 350 degrees F.

5. Arrange the prosciutto slices in a single layer on a baking sheet. Roast until brown and crisp, about 10 minutes. Set aside to cool.

6. Trim the string beans and cut them in half. Blanch the beans in boiling salted water for 3 minutes Drain in a colander and cool under cold running water. Drain thoroughly.

7. Crumble the prosciutto into the potato salad. Add the string beans, olives, and parsley and toss to combine. Leftover salad will keep, covered, in the refrigerator for 1 day.

SERVES 6

PREPPING IN ADVANCE: The prosciutto can be roasted 1 day ahead. Let cool, wrap tightly in plastic wrap, and refrigerate.

Dress the potato salad 1 day in advance as well. Cover and store in the refrigerator. One half hour before serving, finish the salad as directed in step 7.

Roasted Potatoes and Eggplant with Sun-Dried Tomato Salsina

Buttery Yukon potatoes go nicely with rich roasted eggplant and a sun-dried tomato sauce. If Yukon potatoes are not available, red-skinned potatoes can be substituted.

You can make the preparation very easy for yourself: Either roast the egg-plant the day before or roast it at the same time that you roast the potatoes, which should be about 2 hours before serving. That way you can hold the roasted vegetables at room temperature, no refrigeration needed, which is unquestionably the best option when it comes to maintaining flavor and texture.

1½ pounds Yukon gold potatoes

2 tablespoons extra-virgin olive oil, plus ¼ cup

1 teaspoon salt

½ teaspoon freshly ground black pepper

4 ounces sun-dried tomatoes

1 garlic clove, peeled

1 tablespoon balsamic vinegar

1 large eggplant, about 1½ pounds, cubed and roasted (see page 196)

1 tablespoon chopped thyme

3 tablespoons freshly grated Parmigiano-Reggiano cheese

1. Preheat the oven to 400 degrees F. Have ready a large baking sheet.

2. Wash, then cut the potatoes into 1½-inch chunks. Toss them with 2 table-spoons of the olive oil, the salt, and pepper. Spread the potatoes on the baking sheet and roast until golden, 35 to 40 minutes. Let cool on the baking sheet.

3. Soak the sun-dried tomatoes in hot water to cover for 10 minutes. Drain and put in a food processor with the garlic and vinegar. Process until fairly smooth. With the machine running, add the remaining ¼ cup olive oil and process until incorporated.

4. Put the roasted potatoes and eggplant and the sun-dried tomato salsina in a large serving bowl. Add the fresh thyme and Parmigiano and toss to combine. Best served within 2 hours of assembling.

SERVES 6

PREPPING IN ADVANCE: The salsina can be completed 1 day ahead. Transfer it to a bowl, cover tightly, and refrigerate.

The eggplant cubes can also be roasted 1 day in advance. Store, covered, in the refrigerator. Bring to room temperature before using.

Grilled Radicchio with Parmigiano Shavings and Anchovy Croutons

This is a variation on the classic Caesar Salad (page 209), with grilled radicchio replacing the traditional romaine. By grilling radicchio, a red-leafed chicory, you lose some of its slightly bitter taste. You can also pan-sear it, if you like. The radicchio is best grilled shortly before serving. The croutons and cheese, though, can both be prepared ahead of time. And even if you are not all that keen on anchovies, try the croutons once. You won't believe the amount of flavor they add to a salad.

1 small loaf of stale country-style bread or ½ baguette

1 cup extra-virgin olive oil, plus additional for grilling

2 garlic cloves, peeled

4 anchovy fillets packed in oil

3 large heads radicchio

Salt

Freshly ground black pepper

1 piece Parmigiano-Reggiano cheese, 3 ounces

Juice of 2 lemons

1. Preheat the oven to 325 degrees F.

2. Cut the bread into 1-inch cubes. (You will need 4 cups.)

3. In a food processor, combine 1 cup of the olive oil, the garlic cloves, and anchovies and process to a paste. Scrape the paste into a wide bowl, add the bread cubes, and toss to coat. Spread the bread cubes on a baking sheet and bake, turning them halfway through baking, until the croutons are golden and crisp, about 30 minutes. Let cool.

4. Preheat the grill or heat a large skillet or grill pan on the stove top.

5. Remove the core from each head of radicchio and separate the leaves. Toss the leaves with a little extra-virgin olive oil and salt and pepper to taste.

Place the leaves on the rack of the grill over a medium-hot fire and grill just until they start to wilt, about 3 minutes, turning as needed. Remove as done with long-handled tongs and let cool.

If pan-searing or grilling on the stove top: Place as many leaves as will fit without crowding in the pan or on the grill pan and cook over high heat until they start to wilt, turning as needed. Remove with tongs and let cool.

6. Put the grilled radicchio in a large bowl and juice the lemons, through a strainer, over it.

7. Using a vegetable peeler or box grater, cut the Parmigiano into shavings and add them to the radicchio. Add the croutons and a grinding of fresh black pepper to taste. Transfer the salad to a platter and serve immediately.

SERVES 6

PREPPING IN ADVANCE: The anchovy croutons can be made 4 hours ahead. Cover and store at room temperature.

The Parmigiano shavings can also be cut on the morning of the day you plan to serve the salad. (They can be fragile, so handle them delicately.) Store, tightly covered, in the refrigerator. Remove 30 minutes or so before using to let them come to full flavor before adding them to the salad.

Roasted Butternut Squash with Mint and Brown Sugar Sauce

This is a colorful combination for fall dining and makes a good accompaniment to turkey or lamb. The squash rounds are very tasty as a leftover, too: Slip them into sandwiches—as in post-Thanksgiving turkey sandwiches—or cut them up and add them to a pasta salad, along with a salty cheese, like ricotta salata.

1 garlic clove

2 tablespoons extra-virgin olive oil

¼ cup apple cider vinegar

3 tablespoons light brown sugar

1 butternut squash, 3½ pounds, peeled, seeded, cut into ½-inch-thick slices, and roasted (see page 200)

¼ cup coarsely chopped mint leaves

1. Peel and slice the garlic clove.

2. In a large skillet, heat the olive oil with the garlic and cook, stirring, until it starts to brown. Add the vinegar and brown sugar. Bring the mixture to a boil and cook over high heat until reduced by half.

3. Add the roasted butternut squash slices and toss to coat. Transfer the squash to a serving bowl and sprinkle the mint leaves on top.

SERVES 6

PREPPING IN ADVANCE: The squash can be roasted 4 hours ahead. Let cool, cover, and hold at room temperature.

Make the sauce and finish the dish as directed in step 3 just before serving.

Fresh Tomato Salad with Mint Pesto

Classic Pesto (page 362) is made with basil. Mint, which is in the same family, also makes a tasty sauce. Use it as a dressing, as we do here, or as a dip for steamed vegetables, or as a spread on sandwiches.

There are a couple of key factors to serving marvelous-tasting tomatoes: Start with the best tomatoes you can find, preferably luscious and truly ripe, and do not under any circumstances refrigerate them before using.

FOR THE MINT PESTO

1 cup firmly packed mint leaves

2 garlic cloves

2 tablespoons pine nuts (pignoli)

1 teaspoon salt

½ teaspoon freshly ground black pepper

½ to ⅔ cup extra-virgin olive oil

6 medium-sized ripe beefsteak tomatoes

1. Wash the mint leaves and pat them dry.

2. In a food processor, combine the mint leaves, garlic, pine nuts, salt, and pepper. With the machine running, gradually add the olive oil in a thin stream. Add just enough oil (about ½ cup) so that the sauce has a consistency that can be spooned.

3. Wash, core, and slice the tomatoes ¼ inch thick. Arrange the tomato slices, overlapping them slightly, on a serving platter. With a spoon, drizzle the pesto over the tomatoes. The salad can stand up to 1 hour at room temperature before serving.

SERVES 6

PREPPING IN ADVANCE: The pesto can be made 1 day ahead of time. Spoon it into a container, cover, and refrigerate.

Tomato Salad

At the height of summer, it is always fun to use heirloom tomatoes in this glorious combination. If you haven't a farmer's market nearby where heirlooms are sometimes available, no matter. Simply choose the reddest, ripest tomatoes you can find. Good-quality olive oil is a plus here, too, but you don't have to go overboard. The point of this simple salad? Delicious ingredients, in season, simply prepared. Serve this with almost anything you like. A crust of wonderful bread will do.

3 large ripe beefsteak tomatoes

1 red onion

1 cup loosely packed basil leaves

Salt

Freshly ground black pepper

Extra-virgin olive oil

1. Wash the tomatoes and pat them dry. Peel, trim, and finely dice the red onion. Rinse the basil leaves, pat them dry, and chop.

2. Cut the tomatoes into ¼-inch-thick wedges and put them in a shallow serving bowl. Scatter the red onion and basil over the top and season with salt and pepper to taste. Just before serving, drizzle olive oil over the salad, toss gently to coat, and serve.

SERVES 6

PREPPING IN ADVANCE: Wash the tomatoes and let them drain in a colander at room temperature.

Rinse the basil leaves, pat them dry, and store in a plastic bag in the refrigerator.

Given how very simple this salad is to prepare, wait to finish preparing the ingredients and combining them until serving time. A salad like this tastes best fresh.

Cherry Tomato, Sautéed Leek, and Pine Nut Salad

Silky sautéed leeks, lots of toasted pine nuts, and firm whole cherry tomatoes make this colorful and a good accompaniment for simply grilled fish or poultry. We are partial to pairing it with salmon, although that is only one of the many possibilities a salad like this presents. Match it as you like, with a whole host of other salads even, but don't expect there to be leftovers, because there won't be.

1 cup pine nuts (pignoli)

3 large leeks

½ cup extra-virgin olive oil

1 pint cherry tomatoes

3 tablespoons coarsely chopped tarragon

Juice of 1 lemon

SERVE WITH: Roasted Salmon (page 312).

1. Preheat the oven to 325 degrees F.

2. Spread the pine nuts on a baking sheet and toast them, stirring occasionally, for about 5 minutes, until golden brown. Let cool.

3. Remove the tough outer leaves and root end on each of the leeks. Cut the white and pale green part of the leeks into 1-inch rings. Place them in a large colander and wash thoroughly under cold running water to remove all grit and sand. Dry well with paper towels.

4. Heat ¼ cup of the olive oil in a large skillet. Add the leeks and sauté them over medium heat, stirring, until wilted, but do not let them brown. Let cool.

5. In a serving bowl, combine the sautéed leeks, tomatoes, toasted pine nuts, remaining ¼ cup of olive oil, tarragon, and lemon juice and toss gently to combine. Serve within 2 hours of assembling.

SERVES 6

PREPPING IN ADVANCE: The most time-consuming part of this entire recipe is the thorough washing, slicing, and drying of the leeks. Do that the day before. Put the slices in a bowl, cover tightly, and refrigerate.

Sauté the leeks and assemble the salad as directed in steps 4 and 5.

Yam and Fennel Salad

Yams and fennel are not often combined. Each is, however, a traditional fall vegetable. Here we roast them, combine them, and suggest you serve them with another fall tradition, turkey—specifically, our Spicy Marinated Roasted Turkey Breast (page 340). You will be surprised at just how compatible the flavors and textures are. In addition, the vegetables can be readied and even roasted in advance—a big plus when it comes to holiday menus.

1 garlic clove

½ cup extra-virgin olive oil

Pinch of ground cinnamon

4 medium yams

1 fennel bulb, about 1 pound

3 tablespoons sherry vinegar

Chopped flat-leaf parsley, for garnish

1. Preheat the oven to 400 degrees F. Have ready 2 large baking sheets.

2. Peel and finely dice the garlic. Put the garlic in a small bowl or container and stir in the olive oil and cinnamon.

3. Peel the yams and cut them into ½-inch-thick rounds. Arrange the yam slices on one of the baking sheets.

4. Trim the fennel bulb, cutting off the fronds and stem end, and cut it lengthwise into thin slices. Place the fennel on the other baking sheet.

5. Divide the seasoned oil between the yams and fennel, drizzling it over the slices on each sheet. Roast the vegetables for 30 to 45 minutes, or until the edges of the yams and fennel caramelize. Let cool.

6. Combine the roasted vegetables in a large bowl, toss with the vinegar, and sprinkle the parsley on top. Serve within 2 hours of assembling.

SERVES 6

PREPPING IN ADVANCE: Both the fennel and yams can be cut up the day before serving. Store separately in plastic bags in the refrigerator.

You can roast the vegetables up to 4 hours before serving. Let cool, cover lightly, and hold at room temperature.

Up to 2 hours before serving, finish the dish as directed in step 6.

Roasted Yams with Curried Apples

We've candied yams with honey, and added a twist or two. Harissa, a Tunisian hot chile sauce available in specialty markets, adds a kick of heat, and citrus lends aroma. You will save yourself the chore of having to wash sticky baking sheets if you line them with parchment paper before roasting the yams and apples. If you don't have it, consider lining them with foil, shiny side down, instead.

3 large yams, about 1 pound each

¼ cup honey

¼ cup plus 2 tablespoons extra-virgin olive oil

3 tablespoons orange juice

1 tablespoon harissa

2 Granny Smith apples, 12 ounces each

1 teaspoon curry powder

½ teaspoon ground turmeric

½ teaspoon ground cinnamon

1 tablespoon freshly grated orange zest

1. Preheat the oven to 400 degrees F. Line 2 baking sheets with parchment paper or aluminum foil, shiny side down.

2. Peel, quarter, and slice the yams ½ inch thick.

3. In a shallow bowl, combine 3 tablespoons of the honey, 3 tablespoons of the olive oil, the orange juice, and harissa, stirring well to dissolve the honey. Add the sliced yams and toss to coat.

4. Core the apples and cut them into ½-inch-thick wedges.

5. In another shallow bowl, combine the remaining 3 tablespoons of olive oil, the remaining 1 tablespoon of honey, the curry powder, turmeric, and cinnamon and stir to blend. Add the apples and toss to coat.

6. Spread the yams on one baking sheet, the apples on the other. Roast the apples for 20 minutes; the yams, about 30 minutes, until tender. Let each cool on the baking sheet.

7. Combine the yams and apples in a serving bowl and garnish with the orange zest. Best served within 1 hour of assembling.

SERVES 6

PREPPING IN ADVANCE: Both the yams and apples can be cut up 1 day ahead. Store separately in plastic bags in the refrigerator.

The yams and apples can be roasted 4 hours in advance of serving. Let cool, cover lightly, and hold at room temperature.

Up to 1 hour before serving, complete the dish as directed in step 7.

Grilled Whole Baby Zucchini with Fresh Tomato and Herb Salsa

Zucchini is, at best, a bland foil for all kinds of fuller flavored ingredients. Here baby zucchini has a tender crispness that is offset by a sprightly tomato salsa. Baby pattypan squash can be used in place of the zucchini or in addition to it. A wire cooling rack placed on top of the grill makes it easier to cook the tiny squash and prevents them from falling into the coals. Or use a grill basket.

1. Make the salsa: Wash the tomatoes and cut in half from top to bottom. Slice the tomatoes ¼ inch thick, then cut the slices into fine dice. Peel, trim, and mince the garlic.

2. In a bowl, stir together the tomatoes, garlic, herbs, scallions, and vinegar and add salt and pepper to taste.

3. Preheat the grill or the broiler.

4. Wash the zucchini and pat it dry. In a bowl, toss the zucchini with the olive oil and salt and pepper to taste.

FOR THE SALSA

1 pound ripe tomatoes

1 garlic clove

2 tablespoons chopped dill

2 tablespoons chopped flat-leaf parsley leaves

1 tablespoon chopped oregano

1 cup chopped scallions (green and white parts; about 1 bunch)

1 teaspoon balsamic vinegar

Salt

Freshly ground black pepper

1½ pounds baby zucchini

2 tablespoons extra-virgin olive oil

Salt

Freshly ground black pepper

5. To grill the zucchini: Arrange them on the rack over a medium-hot fire and grill them, turning with tongs to ensure even cooking, until lightly charred. Arrange the hot zucchini on a serving platter.

To broil: Arrange the zucchini on a baking sheet and broil, about 6 inches from the heat, for 4 minutes. Transfer to a serving platter.

6. Serve the salsa in a bowl alongside the platter of grilled zucchini.

SERVES 6

PREPPING IN ADVANCE: The zucchini can be cooked 4 hours ahead. Let cool, cover lightly, and hold at room temperature.

The salsa is best made the morning of the day you plan to serve it. Cover and refrigerate. Remove 1 hour before serving to allow it to come to room temperature.

PASTA

Cavatappi with Roasted Tomatoes
and Fresh Ricotta

Couscous with Moroccan Vegetables

Farfalle with Sautéed Greens,
Lemon, and Pecorino
Romano Cheese

Fusilli with Pesto, Sautéed Leeks,
and Oyster Mushrooms

Gemelli with Spinach, Radicchio,
Escarole, and Aged Provolone

Orecchiette with Broccoli and
Cauliflower in Saffron Sauce

Orecchiette with Roasted Vegetables,
Fresh Herbs, and Asiago Cheese

Penne with Roasted Shallots
and Porcini Mushroom Glaze

Penne with Tomato Cream Sauce,
Pancetta, and Basil

Mezzi Rigatoni with Parsley Pesto
and Roasted Peppers and
Red Onions

Rigatoni with Three-Cut
Tomato Sauce, Anchovies,
and Black Olives

Rigatoni with Hot Sausage,
Tomatoes, and Broccoli Rabe

Penne with Cucumbers,
Tomatoes, and Feta Cheese

Fusilli with Spicy Eggplant,
Spinach, and Black Olives

Ziti with Bacon, Arugula,
and Tomatoes

Ziti with Grilled Zucchini
and Red Peppers and
Aged Goat Cheese

SOME THOUGHTS ON COOKING PASTA FOR PASTA SALAD

When forced by circumstances, you can cook pasta for room-temperature pasta salads 3 hours ahead of time. The pasta should be cooked al dente, "firm to the bite." Since there are so many brands and shapes of pasta in the market, it is best to follow the cooking time on the package. (Never use fresh pasta for pasta salads.) Be sure to stir the pasta frequently and 1 or 2 minutes before the end of the cooking time, taste it for doneness.

When done, drain the pasta in a colander and shake it until it is as dry as possible. Then spread it in a layer on a baking sheet or put it in a wide shallow container, and let it stand until it comes to room temperature. Stir the pasta every now and then to prevent it from clumping. When cool, cover it.

You can also drizzle the drained but still-hot pasta with a little olive oil to prevent it from sticking together. Toss to coat the pasta, and let it cool to room temperature. Then cover.

Cooked pasta, oiled or not, can be held at room temperature for 3 hours. If you must cook the pasta well in advance and need to refrigerate it overnight, make sure that it is well covered to prevent it from drying out. Bring it to room temperature before using in a salad.

Cavatappi with Roasted Tomatoes and Fresh Ricotta

The pure white of the ricotta cheese nesting among the red and green in this pasta make this presentation very festive. Be sure to reserve a few basil leaves so that you can scatter them over the dish, here and there, for a look of casual perfection.

1. Make the sauce: Peel, trim, and thinly slice the garlic.

2. In a blender or food processor, using the on/off button, coarsely chop the roasted tomatoes in batches. (Or chop them by hand.)

3. In a large skillet, sauté the garlic in the olive oil over medium heat, stirring, until softened, but do not let it brown. Stir in the chopped tomatoes, chicken broth, marjoram, and oregano. Cook over low heat, stirring occasionally, for about 30 minutes, until the sauce is very thick and rich. Remove the pan from the heat and let cool.

4. Meanwhile, bring a large pot of salted water to a boil. Add the pasta, stir to separate, and cook over high heat for 8 to 10 minutes, until al dente. (Or follow the cooking directions on the package.) Drain in a colander. To prevent the pasta from sticking together, spread it out on a large baking sheet or platter and let it cool, about 15 minutes. Cover and hold at room temperature for up to 3 hours.

THE SAUCE

3 garlic cloves

40 roasted plum tomato halves (see page 197)

¾ cup extra-virgin olive oil

1 cup chicken broth

1 teaspoon crumbled dried marjoram

1 teaspoon crumbled dried oregano

1½ pounds cavatappi (corkscrew-shaped pasta, about 1½ inches long)

1 pound whole-milk ricotta cheese

1 cup torn basil leaves, with a few reserved for garnish, if desired

5. In a medium bowl, whip the ricotta with a fork until creamy.

6. In a large serving bowl, preferably ceramic, combine the pasta, sauce, and all but a few of the basil leaves, tossing gently to combine.

7. Make a well in the center of the pasta salad and spoon the ricotta into it. (Or, if desired, serve the ricotta in a small bowl for passing at the table.) Scatter the reserved basil leaves over the salad and serve.

SERVES 6

PREPPING IN ADVANCE: The sauce can be completed 1 day ahead through step 3. Transfer it to a bowl, cover, and refrigerate. Let come to room temperature before using.

The pasta can be cooked and held at room temperature for up to 3 hours before using. See page 239 for directions.

Couscous with Moroccan Vegetables

This makes a fantastic centerpiece on a buffet table, and while the recipe is admittedly elaborate, it can be deconstructed so that even the busiest of cooks can do it with ease. Prepare the recipe in stages: Roast the vegetables the day before. Toast the almonds, a garnish, ahead of time, too. Cooking the couscous does have to be done at the last minute, but it is not difficult, and by that time you are in the home stretch, as it were! When you bring this exotic platter to the table, you will realize just how worthwhile all your efforts have been. This is gala company fare, of the very best kind.

A final note: We call for parchment paper for lining the baking sheets you will use to roast the vegetables. This is not an industrial conceit on our part. It will make cleanup a lot easier.

2 medium carrots

2 medium zucchini

1 small butternut squash

¼ cup sliced almonds, for garnish

1 cup pitted prunes (see Note, page 244)

1 cup orange juice

¼ cup honey

2 teaspoons ground ginger

1 teaspoon ground cinnamon

1 teaspoon cayenne

1 teaspoon sweet paprika

1½ teaspoons salt

1¼ cups plus 1 teaspoon extra-virgin olive oil

2 medium red onions

1 pound plain couscous (do not use a flavored couscous)

2 cups water

½ teaspoon saffron threads

¼ teaspoon ground turmeric

1. Preheat the oven to 400 degrees F. Line 4 baking sheets with parchment paper.

2. Prepare the vegetables: Peel the carrots and cut them into 1-inch cubes. Wash, trim, and cut the zucchini into 1-inch cubes. With a vegetable

peeler, remove the skin on the butternut squash, cut in half, scoop out the seeds, and cut into 1-inch cubes.

3. In a small baking pan, toast the almonds, without oil, until golden.

4. Soak the prunes in the orange juice for 1 hour.

5. In a wide bowl, combine the honey, ginger, ½ teaspoon of the cinnamon, cayenne, paprika, and ½ teapoon of the salt. Add 1 cup of the olive oil and whisk to blend. Place the cubed carrots, zucchini, and butternut, one vegetable at a time, in the spice blend and stir to coat lightly. Transfer the cubes to the baking sheets, arranging them in one layer, and keeping the zucchini on a separate baking sheet. Place in the oven. After 20 minutes, turn the vegetables and rotate the pans top to bottom. The zucchini will take 20 minutes to cook. The carrots and butternut squash will take 40 minutes. Remove the vegetables as they are done, and let cool on the baking sheets.

6. Peel the red onions and cut them into 1-inch-thick wedges.

7. Heat ¼ cup of the remaining olive oil in a skillet over medium heat. Add the red onion wedges, turning, and cook until they start to brown, about 10 minutes. Add the prunes and orange juice. Lower the heat and continue cooking until the onions are soft and the orange juice is syrupy, about 20 minutes. Stir in the remaining ½ teaspoon of cinnamon and set aside to cool.

8. Place the couscous in a heatproof bowl and add the remaining 1 teaspoon olive oil. Stir to coat the grains.

9. Bring the water to a boil in a small saucepan and add the remaining 1 teaspoon salt, saffron, and turmeric. Simmer for a few minutes to infuse, then pour the mixture over the couscous. Cover the bowl and let stand ½ hour.

10. To assemble the couscous, first fluff it with a fork or with your fingertips. Spread the couscous, mounding it slightly in the center, in a wide, shallow serving bowl. Sprinkle with the toasted almonds.

11. In a large bowl, combine all the roasted vegetables with the prune and onion mixture, and toss gently to combine. Mound the roasted vegetables in the center of the couscous and serve.

S E R V E S **6**

PREPPING IN ADVANCE: The carrots, zucchini, and squash can all be roasted 1 day ahead. Let cool, cover, and refrigerate. Remove from the refrigerator 1 hour before using to let them come to room temperature.

The almonds can be toasted 1 day ahead, too. Let cool and store in a covered container at room temperature.

NOTES: The same amount of dried apricots or currants can be substituted for the prunes, if desired.

For obvious reasons, texture being the principal one, we do not recommend trying to store this dish to serve later as a leftover. It does not keep.

Farfalle with Sautéed Greens, Lemon, and Pecorino Romano Cheese

This is a recipe that uses the magnificent leaves, the greens, of the beet. For ways to prepare the roots, see pages 205 and 275.

1. Cut off the stems of the arugula and spinach. Wash the leaves well, pat dry, and coarsely chop.

2. Wash the beet greens. Cut off the stems, chop them, and reserve. Coarsely chop the greens.

3. Peel, trim, and finely chop the garlic. Grate the zest of the lemon; reserve the lemon for juice.

2 cups firmly packed arugula leaves

2 cups firmly packed spinach leaves

2 cups firmly packed beet greens

2 garlic cloves

Grated zest and juice of 2 large lemons

½ cup extra-virgin olive oil

3 tablespoons unsalted butter

½ cup chicken broth

1½ pounds farfalle (bow ties)

1 cup grated Pecorino Romano cheese

4. In a large skillet, sauté the garlic in the olive oil over medium heat, stirring, until softened, but do not let it brown. Add the butter and half of the lemon juice and cook for 1 minute. Add the chicken broth, and stir well to combine. Add the beet greens and stems and cook for 3 minutes. Next add the arugula and spinach, a little at a time, letting each addition wilt before adding the next. Cover and cook over medium heat for 5 minutes. Remove the pan from the heat, and remove the cover. Let cool.

5. In the meantime, bring a large pot of salted water to a boil. Add the pasta, stir to separate, and cook over high heat for 10 minutes, until al dente. Drain in a colander. To prevent the pasta from sticking together, spread it out on a large baking sheet or platter and let it cool, about 15 minutes. Cover and hold at room temperature for up to 3 hours.

6. Transfer the pasta to a large porcelain serving bowl. Add the sautéed greens and toss well to combine. Add the Pecorino Romano, a little at a time, tossing to combine; add the lemon zest, the remaining lemon juice, and toss again. Serve within 2 hours.

SERVES 6

PREPPING IN ADVANCE: The sautéed greens can be prepared 3 hours ahead through step 4. When cool, cover, and hold at room temperature.

Fusilli with Pesto, Sautéed Leeks, and Oyster Mushrooms

Pesto makes this salad a lovely shade of green. The leeks and oyster mushrooms give it pastel variation. Serve it on a white platter for maximum effect. Remember that pesto turns black if left to stand at room temperature, which makes this combination a mandatory dress-and-serve.

2 medium leeks

½ pound oyster mushrooms

2 tablespoons extra-virgin olive oil

½ cup chicken broth

½ teaspoon freshly ground black pepper

1½ pounds fusilli

Classic Pesto (page 362)

1. Trim the root ends and most of the greens off the leeks and discard. Cut the leeks in half lengthwise and rinse well under running water. Slice each leek half into ¼-inch-thick slices. Put the slices in a colander and rinse well under running water to remove all grit and sand. Drain well in the colander.

2. Rinse the mushrooms and chop very coarsely.

3. In a large skillet, sauté the leeks in the olive oil over very low heat, stirring, until limp. Add the oyster mushrooms, stir well, then add the chicken broth and pepper. Cover and cook for 15 minutes. Remove the cover, increase the heat to high, and cook, stirring often, until the juices evaporate. Remove the pan from the heat and let the sauce cool.

4. In the meantime, bring a large pot of salted water to a boil. Add the pasta, stir to separate, and cook for 10 minutes, until al dente. (Or follow the cooking directions on the package.) Drain the pasta in a colander. To prevent the pasta from sticking together, spread it out on a large baking sheet

or platter and let it cool, about 15 minutes. Cover and hold at room temperature for up to 3 hours.

5. Turn the pasta into a large serving bowl, add the pesto and the leek and mushroom sauce, and toss well to combine. Serve immediately.

SERVES 6

PREPPING IN ADVANCE: The leek and mushroom sauce can be made 1 day ahead. Let cool, cover, and refrigerate. Bring to room temperature before combining with the pasta and pesto.

Gemelli with Spinach, Radicchio, Escarole, and Aged Provolone

When provolone is young, the cheese is fine and soft, best used as a table cheese. After about a year, it becomes drier and pungent, acquiring a strong, concentrated flavor that is reminiscent of Parmigiano but much sharper. The sautéed greens bring a slightly bitter but mellow flavor that tempers the provolone.

Gemelli, which means "twins" in Italian, are intertwined twists of pasta. They are a little different and because of that bring something extra to this salad. Most supermarkets have them, but if yours doesn't, use fusilli.

2 heads radicchio, about 6 ounces each

2 cups firmly packed spinach leaves

2 cups firmly packed escarole leaves

2 garlic cloves

¾ cup extra-virgin olive oil

1½ pounds gemelli

1 cup coarsely grated aged provolone

1 teaspoon freshly ground black pepper

1. Separate the leaves of each radicchio from the core, and discard the core. Wash the leaves, pat dry, and coarsely chop.

2. Wash the spinach and escarole. Cut the stems off the spinach. Pat the greens dry and coarsely chop. Peel, trim, and thinly slice the garlic.

3. In a large skillet, cook the garlic in the olive oil over low heat, stirring, until softened, but do not let it brown. Add the radicchio, spinach, and escarole and cook them, turning with long kitchen tongs, until wilted. Remove the pan from the heat and let cool.

4. Bring a large pot of salted water to a boil. Add the pasta, stir to separate, and cook over high heat for 10 minutes, until al dente. (Or follow the cooking directions on the package.) Drain the pasta in a colander. To prevent the pasta from sticking together, spread it out on a large baking sheet or platter and let it cool, about 15 minutes. Cover and hold at room temperature for up to 3 hours.

5. Transfer the pasta to a large ceramic pasta bowl. Add the sautéed greens with the oil and any juices in the pan, and mix thoroughly. Add the provolone and pepper and toss well to combine. Serve within 2 hours.

SERVES 6

PREPPING IN ADVANCE: The sautéed greens can be prepared 2 hours ahead. When cool, cover and hold at room temperature.

Orecchiette with Broccoli and Cauliflower in Saffron Sauce

This pasta is very tasty. It's an ideal dish for a lunch gathering or informal dinner. It will require your attention, though. So plan to cook the pasta up to 3 hours ahead and the cream sauce and vegetables 1 hour in advance of serving. *Orecchiette*, meaning "little ears" in Italian, are wonderfully suited for "holding" the sauce. If you aren't able to find this specific shape, use small shells.

1. In a small, dry skillet toast the pine nuts over medium heat, stirring constantly, until fragrant. Transfer to a dish to cool.

2. Peel, trim, and finely dice the onion. Peel, trim, and mince the garlic.

3. In a large skillet, cook the onion in the olive oil over low heat, stirring, until translucent. Add the garlic, saffron, and white wine and cook, stirring, for a few more minutes to blend. Add the chicken broth, bring it to a boil, and cook for 5 minutes. Stir in the cream and cook until slightly thickened, about 3 minutes. Turn off the heat and let the sauce cool to room temperature.

¼ cup pine nuts (pignoli)

½ white onion

2 garlic cloves

½ cup extra-virgin olive oil

½ teaspoon saffron threads

2 tablespoons white wine

½ cup chicken broth

1 cup heavy cream

1 large head broccoli, about 1 pound

½ large head cauliflower, about 1 pound

6 cups water

2 teaspoons salt

1½ pounds orecchiette ("little ears")

1 teaspoon freshly ground black pepper

4. Cut the florets off the head of broccoli and trim into bite-sized pieces. Cut the cauliflower into bite-sized florets.

5. In a large saucepan, bring the water to a boil with the salt. Add the broccoli and cauliflower florets and blanch for about 3 minutes. Drain in a colander and rinse thoroughly under cold water; let drain in the sink.

6. Bring a large pot of salted water to a boil. Add the pasta, stir to separate, and cook over high heat for about 8 minutes, until al dente. (Or follow the cooking directions on the package.) Drain in a colander. To prevent the pasta from sticking together, spread it out on a large baking sheet or platter and let it cool, about 15 minutes. Cover and hold at room temperature for up to 3 hours.

7. Put the pasta in a large bowl, add the cauliflower and broccoli florets, and toss lightly. Stir in the saffron sauce, add the toasted pine nuts and pepper, and toss to combine. Serve within 1 hour.

SERVES 6

Orecchiette with Roasted Vegetables, Fresh Herbs, and Asiago Cheese

The medley of vegetables in this recipe should be juicy and well cooked, almost disintegrating, and not resistant to the tooth at all. The herbs, on the other hand, are used raw, which makes for wonderful contrast. If you roast the vegetables ahead of time, which you can do, assembling this extravaganza is downright fun.

1 cup roasted bell pepper quarters (see page 193)

1½ cups roasted zucchini slices (see page 201)

24 roasted plum tomato halves (see page 197)

3 garlic cloves

1 cup loosely packed basil leaves

½ cup flat-leaf parsley leaves

1 teaspoon dried hot pepper flakes

½ cup extra-virgin olive oil

1 teaspoon freshly ground black pepper

1½ pounds orecchiette ("little ears")

1 cup grated Asiago cheese

1. Cut the pepper quarters into ¼-inch-wide strips; cut the zucchini slices in half.

2. In a large bowl, mash the tomatoes to a coarse pulp.

3. Peel, trim, and slice the garlic. Rinse, pat dry, and coarsely chop the basil and parsley leaves.

4. In a large saucepan, sauté the garlic and hot pepper flakes in the olive oil. (It is too much oil for the garlic, but the oil is part of the sauce.) When the garlic is softened, but not browned, add the mashed tomatoes and ground pepper. Cover and cook over very low heat for 15 minutes. Turn off the heat, add the roasted zucchini and roasted pepper ribbons, and combine well. Let the sauce cool to room temperature.

5. Bring a large pot of salted water to a boil. Add the pasta, stir to separate, and cook over high heat for about 8 minutes, until al dente. (Or follow the cooking directions on the package.) Drain the pasta in a colander. To prevent the pasta from sticking together, spread it out on a large baking sheet or platter and let it cool, about 15 minutes. Cover and hold at room temperature for up to 3 hours.

6. Transfer the pasta to a large serving bowl. Add the sauce, Asiago, and chopped herbs. Toss thoroughly to combine, and serve.

SERVES 6

PREPPING IN ADVANCE: The sauce can be completed 2 hours ahead. When cool, cover, and hold at room temperature.

Penne with Roasted Shallots and Porcini Mushroom Glaze

This pasta salad is particularly nice for company because fresh porcini mushrooms, available only in the fall, are special. The wait for them is worth it. Use cremini, shiitake, or a combination of the two at other times. If you are serving this for a special occasion, roast tenderloin, with or without a peppercorn crust, is the ideal accompaniment. Because of the cream in the mushroom glaze, this pasta, special as it is, does not keep.

1. Position a rack in the upper third of the oven. Preheat the oven to 350 degrees F.

2. Peel and trim the shallots. Toss the shallots with 2 tablespoons of the olive oil and salt and several grinds of pepper to taste. Spread them on a small baking sheet and roast for 45 minutes. Remove and let cool.

8 ounces shallots
(about 8 medium shallots)

½ cup extra-virgin olive oil
plus 2 tablespoons

Salt

1 teaspoon freshly ground black
pepper, plus extra for seasoning

8 ounces fresh porcini mushrooms

2 garlic cloves

½ cup dry white wine

¼ teaspoon ground nutmeg

2 teaspoons thyme leaves

⅔ cup heavy cream

1 pound penne

½ cup freshly grated
Pecorino Romano cheese

SERVE WITH: Roast Filet of Beef with Peppercorn Crust (page 344).

3. Trim the ends off the stems of the mushrooms and discard. Rinse the mushrooms well and thinly slice them from top to bottom.

4. Peel, trim, and slice the garlic.

5. In a large skillet, cook the garlic in ½ cup olive oil over low heat, stirring, until softened, but do not let it brown. Add the sliced mushrooms and sauté them, stirring, until they begin to release water. Add the wine and increase the heat to medium. Add the 1 teaspoon freshly ground black pepper, nutmeg, and thyme. Lower the heat, cover the pan, and cook for 20 minutes. Add the cream, stir well, and cook for 2 minutes. Remove the pan from the heat and let cool.

6. Bring a large pot of salted water to a boil. Add the pasta, stir to separate, and cook over high heat for 10 minutes, until al dente. (Or follow the cooking directions on the package.) Drain the pasta in a colander. To prevent the pasta from sticking together, spread it out on a large baking sheet or platter and let it cool, about 15 minutes. Cover and hold at room temperature for up to 3 hours. Transfer the cooled pasta to a large serving bowl.

7. On a cutting board, coarsely chop the roasted shallots. Add them to the pasta, add the mushroom glaze, and toss well. Add the cheese and toss again. Adjust the seasonings. Serve within 1 hour.

SERVES 6

Penne with Tomato Cream Sauce, Pancetta, and Basil

Cream, in this case half-and-half, adds an ineffable, luxurious quality to any pasta sauce. It works its magic here in a simple, summery combination that is as pretty as it is comforting. A big bowl of this on a buffet table alongside a platter of roasted chicken or a selection of vegetable salads, a wonderful bread or two, a cut of cheese, and you have the makings of a feast. Another advantage: Both the pasta and the base of the sauce can be made in advance.

2 pounds plum tomatoes

2 garlic cloves

6 ounces pancetta (Italian bacon)

1 cup loosely packed basil leaves

½ cup extra-virgin olive oil

1 teaspoon salt

1 teaspoon freshly ground black pepper

½ teaspoon dried hot pepper flakes

¼ teaspoon freshly ground nutmeg

1½ pounds penne

1 cup half-and-half

½ cup freshly grated Parmigiano-Reggiano cheese

1. Wash, trim, and dice the tomatoes. Peel, trim, and thinly slice the garlic. Dice the pancetta into ¼-inch cubes. Rinse and pat the basil leaves dry.

2. In a large skillet, sauté the pancetta in the olive oil over low heat, stirring, for 5 minutes. Add the garlic and sauté, stirring, until softened, but do not let it brown. Add the tomatoes, salt, black pepper, pepper flakes, and nutmeg. Cover the pan and cook, stirring once or twice, for 30 minutes. Remove the pan from the heat and let the sauce cool to room temperature.

3. Bring a large pot of salted water to a boil. Add the pasta, stir to separate, and cook over high heat for 10 minutes, until al dente. (Or follow the cooking directions on the package.) Drain the pasta in a colander. To prevent the pasta from sticking together, spread it out on a large baking sheet or platter and let it cool, about 15 minutes. Cover and hold at room temperature for up to 3 hours. Turn the pasta into a large ceramic serving bowl.

4. Mix the half-and-half into the tomato sauce and stir until well blended. Pour the sauce over the pasta and toss a few times to combine. Blend in the Parmigiano and toss again. Add the basil leaves and toss gently to distribute them. Best served within 1 hour of finishing.

SERVES 6

PREPPING IN ADVANCE: The sauce can be made 1 day ahead through step 2. When cool, transfer it to a bowl, cover, and refrigerate. Bring it to room temperature; then finish it as directed in step 4.

Mezzi Rigatoni with Parsley Pesto and Roasted Peppers and Red Onions

There is a splendid marriage of the singular flavor of caramel (from two different roasted vegetables) and fresh herbs in this colorful salad. Make this very easy for yourself and prepare both the roasted peppers and onions in advance. In fact, the pesto is a make-ahead, too. For the best flavor and most vibrant colors, and there are a lot of lovely ones here, assemble it before serving.

2 red onions

2 tablespoons extra-virgin olive oil

¼ teaspoon salt

¼ teaspoon freshly ground black pepper

1½ pounds mezzi rigatoni (half the size of the regular)

3 red bell peppers, roasted, skinned, seeded, cored, and cut into strips (see page 193)

Parsley Pesto (page 363)

½ cup freshly grated Pecorino Romano cheese

1. Preheat the oven to 400 degrees F.

2. Peel, trim, and slice the onions crosswise into ¼-inch-thick rings. Separate the rings, put in a bowl, and add the oil, salt, and pepper. Toss to coat. Spread the onions in a single layer on a baking sheet and roast 30 minutes, or until the edges start to brown and crisp. Let cool on the baking sheet.

3. Bring a large pot of salted water to a boil. Add the pasta, stir to separate, and cook over high heat for 10 minutes, until al dente. (Or follow the cooking directions on the package.) Drain the pasta in a colander. To prevent the pasta from sticking together, spread it out on a large baking sheet or platter and let it cool, about 15 minutes. Cover and hold at room temperature for up to 3 hours.

4. Turn the pasta into a large serving bowl. Add the pesto, the pepper strips, roasted red onion rings, and cheese and toss well to combine. Best served within 1 hour of finishing.

SERVES 6

PREPPING IN ADVANCE: The peppers and onions can be roasted in advance and stored in the refrigerator.

The pesto, too, can be made ahead. Bring all to room temperature before using in the salad.

Rigatoni with Three-Cut Tomato Sauce, Anchovies, and Black Olives

If the bold flavors of Provençal or Mediterranean cooking appeal to you, you must make this salad. And if you are given to eating anchovies, you have a treat in store. If you are wondering why we cut the tomatoes in the sauce here in three different ways, the answer is simple: It has everything to do with texture—wonderful texture.

4 pounds plum tomatoes

3 garlic cloves

8 anchovy fillets packed in olive oil

1 cup loosely packed basil leaves

½ cup extra-virgin olive oil

½ teaspoon dried hot pepper flakes

1 teaspoon salt

1½ pounds rigatoni

1 cup pitted kalamata olives

1 cup freshly grated Parmigiano-Reggiano cheese

1. Wash and core the tomatoes. Divide them into 3 piles. Chop the first pile very fine. Cut the second pile into about ½-inch slices; cut the remaining tomatoes lengthwise into quarters.

2. Peel, trim, and thinly slice the garlic. Mince the anchovies. Rinse and pat the basil leaves dry.

3. In a large skillet, cook the garlic in the olive oil over low heat, stirring, until softened, but do not let it brown. Add the anchovies, and stir well. Add the tomatoes, pepper flakes, and salt, and cook, covered, for 30 minutes.

4. Uncover the pan, make a well in the center of the tomatoes for the juice to collect, and cook, uncovered, for 30 minutes, until almost dry. During the last half hour of cooking, moisten the crown of tomatoes now and then with the juice. Remove the pan from the heat and let the sauce cool to room temperature.

5. Bring a large pot of salted water to a boil. Add the pasta, stir to separate, and cook over high heat for 10 minutes, until al dente. (Or follow the cooking directions on the package.) Drain the pasta in a colander. To prevent the pasta from sticking together, spread it out on a large baking sheet or platter and let it cool, about 15 minutes. Cover and hold at room temperature for up to 3 hours.

6. Turn the pasta into a large ceramic serving bowl. Add the sauce, olives, and basil and toss well. Add the Parmigiano and toss again. Best served within 1 hour of finishing.

SERVES 6

PREPPING IN ADVANCE: The sauce can be completed up to 2 days ahead through step 4. Transfer it to a bowl, cover, and refrigerate. Bring to room temperature before using in the salad.

Rigatoni with Hot Sausage, Tomatoes, and Broccoli Rabe

Extra-virgin olive oil plays a large part in the success of the sauce here. Use a good one. Aside from that, all the remaining ingredients in this pleasing, colorful combination are easy to find. In fact, you can prepare each of the separate components—the sauce, broccoli rabe, and pasta—in advance, which makes putting this together, even on the busiest of days, eminently doable.

2 pounds plum tomatoes

2 garlic cloves

1 pound broccoli rabe

1 pound hot Italian sausage

1 cup extra-virgin olive oil

1 teaspoon salt

½ cup chicken broth

1½ pounds rigatoni

1 cup freshly grated Parmigiano-Reggiano cheese

1. Wash, trim, and finely dice the tomatoes. Peel, trim, and slice the garlic. Wash the broccoli rabe well and trim the thick parts of the stems, if any; pat dry.

2. Remove the casings on the sausage and, with your fingers, crumble the meat into small chunks.

3. In a large skillet, cook the garlic in ½ cup of the olive oil over low heat, stirring, until softened, but do not let it brown. Add the sausage and cook, stirring, for 5 minutes, or until it loses its color. Add the tomatoes and salt, stir to combine, and cover the pan; cook, stirring once or twice, for 45 minutes. Remove the pan from the heat and let the sauce cool to room temperature.

4. In a medium skillet, cook the broccoli rabe in the remaining ½ cup of olive oil over low heat, stirring, for 2 or 3 minutes. Add the chicken broth, and cook, covered, for 10 minutes. Remove the pan from the heat and let cool to room temperature.

5. Bring a large pot of salted water to a boil. Add the pasta, stir to separate, and cook over high heat for 10 minutes, until cooked but al dente. (Or follow the cooking directions on the package.) Drain the pasta in a colander. To prevent the pasta from sticking together, spread it out on a large baking sheet or platter and let it cool, about 15 minutes. Cover and hold at room temperature for up to 3 hours.

6. Turn the pasta into a large ceramic serving bowl. Add the tomato sauce. Drain the broccoli rabe well of any liquid and add to the pasta; toss well to combine. Add the Parmigiano and toss once more. Best served within 1 hour of finishing.

SERVES 6

PREPPING IN ADVANCE: The tomato-sausage sauce can be completed 1 day ahead. When cool, transfer it to a bowl, cover, and refrigerate. Let come to room temperature before serving.

The broccoli rabe can be cooked several hours ahead on the day of serving. When cool, cover, and reserve at room temperature.

Penne with Cucumbers, Tomatoes, and Feta Cheese

This is a superb pasta for a hot summer's day because two of the main ingredients—the cucumbers and tomatoes—are used raw, helping to make the salad especially crisp and refreshing. Good olive oil is key here; it is a major component in the dressing.

Don't make this in advance. In fact, don't even think about it. The point of using raw vegetables and lots of mint is that they be fresh tasting and at their peak flavor, which means that they should also be at room temperature.

5 large ripe beefsteak tomatoes

3 large cucumbers

3 garlic cloves

1 cup packed mint leaves

1 cup extra-virgin olive oil

1 teaspoon dried hot pepper flakes

3 tablespoons red wine vinegar

1½ pounds penne or *tortiglioni*

½ cup pitted kalamata olives

1 pound feta cheese

At Mangia, we like to make this with *tortiglioni*, a narrow rigatoni. If you can find it, try it. Otherwise, penne works just fine.

1. Wash, core, and chop the tomatoes into ½-inch cubes.

2. Peel the cucumbers, quarter lengthwise, and remove the seeds. Cut each piece in thirds, and slice lengthwise into thin slivers. Put the slivers in a bowl of cold water.

3. Peel, trim, and mince the garlic. Rinse the mint leaves, pat them dry, and coarsely chop.

4. In a small skillet, cook the garlic in the olive oil over low heat, stirring, until softened, but do not let it brown. Add the pepper flakes and cook for 1 to 2 minutes. Remove the pan from the heat and let cool to room temperature. Then blend in the vinegar.

5. Bring a large pot of salted water to a boil. Add the pasta, stir to separate, and cook over high heat about 10 minutes, until al dente. (Or follow the cooking directions on the package.) Drain the pasta in a colander. To prevent the pasta from sticking together, spread it out on a large baking sheet or platter and let it cool, about 15 minutes. Cover and hold at room temperature for up to 3 hours.

6. Drain the cucumbers.

7. Turn the pasta into a large ceramic serving bowl. Add the tomatoes, cucumbers, mint, olives, and seasoned olive oil. Toss well until the pasta is uniformly shiny. Crumble the feta into the salad, and toss to combine. Best served within 1 hour of finishing.

SERVES 6 TO 8

Fusilli with Spicy Eggplant, Spinach, and Black Olives

If you are looking for a pasta recipe with something other than tomato sauce, here it is. Roasted eggplant, spinach, black olives, a pinch of hot pepper, and fresh lemon make an unusual combination— and a very good sauce.

2 large whole eggplants, 1½ pounds each

3 garlic cloves

4 cups spinach leaves

½ cup firmly packed parsley leaves

½ cup extra-virgin olive oil, plus additional for filming the pan

1 teaspoon salt

1 teaspoon dried hot pepper flakes

Juice of 3 lemons

1 cup chicken broth

1½ pounds fusilli

1 cup pitted Gaeta olives

½ cup freshly grated Parmigiano-Reggiano cheese

¼ cup drained capers (optional)

1. Position an oven rack in the upper third of the oven. Preheat the oven to 350 degrees F.

2. Prick the eggplants once or twice with a fork and place them on a baking sheet. Roast for about 1 hour. Let cool until they can be handled. Cut the eggplants in half lengthwise, scoop out all the pulp, and put into a bowl. (You should have about 2½ cups.) Discard the skins.

3. Peel, trim, and slice the garlic. Wash and pat the spinach dry; cut off and discard the stems. Chop the leaves coarsely. Rinse the parsley, pat it dry, and chop coarsely.

4. In a large skillet, cook the garlic in ½ cup olive oil over low heat, stirring, until softened, but do not let it brown. Lower the heat, add the eggplant pulp, salt, pepper flakes, and lemon juice and cook for about 5 minutes.

Add the chicken broth and stir well, and cover the pan. Cook the sauce, stirring once or twice, for 15 minutes.

5. In a medium skillet, heat enough olive oil, over medium heat, to just film the pan. Add the chopped spinach leaves and cook 1 or 2 minutes, just until wilted. Remove the pan from the heat and let stand at room temperature.

6. Bring a large pot of salted water to a boil. Add the pasta, stir to separate, and cook over high heat for 10 minutes, until al dente. (Or follow the cooking directions on the package.) Drain the pasta in a colander. To prevent the pasta from sticking together, spread it out on a large baking sheet or platter and let it cool, about 15 minutes. Cover and hold at room temperature for up to 3 hours.

7. Turn the pasta into a large serving bowl. Add the eggplant sauce, spinach, olives, parsley, Parmigiano, and capers, if using, and toss well to combine. Best served within 1 hour of finishing.

SERVES 6

PREPPING IN ADVANCE: The eggplant sauce can be completed several hours ahead on the day it is served. When cool, cover and let stand at room temperature until ready to use.

Ziti with Bacon, Arugula, and Tomatoes

Bacon, lettuce, and tomato is a renowned combination and works every bit as well with pasta as it does between two slices of bread. The lettuce of choice here is definitely arugula. It adds just the right pepperiness and bite.

This dish is perfect for a large gathering, and it is easy to make.

8 slices of bacon

4 large ripe beefsteak tomatoes

3 garlic cloves

2 cups firmly packed arugula leaves

½ cup extra-virgin olive oil

1 teaspoon salt

1 teaspoon freshly ground black pepper

1½ pounds ziti

¾ cup freshly grated Parmigiano-Reggiano cheese

1. Place the bacon in a cold skillet, turn the heat to low, and cook, turning, until crisp. Transfer to paper towels to drain. Reserve 2 tablespoons of the fat. When cool, crumble the bacon into a small bowl; reserve until serving time.

2. Core and quarter each tomato lengthwise. With a small teaspoon, seed the tomatoes. Chop the flesh into small chunks. Peel, trim, and slice the garlic. Wash the arugula and pat it dry.

3. In a large skillet, cook the garlic in the olive oil and bacon fat over low heat, stirring until softened, but do not let it brown. Add the tomatoes, salt, and pepper, increase the heat to medium, and sauté for 2 minutes. Remove the pan from the heat. Add the arugula and stir to combine.

4. Bring a large pot of salted water to a boil. Add the pasta, stir to separate, and cook over high heat for 10 minutes, until al dente. (Or follow the cooking directions on the package.) Drain the pasta in a colander. To prevent the pasta from sticking together, spread it out on a large baking sheet or platter and let it cool, about 15 minutes. Cover and hold at room temperature for up to 3 hours.

5. Turn the pasta into a large ceramic serving bowl. Add the tomato sauce with all the oil, and mix well. Just before serving, add the bacon and Parmigiano and toss to combine. Check the seasonings. Add salt and freshly ground pepper to taste. Best served within 1 hour of finishing.

SERVES 6

Ziti with Grilled Zucchini and Red Peppers and Aged Goat Cheese

There are Greek influences at work here—namely, the goat cheese and mint. This salad is filled with flavor and color and is very easy to like. It goes beautifully with any roast meat, especially butterflied marinated lamb on the grill.

If you cannot find aged goat cheese, substitute finely chopped ricotta salata.

4 large zucchini, about 2½ pounds each

1 cup extra-virgin olive oil

3 large red bell peppers

2 garlic cloves

1 cup loosely packed mint leaves

1 tablespoon dried oregano

1 tablespoon fresh thyme leaves

1½ pounds ziti

1½ cups grated aged goat cheese, such as Kasseri

1 teaspoon freshly ground black pepper

1. Preheat the grill.

2. While the grill heats, trim the zucchini and slice it lengthwise into ½-inch-thick slices. Brush the slices well on both sides with some of the olive oil. When the coals are white, grill the zucchini around the edges of the grill for about 3 minutes on each side; remove and reserve at room temperature. (You can also grill the zucchini on the stove top in a hot grill pan, if desired.)

3. In the center of the grill, where the heat is more intense, grill the peppers, turning them frequently and fast to char them evenly all over. They should be black before you take them off the fire. Put the peppers in a plastic bag and let them steam while you prepare the rest of the sauce.

4. Slice the grilled zucchini lengthwise into ribbons.

5. Peel, trim, and mince the garlic. Rinse the mint leaves, pat them dry, and coarsely chop.

6. In a medium skillet, cook the garlic, oregano, and thyme in the remaining olive oil over low heat, stirring, until the garlic is softened, but do not let it brown. Remove the pan from the heat and let cool.

7. Bring a large pot of salted water to a boil. Add the pasta, stir to separate, and cook over high heat for 10 minutes, until al dente. (Or follow the cooking directions on the package.) Drain the pasta in a colander. To prevent the pasta from sticking, spread it out on a large baking sheet or platter and let it cool, about 15 minutes.

8. Under a trickle of running water, remove the charred skin on the peppers, then stem them. Halve the peppers, remove the seeds and cores, and cut lengthwise into thin strips.

9. Turn the pasta into a large ceramic serving bowl. Add the zucchini, pepper strips, and seasoned oil to the pasta and toss well. Sprinkle with the goat cheese and pepper and toss again. Add the mint and toss gently to combine. Best served within 1 hour of finishing.

SERVES 6

PREPPING IN ADVANCE: The vegetables can be grilled up to 3 hours ahead. Hold at room temperature.

GRAINS AND BEANS

GRAINS

Thai Tabbouleh

Wheat Berries with Roasted Beets and Sage

Saffron Rice with Mangoes and Jalapeño Peppers

Wild Rice and Roasted Corn

Wild Rice with Oven-Burst Grapes, Almonds, and Mint

Buckwheat with Shiitake Mushrooms and Thyme

Barley with Broccoli and Braised Garlic

BEANS

Black Bean Salad with Tomatoes, Feta Cheese, and Chipotle Salsa

Red Beans with Chives and Ricotta Salata

White Beans with Tomato, Roasted Prosciutto, and Sage

White Beans with Peppers and Rosemary

Chickpeas with Broccoli Rabe and Roasted Shallots

Flageolets with Nancy's Peperonata

Lentils with Garlic Sausage and Sage

Lentils with Peppers and Goat Cheese

Thai Tabbouleh

Tabbouleh, made with cracked wheat and lots of fresh herbs, is Middle Eastern in origin. Mangia's version has Asian touches—pickled ginger and cilantro—and a light lime dressing. This is exotic and refreshing, crunchy and comforting, and beautifully green.

1 cup medium-grain bulgur

¼ teaspoon salt

1¼ cups boiling water

2 tablespoons commercially prepared pickled ginger (sushi ginger)

1 small jalapeño pepper

1 medium cucumber

1 large ripe tomato

½ cup chopped mint leaves

½ cup chopped basil leaves

¼ cup chopped cilantro

½ cup chopped scallions (green and white parts)

¼ cup fresh lime juice, or more as needed

2 tablespoons extra-virgin olive oil

Salt

Freshly ground black pepper

1. Place the bulgur in a medium heat-proof bowl and add the salt. Pour the boiling water over the bulgur, cover the bowl, and let the bulgur steep for about 15 to 20 minutes, until the water has been absorbed. Fluff the grains with a fork; set aside to cool. For storing instructions, see page 274.

2. Mince the pickled ginger. Seed and mince the jalapeño. Peel, seed, and dice the cucumber into ¼-inch pieces. Seed and dice tomato. Put the ginger, jalapeño, cucumber, tomato, mint, basil, cilantro, and scallions in a large serving bowl.

3. Add the bulgur to the bowl, and then the lime juice and olive oil. Toss well to combine, and season with salt and pepper to taste. Best served within 2 hours of finishing.

SERVES 6

NOTE: Due to the number of raw ingredients, this salad does not keep.

PREPPING IN ADVANCE: The salad may be partially prepared 4 hours ahead. In step 2, combine the ginger, jalapeño, cucumber, and scallions in a bowl. Add the bulgur, cover, and refrigerate. One hour before serving, remove the salad from the refrigerator. Add the tomato, herbs, lime juice, and olive oil and toss well to combine. Season with salt and pepper and serve.

ON COOKING AND STORING GRAINS IN ADVANCE

Each of the grains in the recipes that follow can be prepared in advance of serving. Cook as directed and let cool. Transfer to an airtight container, cover, and refrigerate for up to 2 days. Remove from the refrigerator 1 hour before assembling the salad to allow it to come to room temperature.

Wheat Berries with Roasted Beets and Sage

Wheat berries are unprocessed whole kernels of wheat. When cooked, they maintain their berry shape and have a chewy texture that plays nicely off cubed roasted beets in this salad. Save the beet greens for Farfalle with Sautéed Greens, Lemon, and Pecorino Romano Cheese (page 245).

This is colorful and pretty. You can prepare the two main components—the wheat berries and beets—in advance, making this easy to put together. If you are looking to add to your list of healthier salads, this is a good place to start.

1½ cups wheat berries

3 cups water

Pinch of salt

4 medium beets

2 medium red onions

¼ cup extra-virgin olive oil

2 tablespoons chopped sage leaves

Freshly ground black pepper

1. In a saucepan, combine the wheat berries, water, and a pinch of salt. Bring the water to a boil over medium heat and simmer for about 1 hour, until the berries are tender. Drain and let cool. For storing instructions, see the box opposite.

2. Preheat the oven to 400 degrees F.

3. Wash the beets and trim off the stem and root ends. Wrap the beets in a sheet of aluminum foil, place on a baking sheet, and roast about 40 minutes, until the beets "give" when pierced with a knife. Remove from the oven and let cool in the foil, about 1 hour.

4. Peel, trim, and slice the onions ¼ inch thick.

5. In a small skillet, heat 3 tablespoons of olive oil over medium heat, add the onions, and sauté, stirring, for 5 minutes. Reduce the heat to low and cook, stirring often, for 15 minutes more. Add the chopped sage and cook 10 minutes. Set aside to cool.

6. When the beets are cool enough to handle, peel off the skins with a paring knife. Cut the beets into ½-inch cubes and put in a serving bowl.

7. Add the red onion mixture to the beets, and stir to combine. Add the wheat berries and the remaining 1 tablespoon of olive oil. Season with salt and pepper to taste, toss gently, and serve.

SERVES 6

NOTE: The salad is best served within 2 hours, but it keeps, covered, in the refrigerator for 1 day.

PREPPING IN ADVANCE: Both the wheat berries and beets can be cooked ahead. Roast the beets, let cool, cover, and store in the refrigerator 1 day in advance.

Saffron Rice with Mangoes and Jalapeño Peppers

Extraordinary color and tropical flavors distinguish this rice salad. You will need really ripe mangoes for it. Here's how to tell if one is ready to use or not: The flesh should feel soft when pressed, and the mango should have a sweet, fruity aroma. To ensure that the mangoes are ready when you want them, buy them ahead of time and let them ripen on your counter—a matter of a few days, usually.

2½ cups water

½ cup tomato puree

1 teaspoon salt

¼ teaspoon saffron threads

1½ cups long-grain rice

2 ripe mangoes

2 small jalapeño peppers

½ cup cilantro sprigs

2 teaspoons grated fresh ginger

1 tablespoon grated orange zest

Juice of 1 orange

2 tablespoons extra-virgin olive oil

½ teaspoon freshly ground black pepper

1. In a medium saucepan, combine the water, tomato puree, salt, and saffron and bring to a boil over medium-high heat. Boil for several minutes, add the rice, and stir once. Cover the pan, reduce the heat to low, and simmer until the liquid is absorbed and the rice is still firm, about 15 minutes. Turn the rice out into a bowl and set aside to cool. For storing instructions, see page 274.

2. Place a mango, stem end up, on a cutting board with the narrow side facing you. Cut through the flesh, from top to bottom, on either side of the stem. (This will give you 2 halves of flesh per mango and eliminate the large pit that runs the length of the fruit.) With a sharp paring knife, peel

the skin off the 2 halves. Slice each half lengthwise into ½-inch wedges, then cut each wedge in half again. Do the same with the remaining mango.

3. Seed and finely chop the jalapeño peppers. Coarsely chop the cilantro sprigs.

4. In a large serving bowl, combine the saffron rice, mangoes, jalapeño peppers, cilantro, ginger, and orange zest. Pour the fresh orange juice into the bowl and add the olive oil. Toss to combine, add the pepper, and adjust the seasonings to taste. Plan on serving this the same day for best flavor.

SERVES 6

NOTE: Because of the number of raw ingredients in this salad, it does not keep.

PREPPING IN ADVANCE: The mangoes can be cut up and stored, covered, in the refrigerator up to 2 hours ahead.

Wild Rice and Roasted Corn

Wild rice is not a grain, but an aquatic grass seed native to North America. Hand harvesting makes it expensive, but the yield makes it worth it: It triples in volume when cooked. With a chewy texture and nutty taste, it is especially appealing combined with corn and peppers, both of which are native to the Western Hemisphere, too. This is an American salad through and through, with character and brio. Instead of making another potato salad for next year's Fourth of July picnic, why not take this? The major components can all be prepared in advance.

1 cup wild rice

3 cups water

1½ teaspoons salt

4 ears fresh corn

3 tablespoons extra-virgin olive oil, plus extra for roasting

½ teaspoon freshly ground black pepper, plus additional for seasoning

2 scallions

1 teaspoon chopped thyme sprigs

1 large red bell pepper, cut into strips and roasted (page 193), omitting the rosemary

2 tablespoons balsamic vinegar

1. In a medium saucepan, combine the wild rice, water, and 1 teaspoon of the salt. Bring the water to a boil over medium-high heat. Cover, and cook over low heat until the grains start to swell but are still firm to the bite, about 45 minutes. Drain, transfer to a wide, shallow bowl, and let cool. For storing instructions, see page 274.

2. Preheat the oven to 400 degrees F.

3. Shuck the corn and remove the silk. Holding each ear of corn upright on a cutting board and starting from the tip, slice off the kernels, cutting as close to the cob as possible. Place the corn in a bowl and add a drizzle of

olive oil, the ½ teaspoon salt, and pepper; toss to coat. Place on a baking sheet and roast until the kernels start to brown slightly at the edges, about 15 minutes. Let cool.

4. Trim off the dark green top and root end on each scallion and slice thin, using the green and white parts. Remove the leaves from the thyme sprigs and coarsely chop.

5. Put the wild rice, roasted corn and pepper strips, scallions, and thyme in a large serving bowl. Add the 3 tablespoons of olive oil and balsamic vinegar. Toss to combine, season with salt and pepper to taste, and serve.

SERVES 6

NOTE: The salad keeps, covered, in the refrigerator for 24 hours.

PREPPING IN ADVANCE: The corn and bell pepper can be roasted at the same time, if desired, 1 day ahead. Let cool, place in separate bowls, cover, and refrigerate.

Wild Rice with Oven-Burst Grapes, Almonds, and Mint

At Mangia we roast fruit. Here it is grapes, a wonderful touch that softens their texture, "bursting" them as it concentrates their sweetness. With toasted almonds and fresh mint, this salad is finished with nothing more than cinnamon-scented olive oil.

1 cup wild rice

3 cups water

1 teaspoon salt

1 cup seedless red grapes

1 cup seedless green grapes

2 tablespoons extra-virgin olive oil, plus additional for roasting

¼ cup sliced almonds

½ cup mint leaves

1 teaspoon ground cinnamon

1. In a medium saucepan, combine the wild rice, water, and salt and bring the water to a boil over medium-high heat. Cover and cook over low heat until the grains start to swell but are still firm to the bite, about 45 minutes. Drain, transfer to a wide, shallow bowl, and set aside to cool. For storing instructions, see page 274.

2. Preheat the oven to 400 degrees F.

3. Wash the grapes and dry them. Put in a bowl, and drizzle with olive oil—just enough to gloss them. Place the grapes on a baking sheet and bake until the skins burst, about 10 minutes. Let cool on the baking sheet.

4. While the grapes are roasting, toast the sliced almonds, without oil, until lightly golden, about 10 minutes, in a small baking pan. Remove and let cool.

5. Rinse the mint leaves and pat dry. Chop very coarse.

6. In a large serving bowl, combine the wild rice, roasted grapes, mint, and almonds. Add the 2 tablespoons of olive oil and cinnamon and toss well to combine. Adjust the seasonings and serve.

SERVES 6

NOTE: The salad keeps, covered, in the refrigerator for 1 day.

PREPPING IN ADVANCE: The almonds can be toasted 2 days ahead. Let cool, cover, and store at room temperature.

The rice can be cooked 1 day ahead. Let cool, cover, and store in the refrigerator.

The grapes can be roasted 2 hours ahead. Hold, covered, at room temperature.

Buckwheat with Shiitake Mushrooms and Thyme

Buckwheat is in the same plant family as rhubarb, which is grown for its stalks. Buckwheat, on the other hand, is grown for its seeds and is cultivated in countries where the soil is too poor and the climate too cold for other cereals to grow. The whole grains can be boiled like rice or baked in sweet puddings. Buckwheat flour figures in the wonderful Russian pancakes called blini.

Here the grain is toasted, paired with shiitake mushooms, and glossed with porcini oil. This fragrant oil really makes the salad; there is no substitute for it in this recipe.

1 large egg white

1 cup whole buckwheat groats (kasha)

2 cups boiling water or chicken broth

2 teaspoons salt

2 tablespoons extra-virgin olive oil

4 ounces shiitake mushrooms

1 medium red onion

1 tablespoon chopped thyme leaves

½ teaspoon freshly ground black pepper

1 tablespoon porcini mushroom oil

1. Beat the egg white lightly. In a bowl, combine the egg white and buckwheat groats; stir until the groats are completely coated.

2. Heat a medium skillet over medium heat until hot. Add the buckwheat and stir with a wooden spoon until it is dry and all the grains are separate. Add the boiling water or broth and 1 teaspoon of the salt. Cover and reduce the heat to low. Cook about 10 minutes. Remove the pan from the heat, spoon the buckwheat into a shallow bowl, and let cool. For storing instructions, see page 274.

3. Thinly slice the shiitake mushrooms. Peel, trim, and thinly slice the red onion.

4. Heat the olive oil in a skillet. Add the onion and sauté it, stirring, until translucent. Add the shiitakes and cook several minutes longer, until they start to wilt. Sprinkle with the thyme, the remaining 1 teaspoon of salt, and pepper.

5. Fold the cooked mushrooms and onions into the buckwheat. Add the porcini oil, toss to combine, and serve.

SERVES 6

NOTE: The salad keeps, covered, in the refrigerator for 1 day.

PREPPING IN ADVANCE: The salad can be completed several hours ahead of serving. Cover loosely and hold at room temperature.

Barley with Broccoli and Braised Garlic

We not only roast garlic at Mangia (page 374), but we also braise it, which brings out its sweetness and softens its texture in different ways. One of the residual effects, of course, is all the lovely garlic-flavored olive oil you have on hand after braising it. Use it in salad dressings, as a cooking oil, or for drizzling over focaccia or other chewy breads.

Along with the barley, you will find familiar Asian overtones here—a touch of sesame oil, some red pepper flakes, and crisp broccoli florets. Fish would make a very fine accompaniment, roasted, poached, or, easiest of all, steamed.

2½ cups water

2 teaspoons plus 1 pinch salt

1 cup pearl barley

1 head broccoli, 1 pound

½ cup garlic cloves

¾ cup plus 2 tablespoons extra-virgin olive oil

1 teaspoon dried hot pepper flakes

2 tablespoons Asian sesame oil

½ teaspoon sweet paprika

1. In a medium saucepan, bring the water to a boil. Add 1½ teaspoons of the salt and the barley. Return the water to a boil, lower the heat, and simmer until the barley is tender, 35 to 40 minutes. Drain in a colander. For storing instructions, see page 274.

2. Trim the broccoli into florets, discarding the stems.

3. Bring a second saucepan of water to a boil. Add ½ teaspoon salt and the broccoli florets. Blanch several minutes, drain in a colander, and run under cold water. Drain well.

4. Peel the garlic cloves, put them in a small saucepan, and cover with ¾ cup olive oil. Simmer the garlic over medium-low heat, braising it, until golden brown and soft, about 15 minutes. Transfer the cloves to a plate with a slotted spoon. Drain off all but 2 tablespoons of the oil. Let the reserved oil cool, pour it into a jar, and store in the refrigerator for future use.

5. Heat 2 tablespoons oil in the skillet until hot. Add the blanched broccoli florets, hot pepper flakes, and a pinch of salt. Cook several minutes, tossing the florets to coat them with the seasoned oil and pepper; then set aside to cool.

6. In a serving bowl, combine the barley, broccoli, and braised garlic. Add the sesame oil and paprika and toss gently to combine. Best served within 1 hour of finishing.

SERVES 6

PREPPING IN ADVANCE: The braised garlic can be made 2 days ahead. Let cool, transfer the oil and garlic cloves to a container, cover, and store in the refrigerator.

BEANS

Black Bean Salad with Tomatoes, Feta Cheese, and Chipotle Salsa

Wonderful on its own with a warm tortilla or two, with meat or fish, or a selection of vegetable salads, this looks especially appealing on a plain white platter—which is just how we serve it at Mangia. If you cook the beans ahead of time, the rest of the preparation is simple.

2 cups dried black beans, picked over

1 medium red onion

1 large tomato

1 chipotle chile in adobo sauce (with a little of the sauce)

¼ cup extra-virgin olive oil

2 tablespoons fresh lemon juice

1 garlic clove

4 ounces feta cheese

Salt and freshly ground black pepper

1. Soak the beans in water to cover overnight. The next day, drain them. Put the beans in a medium saucepan and add water to cover. Bring the water to a boil over high heat, skim off the foam on the surface, and reduce the heat to medium-low. Cover and cook for 45 minutes to 1 hour, until tender. Drain the beans in a colander and let cool. For storing instructions, see page 288.

2. Peel, trim, and halve the onion; slice the halves into ¼-inch half moons. Cut the tomato into ¼-inch dice.

3. Place the chipotle chile, olive oil, lemon juice, and garlic in a food processor and blend until the salsa is smooth.

4. In a serving bowl, combine the black beans with the salsa; then add the tomato and red onion. Crumble the feta into the bowl and toss gently. Adjust the seasonings, and serve.

SERVES 6

NOTE: Although the salad is best served within 1 hour of finishing, it keeps, covered, in the refrigerator for 1 day.

PREPPING IN ADVANCE: The salsa can be completed 1 day ahead. Transfer it to a container, cover, and store in the refrigerator.

ON COOKING AND STORING DRIED BEANS IN ADVANCE

The quality and length of time dried beans have been stored determine how long it will take to cook them. Because it is impossible to know either of those factors, we suggest that you use the cooking times in the recipes that follow as guidelines and start checking the beans for doneness about 10 minutes before the end of the cooking time. Know that beans double in volume when cooked.

When the beans are done, remove the pan from the heat, remove the cover, and let the beans cool in the cooking liquid. Store them in the cooking liquid in the refrigerator for up to 2 days. To use, drain and proceed with the recipe. (The cooking liquid is delicious and can be used in soups.)

Red Beans with Chives and Ricotta Salata

Ricotta salata cheese is made from sheep's milk and is similar to feta but with a creamier consistency. It is slightly sweet in flavor and makes a nice complement to the vegetables and beans in this colorful salad.

When assembling this for serving, toss it gently. You want to maintain the shape of the individual components because together they are interesting, and appealing.

1 cup dried red kidney beans, picked over

1 shallot

4 or 5 whole cloves

3 or 4 thyme sprigs
plus ½ teaspoon chopped thyme

1 bay leaf

1 large onion

1 stalk celery

1 carrot

1 medium Yukon gold potato

3 tablespoons extra-virgin olive oil

1 teaspoon sweet paprika

½ teaspoon ground cumin

¼ cup snipped chives
(in ½-inch lengths)

2 ounces ricotta salata cheese

1 tablespoon sherry vinegar

1. Soak the beans in water to cover overnight. The next day, drain them. Peel the shallot and stud it with the cloves.

2. In a large saucepan, combine the beans, shallot, cloves, thyme sprigs, and bay leaf; add water to cover. Bring the water to a boil over high heat, skim off the foam on the surface, and reduce the heat to medium-low. Cover and cook for 45 minutes to 1 hour, or until tender. Drain the beans in a colander, and remove the shallot, bay leaf, and thyme sprigs. Let cool. For storing instructions, see page 288.

3. Peel, trim, and cut the onion into ½-inch dice. Cut the celery and carrot into ½-inch dice. Peel and cut the potato in the same manner.

4. In a skillet, heat the olive oil over medium heat. Add the diced onion, celery, and carrot, and cook, stirring, until wilted. Add the diced potato. Lower the heat, add the paprika, cumin, and chopped thyme and cook, stirring occasionally, until the potatoes are golden and cooked through, about 30 minutes. Set aside to cool.

5. Cut the ricotta salata into ½-inch dice.

6. In a large serving bowl, combine the beans with the potato mixture, tossing gently to combine. Add the ricotta salata and chives and toss once more. Drizzle the sherry vinegar over the salad, and serve.

SERVES 6

NOTE: Although the salad is best served within 2 hours, it keeps, covered, in the refrigerator for 1 day.

PREPPING IN ADVANCE: If you would like to make this salad completely in advance, do so on the morning of the day you plan to serve it. Cover and refrigerate. Remove 1 hour before serving.

White Beans with Tomato, Roasted Prosciutto, and Sage

Roasted prosciutto adds a lovely saltiness and crunch to the yielding, tender texture of the beans in this salad. A lot of fresh sage adds singular color and aroma.

1½ cups dried great Northern beans or cannellini beans, picked over

1 small onion

4 whole cloves

1 bay leaf

1 thyme sprig

3 cups water

2 garlic cloves

6 plum tomatoes

2 tablespoons extra-virgin olive oil

½ cup chopped sage leaves

1 teaspoon salt

3 ounces thinly sliced prosciutto

Freshly cracked black pepper (see Note, page 167)

1. Soak the beans in water to cover overnight. The next day, drain them. Peel the onion, and stud it with the cloves.

2. In a large saucepan, combine the beans, onion, bay leaf, sprig of thyme, and water. Bring the water to a boil over high heat, skim off the foam on the surface, and reduce the heat to medium-low. Cover and cook for about 45 minutes, until the beans are tender. Drain the beans in a colander and remove the onion, bay leaf, and thyme sprig. Let cool. For storing instructions, see page 288.

3. Preheat the oven to 400 degrees F.

4. Peel, trim, and mince the garlic. Wash and core the tomatoes. Grate them, one at a time, on the largest holes of a box grater.

5. In a skillet, heat the olive oil, add the garlic, and sauté, stirring, until it starts to brown. Add the sage and cook for 2 minutes. Add the grated tomatoes, stir to combine, and add the salt. Simmer, stirring once, for 15 minutes. Remove from the heat and let cool.

6. Spread the prosciutto out in a single layer on a baking sheet. Roast until crisp, about 10 minutes. Let cool.

7. In a large bowl, combine the beans and tomato-sage sauce. Crumble the prosciutto into the bowl, season with freshly cracked pepper, and serve.

SERVES 6

NOTE: Although the salad is best served within 3 hours, it keeps, covered, in the refrigerator for 1 day.

PREPPING IN ADVANCE: The tomato-sage sauce can be completed 1 day ahead. Let cool, cover, and store in the refrigerator.

For the best texture, roast the prosciutto and add it to the salad just before serving.

White Beans with Peppers and Rosemary

Look for sweet white runner beans in specialty markets. These are large beans, almost one inch in length. They have a sweet taste and wonderful, creamy texture when cooked. Because of their size, they require a longer cooking time than other dried beans, at least 1 hour, or more if they have been stored for a while. They are the right bean, though, totally compatible with the roasted peppers and fresh rosemary in this recipe. If you cannot find them, great Northern beans are a substitute.

1 cup dried white runner beans or great Northern beans, picked over

3 cups water

2 garlic cloves

¼ cup extra-virgin olive oil

1 teaspoon dried hot pepper flakes

1 teaspoon salt

2 medium red bell peppers, cut into strips and roasted (see page 193)

2 tablespoons chopped fresh rosemary

Freshly ground black pepper to taste

1. Soak the beans in water to cover overnight. The next day, drain them.

2. In a saucepan, combine the beans and water. Bring the water to a boil over high heat, skim off the foam on the surface, and reduce the heat to medium-low. Cover and cook until the beans are tender, about 1 hour. Drain the beans in a colander and let cool. For storing instructions, see page 288.

3. Peel, trim, and mince the garlic.

4. In a skillet over medium heat, heat the olive oil, add the garlic and pepper flakes, and cook, stirring, just until the garlic starts to color. Add the salt and stir to combine.

5. In a serving bowl, combine the beans, seasoned olive oil, roasted pepper strips, and rosemary; toss gently to combine. Adjust the seasonings to taste and serve.

SERVES 6

NOTE: The salad keeps, covered, in the refrigerator for 1 day.

PREPPING IN ADVANCE: Roast the pepper strips in advance. Let cool, cover, and store in the refrigerator.

Chickpeas with Broccoli Rabe and Roasted Shallots

Creamy chickpeas, bitter broccoli rabe, sweet shallots, and a snappy red pepper puree—the combination looks great and tastes good, too. In case you are thinking you might like to use canned chickpeas as a way of saving time, we don't recommend it. The texture of soaked, slowly simmered chickpeas is what you want here.

1. Soak the chickpeas in water to cover overnight. The next day, drain them.

8 ounces dried chickpeas, picked over

2½ cups water

8 large shallots

¾ cup extra-virgin olive oil, plus extra for roasting

Salt and freshly ground black pepper

1 pound broccoli rabe

1 large red bell pepper, roasted, peeled, seeded, and cored (see page 193)

½ teaspoon ground cumin

½ teaspoon sweet paprika

¼ teaspoon cayenne

1 teaspoon fresh lemon juice

2. In a saucepan, combine the chickpeas and water. Bring the water to a boil over high heat, skim off the foam on the surface, and reduce the heat to medium-low. Cover and cook until the chickpeas are tender, about 1 hour. Drain in a colander and let cool. For storing instructions, see page 288.

3. Preheat the oven to 400 degrees F.

4. Peel and trim the shallots. Toss them in a bowl with a drizzle of olive oil and salt and pepper to taste. Place the shallots on a baking sheet and roast until soft, about 40 minutes. (The skins will darken and the edges will start to char.) Remove and let cool.

5. Wash the broccoli rabe and trim off the bottom 2 inches of stem. Bring a medium pot of salted water to a boil. Add the broccoli rabe and blanch for several minutes. (Blanching rabe before sautéing it removes some of its natural bitterness.) Remove from the pot and cool under cold running water to stop the cooking. Blot excess water with a towel.

6. Heat the ¼ cup of the olive oil in a large skillet over high heat. Add the broccoli rabe and cook for several minutes, stirring and lifting the rabe with tongs, until it is uniformly wilted. Season with salt to taste and set aside.

7. In a food processor, blend the roasted pepper with the cumin, paprika, cayenne, and ½ cup of remaining olive oil until pureed.

8. In a large serving bowl, combine the chickpeas, red pepper puree, sautéed broccoli rabe, and roasted shallots, and toss gently to combine. Best served within 2 hours of finishing.

SERVES 6

PREPPING IN ADVANCE: The shallots can be roasted 24 hours ahead. Let cool, cover, and store in the refrigerator.

The red pepper puree can also be prepared 24 hours ahead. Transfer it to a container, cover tightly, and store in the refrigerator.

Sauté the broccoli rabe 1 hour before assembling the salad.

Flageolets with Nancy's Peperonata

Flageolets are actually immature pod beans that are picked and removed from their pods when still green. Originally cultivated in the Americas, they were adopted by the French in the nineteenth century. Their taste, like their color, is delicate. They go beautifully with the assertive flavors of peperonata, which, as the word suggests, includes bell peppers, lots of tomatoes, garlic, and several surprises Nancy likes to add to the pot. Peperonata is also delicious just as is on chewy, crusty bread.

1. Soak the beans in water to cover overnight. The next day, drain them. Peel the onion and stud it with the cloves.

2. In a saucepan, combine the beans, onion, bay leaf, and water. Bring the water to a boil over high heat, skim off the foam on the surface, and reduce the heat to medium-low. Cover and cook about 50

1½ cups dried flageolet beans or great Northern beans, picked over

½ onion

4 whole cloves

1 bay leaf

2 cups water

FOR THE PEPERONATA

1 medium onion

2 garlic cloves

1 stalk of celery

¼ cup extra-virgin olive oil

½ teaspoon dried thyme

½ teaspoon dried oregano

½ teaspoon dried marjoram

½ cup coarsely chopped basil

3 cups crushed tomatoes

1 tablespoon sugar

1 tablespoon salt

¼ cup red wine vinegar

¼ cup golden raisins

3 tablespoons drained capers

1 large red bell pepper, roasted, peeled, cored, seeded, and diced (see page 193)

minutes, until the beans are tender. Drain, remove the onion and bay leaf, and let cool. For storing instructions, see page 288.

3. Make the peperonata: Peel, trim, and chop the onion. Peel, trim, and mince the garlic. Trim the celery, then dice.

4. Heat the olive oil in a skillet over medium heat. Add the onion, garlic, and celery and cook for several minutes, until the onion is softened. Add the thyme, oregano, marjoram, basil, and tomatoes. Stir to combine and cook about 10 minutes. Stir in the sugar, salt, red wine vinegar, golden raisins, and capers. Simmer the sauce until it is reduced by one-third, about 25 minutes. Set aside to cool.

5. In a serving bowl, combine the beans with the sauce and diced roasted pepper and stir gently to combine.

SERVES 6

NOTE: Although the salad is best served within 3 hours of finishing, it keeps, covered, in the refrigerator for 1 day.

PREPPING IN ADVANCE: The peperonata can be completed 2 days ahead. Let cool, cover, and store in the refrigerator.

Lentils with Garlic Sausage and Sage

Lentils and sausage is a classic combination. We especially like to use French green lentils here, which have, in fact, only a slight green tint to them. They are smaller than their cousins, brown lentils, and their taste is somewhat grassy, the reason to try them. Look for them in specialty markets.

From a purely practical point of view, lentils, unlike beans, do not need to be soaked in advance of cooking. They also cook in about half the time. This makes a luscious weekend meal, with soup and a great bread.

3 pounds kielbasa

8 ounces French green lentils (*lentilles du Puy*)

2 cups water

1 medium onion

3 garlic cloves

1 carrot

1 stalk of celery

3 tablespoons extra-virgin olive oil

3 tablespoons chopped fresh sage leaves
or ½ teaspoon dried

Freshly ground black pepper

1 teaspoon salt

1. Select a stockpot large enough to hold the sausage, and fill halfway with water. Add the sausage and bring the water to a boil. Lower the heat and simmer the sausage for 1 hour. Let cool in the water.

2. Put the lentils in a saucepan with the 2 cups of water. Bring the water to a boil; then simmer just until tender, about 20 minutes. Do not overcook; the lentils should be somewhat firm to the bite, not mushy. Drain in a colander and let cool. The lentils can be cooked 1 day in advance; when cool, cover and refrigerate.

3. Peel, trim, and finely dice the onion. Peel, trim, and chop the garlic. Peel and cut the carrot into ¼-inch dice; cut the celery in the same manner.

4. In a large skillet, heat the olive oil. Add the carrot, celery, onion, and garlic and cook over medium-low heat, stirring, until the onion is wilted. Add the sage and continue cooking until the vegetables are tender, about 20 minutes. Set aside.

5. In a large bowl, combine the lentils with the sautéed vegetables, tossing to combine well. Add a few grinds of pepper and the salt and adjust the seasonings to taste. Mound the lentils on a serving platter. Slice the garlic sausage into ¼-inch-thick rounds and arrange on top of the lentils. Best served within 2 hours of finishing.

SERVES 6

Lentils with Peppers and Goat Cheese

Tangy goat cheese and sautéed sweet peppers make a winning combination with lentils. This is simple to put together and quick to assemble, and has a subtle French feel to it. Serve with a platter of charcuterie, cold cuts, and a baguette.

1 cup French green lentils
(*lentilles du Puy*)

2 cups water

1 shallot

1 medium yellow bell pepper

1 medium red bell pepper

3 tablespoons extra-virgin olive oil

2 tablespoons sherry vinegar or champagne vinegar

3 ounces goat cheese, such as Montrachet

1. Put the lentils in a saucepan with the 2 cups of water. Bring to a boil; then simmer just until tender, about 20 minutes. Do not over-cook. The lentils should be some-what firm to the bite, not mushy. Drain and let cool. The lentils can be cooked 1 day in advance; when cool, cover and refrigerate.

2. Peel and mince the shallot. Cut the tops off the peppers; remove the seeds, trim off the bottoms, and slice into ¼-inch-wide strips.

3. Heat the olive oil in a skillet over medium heat. Add the shallot and cook, stirring, just until softened. Add the peppers, reduce the heat, and cook, stirring occasionally, until the peppers are tender, about 20 minutes. Return the heat to medium and add the vinegar. Cook briefly, until the vinegar evaporates. Remove the pan from the heat and let cool.

4. In a large serving bowl, combine the pepper strips with the lentils, and toss to combine. Crumble in the goat cheese and serve.

SERVES 6

NOTE: The salad is best served within 1 hour, but it keeps, covered, in the refrigerator for 1 day.

PREPPING IN ADVANCE: The pepper combination can be cooked 1 day ahead. Let cool, cover, and refrigerate.

The Entrée Table

FISH AND SHELLFISH

POULTRY

MEATS

The advantages of serving an entrée at room temperature, deliberately at room temperature, that is, are almost too obvious to enumerate. How many of us have stood in the kitchen finishing a finicky sauce, our guests seated, waiting at the dinner table, only to realize that the meal we had so wanted to serve hot was going to be room temperature anyway?

The convenience factor is undoubtedly among the best reasons we know to serve a room-temperature entrée. The very best reason of all, however, is the flavor. Refrigeration, even for a short time, alters taste and texture. Refrigeration is a must under certain conditions and with certain combinations, like mayonnaise. If, by cleverly timing the preparation, you can avoid refrigerating a dish, and this includes our entrées as well as our salads, do so.

Our entrées are very easy to prepare, with grilling, poaching, pan-frying, and roasting among the preferred methods of cooking. Take Grilled Orange-Marinated Salmon (page 310) or Basil-Parmesan Chicken Salad (page 333); nothing complicated there. Where we feel that a certain entrée would be particularly well suited by a side dish, we suggest it. Otherwise, you are on your own to mix and match. The Salads Table is a great place to start looking for ideas.

Most of our entrée recipes end with the words "Best served within 1 hour of finishing." Our time frame comes from experience: We know that is when the flavors will be at their best. Remember the information; simply store it away. Do not set a kitchen timer as a reminder. The whole point of room-temperature food is that it be easy to make, and just as easy to serve and enjoy.

FISH AND SHELLFISH

Poached Cod with Catalan Sauce

Poached Halibut

Pan-Fried Ancho Chile–Rubbed
   Red Snapper

Grilled Orange-Marinated Salmon

Roasted Salmon

Pan-Fried Cajun Swordfish

Paprika-Glazed Broiled Swordfish

Pan-Fried Tuna Steaks

Tuna Niçoise Salad
   with Parmigiano Croutons

Calamari Salad

Octopus with Red Pepper Salsa

Sea Scallops with Spicy Peanut
   Butter Sauce

Shrimp Puttanesca

Jumbo Shrimp with Cannellini Beans

Lemon-Peppered Shrimp
   with Green Rice

Poached Cod with Catalan Sauce

A simple poaching liquid, the French court bouillon, imparts flavor to cod fillets that are then topped with a Mediterranean-style fresh tomato sauce. You can make the sauce a day in advance if you like. It is also very appealing on roasted pork loin or grilled shrimp.

1. Make the sauce: In a small bowl, soak the ancho chile pepper in warm water to cover until soft, about 15 minutes. Drain, seed, and finely chop.

2. Peel, trim, and mince the garlic. Peel, trim, and chop the onion. Trim and dice the bell pepper. Peel, seed, and chop the plum tomatoes.

3. Heat the olive oil in a large skillet over medium heat. Add the garlic, onion, and bell pepper and cook, stirring, until the onion is translucent. Add the ancho pepper, tomatoes, chicken broth, and cayenne and bring the mixture to a boil.

FOR THE SAUCE

1 dried ancho chile pepper

2 garlic cloves

1 medium onion

1 medium red bell pepper

4 large plum tomatoes

¼ cup extra-virgin olive oil

¼ cup chicken broth

½ teaspoon cayenne

2 tablespoons sherry vinegar

Salt and freshly ground black pepper

FOR THE COURT BOUILLON

1 medium leek

1 medium carrot

½ small fennel bulb

6 cups water

1 cup dry white wine

About 6 flat-leaf parsley sprigs

1 teaspoon coriander seeds

1 teaspoon black peppercorns

2 bay leaves

1 teaspoon salt

2 pounds cod fillets

3 flat-leaf parsley sprigs

Cover, reduce the heat to low, and cook, stirring occasionally, for 30 minutes. Stir in the sherry vinegar and salt and pepper to taste and cook 5 minutes longer. Remove the pan from the heat and let cool.

4. Prepare the court bouillon for poaching the cod: Wash and slice the leek; rough-cut the carrot and fennel. In a nonreactive, deep skillet, combine the water, wine, leek, carrot, fennel, parsley sprigs, coriander seeds, peppercorns, bay leaves, and salt. Bring the mixture to a boil, lower the heat, and simmer for 20 minutes.

5. Meanwhile, cut the cod fillets into 6 equal portions. Add the cod to the simmering liquid and poach it gently for 10 to 12 minutes, or until the fish flakes easily when tested with a fork. With a spatula, remove the cooked cod to a serving platter. Discard the court bouillon.

6. Remove the leaves from the parsley sprigs and mince. Spoon the Catalan sauce over the cod fillets and sprinkle the chopped parsley over it. Best served within 1 hour of finishing.

SERVES 6

PREPPING IN ADVANCE: The sauce can be made 1 day ahead. Let cool, cover, and refrigerate. Remove from the refrigerator 1 hour before saucing the poached fillets.

Poached Halibut

Poaching guarantees moist fish, and here tomatoes, fennel seeds, and white wine provide subtle flavor. If your fish market does not carry halibut fillets, use halibut steaks, cut 1 inch thick. While we like these with Pickled Vegetable Relish (page 368) because it makes such a crisp counterpoint to the halibut, an herbed or spicy mayonnaise works nicely, too. A grain or green salad as an accompaniment, and there is the menu.

1 medium onion

6 large plum tomatoes

2 cups dry white wine

1 teaspoon fennel seeds

1 teaspoon salt

2½ pounds halibut fillets, cut into 6-ounce portions

3 lemons or limes, halved, for garnish

SERVE WITH: Pickled Vegetable Relish (page 368).

1. Peel, trim, and dice the onion.

2. Grate the tomatoes, one at a time, on the largest holes of a box grater, discarding the little bit of skin with pulp attached that remains after grating. (You should have 2 cups grated.)

3. Combine the tomatoes, onion, white wine, fennel seeds, and salt in a large skillet. Bring to a boil; then simmer for 20 minutes.

4. Add the halibut fillets to the simmering liquid and poach them until the fish flakes easily when tested with a fork, 8 to 10 minutes. Transfer with a slotted spoon to a large plate and let cool.

5. To serve, place the fillets on a serving platter and garnish with lemons or limes. Serve with a relish or sauce of choice. Best served within 1 hour of finishing

SERVES 6

Pan-Fried Ancho
Chile–Rubbed Red Snapper

A Mexican spice rub enhances the sweet taste of red snapper. This entrée makes an easy summer meal with a salad and a bottle of crisp wine. Try it with the fresh cucumber and avocado combination we suggest below. You will feel as if you were dining in Veracruz.

2 garlic cloves

2 tablespoons ancho chile powder (available in specialty food markets)

1 teaspoon sweet paprika

1 teaspoon ground cumin

Salt and freshly ground black pepper

¼ cup plus 3 tablespoons extra-virgin olive oil

6 red snapper fillets, 6 to 8 ounces each (skin left on)

3 limes, halved, for garnish

SERVE WITH: Cucumber, Avocado, Scallion, and Lime Salad (page 214).

1. Peel, trim, and mince the garlic. Put the garlic in a shallow bowl, add the chile powder, paprika, cumin, and salt and pepper to taste, and stir to combine. Stir in ¼ cup of the olive oil to make a loose paste.

2. Coat the fillets, one at a time, with the chile paste. Let them marinate for ½ hour in the refrigerator. Remove them 10 minutes before cooking to stand at room temperature.

3. Heat the remaining 3 tablespoons of olive oil in a large skillet over medium heat. (Or, if you are cooking the fillets in batches, use 2 tablespoons of oil per batch.) When the oil ripples, add the fillets, skin side down, and fry for 2 minutes. Turn with a spatula and fry several minutes longer, until the flesh is opaque. With the spatula, transfer the fillets to a serving platter, overlapping them slightly, and garnish with the limes. Best served within 1 hour of finishing.

SERVES 6

Grilled Orange-Marinated Salmon

If you use a charcoal grill, as opposed to a gas or electric one, you know that the optimum moment for grilling depends upon a lot of factors, not the least of which is the weather or the way the fire was built. If you deal with those kinds of vagaries, this is the perfect recipe to make. The salmon can be marinated and grilled ahead; it can even be refrigerated several hours in advance of serving. All you really have to factor in is the half hour that is needed for it to stand at room temperature to come to full flavor.

2 tablespoons fennel seeds, toasted (see Note)

½ cup extra-virgin olive oil

¼ cup freshly squeezed orange juice (2 small oranges)

6 salmon fillets (1½ to 2 inches wide), about 6 ounces each (skin left on)

SERVE WITH: Grilled Fennel, Black Olive, and Golden Raisin Salad (page 215).

1. Crush the toasted fennel seeds in a mortar with a pestle, or in a spice grinder. Transfer to a wide, shallow ceramic or glass dish, such as a pie plate, add the olive oil and orange juice, and stir to combine.

2. Add the salmon fillets to the marinade, turning to coat them all over, and let stand, covered, at room temperature for 1 hour.

3. Place the grill rack 1 to 2 inches from the coals. Preheat the grill until the coals are white.

4. Remove the salmon from the marinade, letting the excess drip off, and discard the marinade. Place the fillets, skin side down, on the grill and cook for 3 to 4 minutes. Turn carefully, with long-handled spring tongs if you have them, and grill for 3 to 4 minutes more, or until the flesh flakes

easily when tested with the tongs or a fork. (You may need to move the fillets slightly toward the side, where the heat is less intense, to prevent burning.) Transfer the fillets to a platter and let cool. (The fillets can also be cooked in a grill pan on top of the stove; place, skin side down, in a dry pan, cook 4 minutes, turn, and cook another 4 minutes.)

5. When the salmon is cool enough to handle, remove the skin. Arrange the fillets on a platter and serve within 1 hour of cooking.

SERVES 6

NOTE: To toast fennel seeds: Heat a dry skillet over medium heat until hot. Add the fennel seeds and toast, stirring constantly, until fragrant, about 3 minutes. Remove from the pan and let cool.

Roasted Salmon

This is a simple, foolproof way, and possibly the best way, to cook salmon.

For a winter dinner, when our suggestion of a cherry tomato salad as an accompaniment might seem a little light, why not make Buckwheat with Shiitake Mushrooms and Thyme (page 282) or Whole Roasted Beet Salad with Orange Moroccan Dressing (page 205), or both. You will have plenty of time to fine-tune a menu, however you wish to do it, because the salmon takes barely a minute to prepare. The oven does the rest.

6 salmon fillets, 6 ounces each, 1½ to 2 inches wide (skin left on)

2 tablespoons extra-virgin olive oil

Salt and freshly ground black pepper

SERVE WITH: Cherry Tomato, Sautéed Leek, and Pine Nut Salad (page 231).

1. Preheat the oven to 425 degrees F. Line a baking sheet with parchment paper.

2. In a small bowl, combine the olive oil with salt and pepper to taste.

3. Brush the seasoned oil on both sides of the salmon fillets, coating them well, then arrange them, skin side down, on the baking sheet. Roast for 8 minutes for fish that is still pink in the center when tested in its thickest part with a fork. (For fish that is cooked through, roast 1 to 2 minutes longer.) Let cool on the baking sheet.

4. When cool enough to handle, remove the skin. To serve, arrange the fillets on a serving platter.

SERVES 6

PREPPING IN ADVANCE: Although it is best served within 1 hour of finishing, the salmon can be roasted several hours ahead. Let cool, cover, and refrigerate. Remove ½ hour to stand at room temperature before serving.

Pan-Fried Cajun Swordfish

The type of paprika you use makes a big difference. Szeged paprika from Hungary imparts a deep red color and round sweetness; here it balances the heat of the cayenne in the spice rub. Make extra rub and keep it in a jar in your cabinet. It is nice used on pork tenderloin, or sprinkled over potatoes before roasting.

1. In a bowl, combine all the ingredients for the spice rub, stirring well.

2. Pour the olive oil into a shallow bowl. Dip the swordfish steaks, one at a time, into the oil, letting the excess drip off; then dredge in the spice rub. Pat the spices evenly onto both sides of the steaks.

3. Heat a 10-inch, heavy-bottomed skillet over medium-high heat. Add the peanut oil and heat until hot. Slip in the swordfish steaks, without crowding. (It may be necessary to cook the fish in 2 batches or in 2 skillets.) Fry the fish for about 3 minutes. Turn and cook 3 minutes more, or until the flesh is white when tested with a fork or is springy but firm to your finger. Transfer to a serving platter and garnish with the lemon slices. Best served within 1 hour of finishing.

SERVES 6

FOR THE SPICE RUB

3 tablespoons sweet paprika

1½ tablespoons salt

1 tablespoon cayenne

1½ teaspoons ground allspice

1½ teaspoons ground cumin

1½ teaspoons dried thyme

1½ teaspoons dried oregano

1½ teaspoons freshly ground black pepper

1½ teaspoons white pepper

1 teaspoon garlic powder

¾ cup extra-virgin olive oil

6 swordfish loin steaks, 6 to 8 ounces each, about 1 inch thick

¼ cup peanut oil

Lemon slices, for garnish

SERVE WITH: Orange and Arugula Salad (page 220).

Paprika-Glazed Broiled Swordfish

We like to use Spanish, not Hungarian, paprika for this recipe because of its smoky flavor. Spanish paprika is not as easy to find, however, and is worth hunting for under the label Pimenton de la Vera. When you find it, buy it.

Paprika loses its punch if kept too long on the shelf. Check before using. It smells pungent when fresh.

3 tablespoons unsalted butter

1 tablespoon salt

1 tablespoon freshly ground black pepper

2 teaspoons Spanish paprika

6 swordfish steaks, 6 to 8 ounces each, about 1 inch thick

Lime wedges, for serving

1. Preheat the broiler.

2. In a small skillet, melt the butter over low heat. Add the salt, pepper, and paprika and stir to combine. Remove from the heat.

3. Place the swordfish steaks on the broiler pan and brush with the seasoned butter. Broil 6 inches from the heat source for about 4 minutes. Turn, brush the second side with the remaining butter, and broil about 4 minutes more, until the fish flakes when tested with a fork or feels springy, but firm to the touch, when pressed with your finger. Transfer the steaks to a serving platter, overlapping them slightly, and garnish with the lime wedges. Best served within 1 hour of finishing.

SERVES 6

Pan-Fried Tuna Steaks

Three different kinds of seeds—cumin, coriander, and fennel—encrust these tuna steaks, which we simply pan-fry. At Mangia, we like our tuna rare, deep red in the center. Follow the suggested timing below should you like it better done. If you have any tuna left over, place small chunks of it on tender lettuce leaves and serve as an hors d'oeuvre.

1 tablespoon cumin seeds

1 tablespoon coriander seeds

1 tablespoon fennel seeds

Salt

Freshly ground black pepper

¾ cup extra-virgin olive oil

6 tuna steaks, 6 to 8 ounces each, about 1 inch thick

Lemon wedges, for serving

SERVE WITH: Sweet-and-Hot Pepper Relish (page 366).

1. In a mortar with a pestle or in a spice grinder, crush the cumin, coriander, and fennel seeds until fine. Add salt and pepper to taste.

2. Brush the tuna steaks on both sides with ¼ cup of the olive oil, coating well. Sprinkle the crushed seed mixture onto both sides of the steaks, pressing it on.

3. In a large heavy skillet, heat the remaining ½ cup olive oil over medium heat, until very hot. Add the fish steaks carefully to prevent the oil from splattering. Do not crowd the pan. Cook approximately 2 minutes, turn with a spatula, and cook 2 minutes more for medium-rare fish. (If you like fish that is rare in the center, then reduce the cooking time by 1 minute; for more thoroughly cooked tuna, add 1 minute.) Remove the steaks to a serving platter and garnish with the lemon wedges. Best served within 1 hour of finishing.

SERVES 6

Tuna Niçoise Salad with Parmigiano Croutons

Our take on the classic recipe from the South of France, with a nod to Italy. It requires some preparation, but you won't regret a minute of it once you take the first bite. And most of it, the individual components, that is, can be done in advance. This is an entrée for the summer solstice, for a dinner in the late lingering twilight, for family and friends.

1. Preheat the oven to 325 degrees F.

2. Make the croutons: Cut the bread into ½-inch cubes and put the cubes in a bowl. Add the olive oil, cheese, pepper flakes, and salt and toss to coat. Spread the croutons on a baking sheet and bake until crisp and golden, about 35 minutes. Let cool.

3. Preheat the grill until hot. Or preheat a grill pan or large cast-iron skillet over medium-high heat on the stove top until it smokes.

FOR THE CROUTONS

4 slices of stale country bread

½ cup extra-virgin olive oil

¼ cup coarsely grated Parmigiano-Reggiano cheese

Pinch of dried hot pepper flakes

½ teaspoon salt

2 pounds tuna steaks, 1 inch thick

½ cup extra-virgin olive oil

Salt

Freshly ground black pepper

8 ounces creamer potatoes

8 ounces string beans, trimmed

1 small red onion

2 medium tomatoes

6 to 8 radicchio leaves

¾ cup chopped basil leaves

1 garlic clove

4 anchovy fillets packed in oil

6 tablespoons extra-virgin olive oil

2 tablespoons red wine vinegar

¼ cup drained capers

4. Brush both sides of the tuna steaks generously with the olive oil and season with salt and pepper. Arrange on the grill, grill pan, or skillet and cook, turning once, for 2 minutes per side for medium. Transfer to a platter and let stand while preparing the rest of the salad.

5. Slice the potatoes ¼ inch thick. Place them in salted water to cover and cook until tender, no more than 10 minutes. Drain in a colander, run under cold water to stop the cooking, and reserve.

6. Cook the string beans in boiling salted water to cover until crisp-tender and bright green, about 4 minutes. Drain, run under cold water to stop the cooking, and reserve.

7. Peel, trim, and slice the red onion into ¼-inch-thick rings. Soak in cold water to cover for 20 minutes. While the onion is soaking, dice the tomatoes. Tear the radicchio leaves coarsely. Chop the basil leaves.

8. Peel, trim, and mince the garlic. Mash the anchovy fillets. In a small bowl, combine the garlic and anchovies with the olive oil and vinegar. Set aside until ready to dress the salad.

9. Slice the grilled tuna into 1½ x ½-inch pieces. Drain the red onion and pat it dry.

10. To serve, combine in a large shallow bowl the radicchio, tomatoes, potatoes, string beans, red onion, basil, and capers. Add the tuna and dressing and toss to combine. Taste and adjust the seasonings, and garnish with the Parmigiano croutons. Best served within 1 hour of finishing.

SERVES 6

PREPPING IN ADVANCE: The croutons can be completed the night before serving. Let cool and store in an airtight container at room temperature.

Cook the potato, beans, and tuna 4 hours ahead. Store separately in covered containers in the refrigerator.

The radicchio can be washed ahead of time. Be sure to dry it well. Store in a resealable plastic bag in the refrigerator.

Remove all the components of the salad from the refrigerator 1 hour in advance to stand at room temperature before assembling.

Calamari Salad

Some very fussy customers cannot live without this simple salad. Our version of this classic is very Italian, with a dash of Tabasco for a lick of heat.

1. Peel, trim, and slice the onion.

2. Pour the water into a 4-quart stockpot and add the sliced onion, lemon half, and bay leaf. Bring the water to a simmer, and simmer for 20 minutes.

1 medium onion

3 quarts water

½ lemon

1 bay leaf

3 pounds cleaned fresh or frozen calamari

2 small garlic cloves

⅓ cup extra-virgin olive oil

Juice of 4 lemons

1½ cups coarsely chopped flat-leaf parsley

Dash of Tabasco

Salt

Freshly ground black pepper

3. Meanwhile, prepare the calamari by separating the tubes and tentacles. Rinse the tubes under cold running water and pull off any quills, if not already removed. Cut the calamari into ¼-inch-thick rings.

4. Add the calamari to the simmering water and cook for 5 minutes. (It will turn opaque.) Drain in a colander, remove the onion, lemon, and bay leaf, and let cool for 10 minutes.

5. While the calamari cools, mince the garlic and put in a large ceramic or glass bowl with the olive oil, juice of the 4 lemons, parsley, Tabasco, and salt and pepper to taste. Add the calamari and toss well to combine. Best served within 1 hour of finishing.

SERVES 6

PREPPING IN ADVANCE: The calamari can be cooked and dressed, omitting the parsley, 4 hours ahead of serving. Cover and refrigerate. Remove from the refrigerator 30 minutes before serving to stand at room temperature. Before serving, add the parsley and toss to combine.

Octopus with Red Pepper Salsa

This salad—an antipasto or main course—has always been very popular at Mangia. Plan ahead when making this: The salad needs to marinate 1 day in advance of serving.

1. Slice the onion and lemons. Peel and then smash 3 of the garlic cloves.

2. Fill a large pot with the water (enough to cover the octopus) and add the smashed garlic cloves, sliced onion and lemons, bay leaves, thyme sprigs, and peppercorns. Bring the water to a boil and simmer for 20 minutes.

3. Add the octopus to the water and simmer for approximately 1 to 1¼ hours, until tender. Drain in a colander, remove the onion, lemons, and seasonings, and let cool.

4. While the octopus cooks, peel, trim, and mince the remaining 2 garlic cloves. Put in a large ceramic or glass bowl and stir in the olive oil and lemon juice.

1 small onion

2 lemons

5 garlic cloves

3 bay leaves

2 thyme sprigs

¼ teaspoon whole peppercorns

3½ pounds cleaned fresh octopus

1 cup extra-virgin olive oil

½ cup fresh lemon juice

FOR THE SALSA

3 medium red bell peppers

6 tablespoons extra-virgin olive oil

2 tablespoons fresh lemon juice

2 tablespoons drained capers

½ cup chopped flat-leaf parsley

Salt

Freshly cracked black pepper (see Note, page 167)

5. When the octopus is cool enough to handle, peel off the purple outer skin from the tentacles. Cut the tentacles into bite-sized pieces and add them to the oil and lemon juice marinade. Stir well to combine, cover, and let marinate in the refrigerator overnight.

6. Before serving, make the salsa: Core, seed, and finely dice the peppers. In a large serving bowl, combine the peppers, olive oil, lemon juice, capers, and parsley; toss to combine well.

7. Drain the octopus. Add it to the salsa and toss. Season with salt and freshly cracked black pepper to taste. Best served within 1 hour of finishing.

SERVES 6

PREPPING IN ADVANCE: The octopus marinates the day before serving. Cover and store in the refrigerator. Remove from the refrigerator to stand at room temperature ½ hour before assembling.

The salsa can be completed several hours ahead. Cover, refrigerate, and remove it with the octopus to stand at room temperature before combining just before serving.

Sea Scallops with Spicy Peanut Butter Sauce

We make this dish at Mangia with "dry" scallops—ones that have not been treated with chemicals. Chemicals tend to add to water weight, and liquid prevents scallops from searing properly. For the same reason, frozen scallops will not work here, either. "Dry" scallops sear well— exactly what you want in this dish.

¼ cup smooth peanut butter

2 tablespoons Asian sesame oil

1 tablespoon Chinese red chili paste (see Note)

2 tablespoons rice vinegar

2 tablespoons honey

½ cup water, as needed

1½ to 2 pounds dry scallops (also called diver scallops)

1 teaspoon salt

½ teaspoon white pepper

3 tablespoons peanut oil

¼ cup roasted peanuts, for garnish

2 tablespoons chopped scallions (green and white parts), for garnish

1. In a food processor, combine the peanut butter, sesame oil, chili paste, rice vinegar, and honey and process until smooth, adding a little of the water, if necessary, to obtain a consistency like heavy cream.

2. Season the scallops on both sides with the salt and pepper.

3. In a large skillet, heat the peanut oil over medium-high heat until hot, but not smoking. Add the scallops and stir-fry them for 3 or 4 minutes, or just until they turn opaque.

4. Add the peanut sauce to the skillet and cook 30 seconds, tossing to coat the scallops. Spoon onto a serving platter and garnish with a sprinkling of the roasted peanuts and scallions. Best served within 1 hour of finishing.

SERVES 6

NOTE: Chinese red chili paste is available at specialty food stores and Asian markets.

PREPPING IN ADVANCE: The dish can be completed up to 1 hour ahead. Hold at room temperature.

Shrimp Puttanesca

This is a slight variation on the renowned Neapolitan seafood and pasta dish. It is wonderful served over plain pasta, too. However you serve it, accompany with it the best crusty bread you can find. And if you want to serve this hot, as opposed to waiting for it to cool to room temperature, which can be difficult because it smells so good, go right ahead.

1. Make the puttanesca sauce: Peel, trim, and finely chop the onion.

2. Heat the olive oil in a large skillet over medium heat until hot. Add the garlic and sauté, stirring, until it just begins to brown. Add the onion, anchovies, and pepper flakes, stir to break up the anchovies; cook several minutes to blend the flavors. Stir in the tomatoes, olives, capers, and oregano and

FOR THE SAUCE

1 medium onion

¼ cup extra-virgin olive oil

1 teaspoon chopped garlic (about 1 large clove)

8 anchovy fillets packed in oil

1 teaspoon dried hot pepper flakes

3 pounds canned chopped peeled plum tomatoes

⅓ cup pitted Gaeta olives

¼ cup drained capers

1 teaspoon chopped fresh oregano or ½ teaspoon dried

½ cup water

¼ cup red wine vinegar

1 teaspoon salt

36 large shrimp (2½ pounds), peeled and deveined

Crusty bread as an accompaniment

cook over medium heat, stirring occasionally, about 10 minutes. Stir in the water and cook another 10 minutes. Stir in the vinegar and cook for 5 minutes. Add the salt.

3. Add the shrimp to the sauce, cover, and cook over medium heat just until the shrimp turn opaque, about 3 minutes. Check the seasonings, and add salt and pepper as desired. Serve in soup plates with lots of crusty bread. Best served within 1 hour of finishing.

SERVES 6

PREPPING IN ADVANCE: The puttanesca sauce can be made 1 day before serving. Let cool, cover, and refrigerate. Reheat until hot, add the shrimp, and cook as directed.

Jumbo Shrimp with Cannellini Beans

This is our twist on the classic Italian salad of tuna and white beans, only far more elegant. On the basis of the ingredients alone—jumbo shrimp, Gaeta olives, and prosciutto—this is an entrée for a special occasion. You will need to start soaking the beans the night before you plan to serve this.

1. Prepare the beans: Soak the beans in water to cover overnight. The next day, drain them and rinse.

FOR THE BEANS

½ pound dried cannellini beans, picked over

1 onion, sliced

1 bay leaf

1 thyme sprig

4 cups water

2. Peel, trim, and slice the onion.

3. In a saucepan, combine the beans, sliced onion, bay leaf, thyme sprig, and water. Bring the water to a boil, cover the pot, and simmer until the beans are tender, but not mushy, about 1 hour. Drain, remove the onion, bay leaf, and thyme sprig, and cool.

4. Make the bean salad: Peel, trim, and chop the garlic. In a large bowl, combine the beans, garlic, olive oil, and lemon juice, tossing gently but thoroughly to combine. Add the olives, parsley, and salt and pepper to taste. Reserve at room temperature.

5. Meanwhile, preheat the oven to 350 degrees F.

6. Arrange the prosciutto in a single layer on a baking sheet and roast until crisp like bacon, about 10 minutes. Let cool.

7. To prepare the shrimp: peel, trim, and mince the garlic and put in a bowl. Add ½ cup of the olive oil, the lemon juice, paprika, salt, and pepper. Add the shrimp, stir to combine, and let marinate for ½ hour.

FOR THE SALAD

1 garlic clove

½ cup extra-virgin olive oil

¼ cup fresh lemon juice

½ cup pitted Gaeta olives

1 cup chopped flat-leafed parsley

Salt

Freshly ground black pepper

3 slices thinly cut prosciutto, about 2 ounces total weight

FOR THE SHRIMP

1 garlic clove

½ cup plus 3 tablespoons extra-virgin olive oil

2 tablespoons fresh lemon juice

2 teaspoons sweet paprika

½ teaspoon salt

½ teaspoon freshly ground black pepper

24 jumbo shrimp, peeled and deveined

8. Heat the remaining 3 tablespoons of olive oil in a large skillet over high heat. When the oil ripples, add the shrimp and cook, tossing, for 3 minutes. Toss well again and cook 3 minutes more, or only until the shrimp turn opaque. Remove the pan from the heat.

9. Crumble the roasted prosciutto into the bean salad. Add the shrimp, toss, and adjust the seasonings if necessary. Spoon the salad onto a serving platter. Best served within 1 hour of finishing.

SERVES 6

PREPPING IN ADVANCE: The bean salad can be completed 1 day ahead through step 4. Cover and refrigerate.

The shrimp can be cooked several hours in advance of serving. Let cool, cover, and hold in the refrigerator.

Remove the shrimp and bean salad ½ hour before serving to stand at room temperature; then combine, adjust the seasonings, and serve.

Lemon-Peppered Shrimp with Green Rice

Jumbo shrimp are the largest and most expensive available. Every bite is worth it. The look of this is magnificent—it's a party dish.

1. Make the rice: In a medium saucepan, bring the water to a boil, add the salt and rice, and stir well. Return the water to a boil, cover, and reduce the heat to the lowest possible setting. Cook for 20 minutes. Drain any excess water. Let the rice cool in the pan to room temperature. (If you are considering making the rice ahead of time, know that refrigerating it will make it tougher. Hold it at room temperature unless you are making it so far in advance that it must be refrigerated.)

2. Wash the arugula and spinach leaves and pat them dry. Put in a food processor with the parsley and cilantro. Add the olive oil and salt and process to a paste.

FOR THE RICE

4 cups water

1 teaspoon salt

2 cups long-grain rice

2 cups arugula leaves

2 cups flat-leaf spinach leaves

½ cup flat-leaf parsley leaves

½ cup cilantro leaves

¼ cup extra-virgin olive oil

1 teaspoon salt

FOR THE SHRIMP

3 tablespoons extra-virgin olive oil

2 tablespoons ground mixed peppercorns (pink, white, black, and green)

2 tablespoons grated lemon zest

Juice of 2 lemons

2 teaspoons salt

24 jumbo shrimp, peeled and deveined

Lime or lemon wedges, for serving (optional)

3. Marinate the shrimp: In a ceramic or glass bowl, stir together the olive oil, ground peppercorns, lemon zest and juice, and salt until combined. Add the shrimp, stir to coat, and marinate in the refrigerator for 30 minutes.

4. While the shrimp marinate, preheat the oven to 500 degrees F and finish the rice. Fold the cilantro-spinach puree into the cooled rice and stir gently but thoroughly to combine. Mound the rice lengthwise on an oval platter.

5. Place the shrimp on a baking sheet and roast for 3 minutes. Turn and cook for 3 minutes more. Arrange the shrimp, tails crossing, on the rice. If desired, garnish the platter with lime or lemon wedges. Best served within 1 hour of finishing.

SERVES 6

PREPPING IN ADVANCE: The rice can be cooked and sauced several hours ahead. Cover and hold at room temperature.

For best flavor, cook the shrimp no more than 1 hour in advance of serving.

POULTRY

Stewed Chicken with Tomatoes,
    Green Olives, and Raisins

Barbecued Chicken with Toasted
    Fennel Seeds

Basil-Parmesan Chicken Salad

Roasted Herb-Stuffed Chicken Breasts

Roasted Chicken Breast Chunks
    with Sesame Dressing

Chipotle Chile Chicken Wings

Roasted Breast of Turkey

Spicy Marinated
    Roasted Turkey Breast

Seared Duck Breast
    with Pear Chutney

Stewed Chicken with Tomatoes, Green Olives, and Raisins

With sweet and salty overtones, this rustic, vegetable-filled chicken stew shares some of the same ingredients—the tomatoes, raisins, and olives—as the renowned Cuban beef dish, *picadillo*. This, of course, can be served hot. As it cools to room temperature, though, is when the flavors, especially in the sauce, are best. They meld together in an indescribably luxurious way.

If you have any sauce left over, use it as the base for a soup. Simply reheat and add cooked beans or pasta.

1 roasting chicken, 4½ pounds

2 chicken breast halves, on the bone, with skin, about 12 ounces each

3 large white potatoes, 1½ pounds

6 thin medium carrots

1 red onion

3 garlic cloves

3 large tomatoes

12 flat-leaf parsley sprigs

12 cilantro sprigs

2 tablespoons extra-virgin olive oil

2 cups chicken broth

1 teaspoon ground cumin

2 small bay leaves

10 whole black peppercorns

1 tablespoon salt

1 cup dark raisins

1 cup pitted green olives

1. Cut the whole chicken into 8 pieces. Wash them, along with the 2 additional breasts, and shake off the excess water. Cut away all fat and extra skin. Reserve.

2. Peel the potatoes, cut each in 8 pieces, and put in a bowl with plenty of water. Peel and trim the carrots and cut into chunks, about 4 per carrot. Add to the bowl with the potatoes.

3. Peel, trim, and cut the onion into large chunks. Peel and trim the garlic.

4. Wash the tomatoes and cut into large chunks.

5. Tie the parsley and cilantro sprigs together with kitchen string.

6. In this order, put the tomatoes, garlic, and onion in a blender or food processor and puree.

7. Drain the potatoes and carrots.

8. In a large, heavy pot, heat the olive oil over medium heat, add the puree, and cook it, partially covered, for about 15 minutes. Add the chicken broth, cumin, bay leaves, herb bouquet, drained vegetables, peppercorns, and salt and stir well. Put the chicken pieces in the sauce and bring the mixture to a boil. Reduce the heat to the lowest possible setting, cover, and simmer for 45 minutes.

9. Add the raisins and olives, stir to combine, and cook for another 15 minutes. Remove the pan from the heat and let the stew cool slightly.

10. With a slotted spoon, place the chicken, vegetables, olives, and raisins on a large platter. Remove the herb bouquet and bay leaves from the sauce and discard.

11. Return the pot to the heat and reduce the sauce over high heat until thick, about 15 minutes. Pour some of the sauce over the chicken. Let stand at room temperature for 1 to 1½ hours before serving.

SERVES 6

Barbecued Chicken
with Toasted Fennel Seeds

Our barbecued chicken is one of the first dishes to disappear at lunchtime, when customers pour through the doors. It is delicious and different—the fennel seeds set it apart.

1 roasting chicken, 3½ pounds

2 chicken breast halves, on the bone, with skin, 8 to 10 ounces each

1 lemon

Salt and freshly ground black pepper

1 quart Nancy's BBQ Sauce (page 366)

½ cup fennel seeds, toasted (see Note, page 311)

1. Cut the whole chicken into 8 pieces. Wash them and the 2 additional chicken breasts, shake off the excess water, and place the chicken in a large bowl.

2. Juice the lemon over the chicken, and let stand at room temperature for ½ hour.

3. Preheat the oven to 375 degrees F.

4. Drain the chicken, pat it dry, and season with salt and pepper to taste. Return it to the bowl, and pour 1½ cups of the BBQ sauce over it; rub the sauce onto each piece.

5. Place the chicken in one layer in a large roasting pan and sprinkle with the toasted fennel seeds. Bake for about 1 hour, basting occasionally with a generous ½ cup of the remaining sauce. The chicken is done when you are able to easily lift a small piece of the meat off the bone with a fork.

6. To serve, arrange the chicken on a platter. Reheat the remaining 2 cups BBQ sauce, pour it into a bowl, and serve with the chicken.

SERVES 6

PREPPING IN ADVANCE: The chicken can be completed up to 2 hours ahead of serving. Cover and hold at room temperature. When you are ready to serve it, there is no need to reheat the sauce unless desired.

Basil-Parmesan Chicken Salad

Nancy, who has been chef at Mangia as it has grown over the years, does the ordering on a daily basis. It is nothing for her to order 300 pounds of chicken *per day*. To say that chicken is popular is an understatement. This salad, in particular, is a hit at lunchtime.

1. In a large heavy pot, bring the water to a boil.

2. Peel, trim, and quarter the onion. Peel, trim, and smash the garlic.

3. Add the onion, garlic, bay leaves, parsley, and salt to the boiling water and boil for about 10 minutes.

4. Carefully slide the chicken breasts into the pot and return the water to a boil. Reduce the heat to low, cover, and poach the chicken for about 15 minutes. Turn off the heat, remove the cover, and let the chicken cool in the liquid.

3 quarts water

1 onion

2 garlic cloves

2 bay leaves

1 small bunch flat-leaf parsley, tied with kitchen twine

1 teaspoon salt

6 chicken breast halves, on the bone, with skin, 4½ pounds total weight

FOR THE DRESSING

2 garlic cloves

2 cups packed basil leaves

1 cup mayonnaise

¾ cup freshly grated Parmigiano-Reggiano

Juice of 1 lemon

1½ teaspoons freshly ground black pepper

1 teaspoon salt

5. When cool enough to handle, remove the chicken from the broth, skin and bone it, and shred into bite-sized pieces. Put in a large bowl. (Be sure to strain and reserve the broth for making soups or sauces.)

6. Make the dressing: Peel, trim, and chop the garlic as fine as possible. Rinse the basil leaves, pat them dry, and chop very fine.

7. In a bowl, combine the garlic and basil with the remaining dressing ingredients. If you would like a smoother sauce, blend all the ingredients in a blender or food processor until saucelike.

8. Spoon the dressing over the chicken, toss well to combine, and transfer to a serving platter. Serve within 1 hour of finishing.

SERVES 6

PREPPING IN ADVANCE: The salad can be completed 1 day before serving. Cover well and store in the refrigerator. Remove to stand at room temperature 30 minutes before serving.

Roasted Herb-Stuffed Chicken Breasts

We serve these herbed breasts on Green Bean Salad (page 217). The colors are pretty together and the flavors compatible. This makes a lovely summer luncheon, and the chicken lends itself to being prepared in advance—always a plus when it comes to summertime entertaining.

1 large white onion

2 garlic cloves

3 tablespoons extra-virgin olive oil

¾ cup dry white wine

⅔ cup fresh bread crumbs

1 tablespoon chopped fresh tarragon

1 tablespoon chopped basil

1 tablespoon chopped flat-leaf parsley

1 teaspoon dried thyme

1½ teaspoons salt

6 chicken breast halves, on the bone, with skin, about 12 ounces each

2 tablespoons unsalted butter, softened

1 teaspoon freshly ground black pepper

1. Position a rack in the middle of the oven. Preheat the oven to 375 degrees F. Line a roasting pan with parchment paper.

2. Peel, trim, and dice the onion and garlic.

3. In a large skillet, sauté the onion in the olive oil over medium heat, stirring, until translucent. Add the garlic and sauté for 1 or 2 minutes, but do not let it brown. Add the wine and reduce it to ¼ cup (about 5 minutes). Add the bread crumbs, herbs, and salt; combine well. Let cool slightly.

4. Wash and pat the chicken breasts dry. With your fingers, separate the skin from the meat. Place about 1½ tablespoons of the herbed stuffing under the skin on each breast, spreading it to cover as much of the meat as possible. Pat the skin back into place.

5. Arrange the breasts, skin side up, in the baking pan. Brush with the softened butter, and grind the black pepper all over. Bake for 45 minutes. Remove and let cool to room temperature.

6. To serve, arrange the chicken breasts on a serving platter. Serve within 1 hour of finishing.

SERVES 6

PREPPING IN ADVANCE: The breasts can be prepared 4 hours ahead through step 4. Cover and refrigerate. Remove the stuffed uncooked breasts from the refrigerator 30 minutes before baking to come to room temperature.

Once baked, the breasts can stand at room temperature up to 1 hour before serving.

Roasted Chicken Breast Chunks with Sesame Dressing

Asian-inspired dishes are very popular at Mangia. This is a superb party dish; its plating alone makes it appealing.

The sauce is first-rate on its own, too, with roasted or steamed vegetables or tofu.

1. Position a rack in the middle of the oven. Preheat the oven to 375 degrees F. Line a roasting pan with parchment paper.

2. On a cutting board, cut the chicken breasts into bite-sized pieces, about the size of a half-dollar.

3. In a large bowl, stir together the olive oil, cayenne, and salt. Add the chicken and stir to coat. Spread the pieces on the roasting pan without crowding. Roast for 20 minutes. Cover loosely with aluminum foil and let cool.

FOR THE CHICKEN

10 skinless, boneless chicken breast halves or cutlets, about 8 ounces each

3 tablespoons extra-virgin olive oil

1 tablespoon cayenne

1 tablespoon salt

2 tablespoons sesame seeds

2 thin medium carrots

2 cups sugar snap peas

4 cups boiling water

2 bunches watercress

1 large red bell pepper

FOR THE DRESSING

¼ cup soy sauce

¼ cup honey

1 tablespoon Asian sesame oil

1 tablespoon sherry vinegar

½ teaspoon cayenne

¼ teaspoon ground allspice

½ cup soy oil

4. While the oven is still on, toast the sesame seeds. Spread them out on a baking sheet and toast until just golden. Be forewarned; they toast very quickly. Let cool.

5. Peel and trim the carrots; then cut into julienne strips. Cook in boiling salted water for about 3 minutes. Drain and let cool.

6. Wash and trim the sugar snap peas, clipping the stem side only. Add a pinch of salt to the 4 cups of boiling water and blanch the snap peas for 1 minute. Drain and let cool.

7. Wash the watercress, pat dry, and cut off any thick stems. Remove the top, bottom, and seeds of the red pepper and cut into thin strips.

8. Make the dressing: Place all the ingredients for the dressing, except the soy oil, in a food processor or blender and blend. With the motor running, gradually add the soy oil in a thin stream and blend until a smooth emulsion is obtained. (Makes about 1 cup.)

9. In a large bowl, combine the chicken, carrots, sugar snap peas, bell pepper, and a scant cup of the dressing, adding more if necessary; toss well to combine.

10. To serve, wreathe the rim of a large platter with the watercress sprigs. Mound the chicken in the middle, and sprinkle with the toasted sesame seeds. Serve within 2 hours of finishing.

SERVES 6

PREPPING IN ADVANCE: The chicken pieces can be roasted and dressed with 1 cup of the dressing 1 day before serving. Cover and refrigerate.

Remove from the refrigerator to stand at room temperature ½ hour before adding the carrots, sugar snap peas, and bell pepper. Plate and garnish as directed in step 10 just before serving.

Chipotle Chile Chicken Wings

A chipotle chile is a smoked jalapeño—a dried chile pepper, in other words. Most of the time, it is reconstituted with oils and vinegars. Sometimes it is ground and made into a sauce, which is quite easy to find in cans in specialty stores and some supermarkets. Its smoky flavor goes well with black beans, soups, corn salad, and chicken. These wings are a good example and a sure-fire hit. Nobody eats just one.

4 ½ pounds chicken wings (about 30)

½ cup honey

Juice of 1 lime

3 tablespoons canned chipotle chile sauce

3 tablespoons bourbon

1 tablespoon ancho chile powder

1 tablespoon salt

1. Preheat the oven to 400 degrees F. Line a baking sheet with parchment paper.

2. Cut the tip off each chicken wing and discard. Rinse the wings and pat dry.

3. In a large bowl, stir the remaining ingredients together well.

4. Add the chicken wings and stir until well combined. With your fingers, make sure that every wing is uniformly coated.

5. Arrange the chicken wings in one layer on the baking sheet and roast for about 45 minutes. Serve hot or within 2 hours of finishing. If holding, cover the wings with foil.

SERVES 6

PREPPING IN ADVANCE: The wings can be prepared through step 4 the night before you plan to serve them. Remove from the refrigerator to stand at room temperature ½ hour before proceeding with step 5 to finish them.

Roasted Breast of Turkey

Almost anything made with turkey is remarkably popular at Mangia, and that includes sandwiches and panini, salads, and soups. Plain roasted turkey begs for big flavor, and is a wonderful foil for many of the condiments and spreads we include in The Accents Table, starting on page 351. So here is how we roast turkey breast that ends up flavorful and moist. Try it at home, and put it into service the same way we do—in a variety of delicious ways.

1 turkey breast half, on the bone, 3 to 5 pounds (see Note)

2 tablespoons unsalted butter, softened

1 teaspoon salt

1 teaspoon freshly ground black pepper

Figure about 15 minutes per pound in a preheated 350 degree F oven. If you don't want to separate the bone from the meat for easy slicing or serving, ask the butcher to do it for you. If you cannot find the larger size we call for below, simply roast two 2- to 3-pound split breasts.

1. Preheat the oven to 450 degrees F. Position the rack in the upper third of the oven.

2. Wash and pat the turkey breast dry. Rub thoroughly with the butter, sprinkle with the salt and pepper, and place, bone side down, in a roasting pan. Roast about 10 minutes to nicely brown the skin. Lower the temperature to 350 degrees F, and roast 15 minutes per pound. Let cool.

3. When the breast has cooled, place it on a carving board, and with a small, sharp carving knife, proceed to remove the backbone by holding the breast firmly, with the backbone facing you. With the tip of the knife, start separating the bone from the meat, always keeping the sharp edge of the knife up against the bone. Work your way down to the ribs, until the bone is loose. Remove and discard. The turkey is ready for using.

NOTE: Breast of turkey, fresh or frozen, is available in any large supermarket. It is sold whole, ranging in size from 5 to 8 pounds, and halved, which is what we have called for here. Half a breast will yield plenty of meat for sandwiches and snacks. If you are planning to serve 6 people, we suggest you buy a whole breast.

PREPPING IN ADVANCE: A breast of turkey can be roasted up to 1 day before serving. Let cool, cover well, and refrigerate. Remove the meat as you need it.

Spicy Marinated Roasted Turkey Breast

Toasting seeds brings out their flavor, and you will be able to identify the cumin and coriander in the Indian marinade we use here. The longer you marinate the turkey, the better: We suggest 24 hours.

You will need several accompaniments to serve with this. The reason we are advocating Yam and Fennel Salad is because it marries beautifully with the turkey. The salad has a pinch of cinnamon in the dressing.

1. Put the turkey breast in a container large enough to hold it snugly. (A large resealable plastic bag works very well for this.)

2. Peel, trim, and dice the onion into small cubes. Peel, trim, and crush the garlic cloves.

1 turkey breast, 5 to 8 pounds

1 red onion

4 garlic cloves

1 tablespoon cumin seeds

1 tablespoon coriander seeds

½ cup extra-virgin olive oil

½ cup white vinegar

2 tablespoons brown sugar

1 teaspoon dried thyme

1 tablespoon salt

1 teaspoon freshly ground black pepper

SERVE WITH: Yam and Fennel Salad (page 232).

3. In a small, dry skillet, toast the cumin and coriander seeds over low heat, stirring constantly, until they turn a shade darker. Remove from the heat and pour into a small bowl.

4. Add the onion, garlic, olive oil, vinegar, brown sugar, thyme, salt, and pepper and stir well to combine. Pour the marinade over the breast, cover the container (or seal the bag), and marinate in the refrigerator for 24 hours before roasting. If the liquid does not cover the breast, turn the turkey occasionally.

5. Roast, bone, and slice the turkey following the directions on page 340. Arrange the slices on a platter. Best served within 1 hour of slicing; hold at room temperature for maximum flavor.

NOTE: Keep sliced turkey, well covered, in the refrigerator for serving or making into sandwiches the next day.

SERVES 6

Seared Duck Breast with Pear Chutney

This is an elegant combination for fall or winter, when you want the aromas of sweet fruit and rich duck cooking to fill your house. The chutney is an integral part of this dish, a must, lending just the right texture and tartness. Your butcher shop or any large specialty food store will bone duck breasts and trim them for you. Don't, for a minute, let that detail stand in the way of your making this. Wild rice or one of the suggestions below would make a fitting accompaniment.

3 whole boned duck breasts, with skin on, split in half, about 3 pounds total weight

2 teaspoons salt

2 teaspoons freshly ground black pepper

6 tablespoons red wine vinegar

Pear Chutney (page 371)

SERVE WITH: White Beans with Peppers and Rosemary (page 293) or Roasted Brussels Sprouts with Red Onion and Thyme (page 206)

1. Using a sharp knife, cut the skin on each duck breast half in a crosshatch pattern, slicing through the skin, but not into the meat. Season with the salt and pepper.

2. Heat 2 large, heavy-bottomed skillets over high heat until very hot. (Cast-iron skillets work very well.) Place the breasts in the pans, skin side down, and cook for about 10 minutes. Drain off the fat.

3. Spoon 3 tablespoons of the vinegar into each skillet, and cook for 1 minute. Turn the breasts, meat side down, and sear for 3 minutes. Remove the pans from the heat, and let the duck breasts come to room temperature. (After standing, the duck breasts will be pink in the center.)

4. Pat the duck breasts dry and place on a cutting board. Cut each crosswise with a sharp knife into ⅛-inch-thick slices. Layer the slices on a large platter and serve with the chutney, either spooned on the end of the platter or in a small serving bowl.

SERVES 6

PREPPING IN ADVANCE: The duck breasts can be prepared 1 hour ahead through step 3. Transfer them to a platter, cover loosely, and let stand at room temperature.

MEATS

Roast Filet of Beef
    with Peppercorn Crust

Yellow Tomatoes Stuffed
    with Lamb Sausage and Orzo

Pork Loin Larded with Garlic and
    Black Pepper in Tomato-Wine Sauce

Roast Filet of Beef
with Peppercorn Crust

Here is the most reliable—the little black dress, if you will—of special-occasion dishes. And this filet becomes even more interesting when served, as we suggest you do below, with Mustard Applesauce spooned alongside the tenderloin slices. If you don't have time to make the applesauce, a good mustard or horseradish cream works, too.

1 trimmed and tied whole filet of beef, 4 or 5 pounds

1 teaspoon salt

¼ cup cracked black peppercorns (see Note, page 167)

Mustard Applesauce (page 369)

Mint sprigs, for garnish

1. Preheat the oven to 400 degrees F. Line a roasting pan with parchment paper.

2. Salt the filet all over. On a cutting board, pat the cracked peppercorns into the meat, distributing them well. Place the meat in the roasting pan and roast for 35 minutes for rare, or until a meat thermometer registers 115 to 120 degrees F when inserted in the middle. (For medium it should read 130 to 140 degrees, and for well-done 150 to 160 degrees.) Transfer the meat to a cutting board, and let cool.

3. To serve, slice the filet into ½-inch slices and place on a round platter. Spoon the Mustard Applesauce next to the slices. Garnish the platter with fresh mint, and serve.

SERVES 6

PREPPING IN ADVANCE: Although it is best served within 1 hour of finishing, the filet can be roasted several hours ahead and held at room temperature. Slice it when you are ready to serve it, not in advance.

Yellow Tomatoes Stuffed with Lamb Sausage and Orzo

Inspired by Nancy's trip to Turkey, these tomatoes will taste even better if they've been grown in your own garden. In that event, use whatever color you have—yellow or red.

1. Bring 2 quarts salted water to a boil in a large saucepan. Add the orzo, stir, and cook 3 minutes, or until al dente. Drain in a colander, run under cold water until cold to stop the cooking, and drain again.

2. Preheat the oven to 375 degrees F. Lightly oil a baking pan large enough to hold 12 tomato halves, without crowding, in one layer.

3. Cut the tomatoes in half and, with a small spoon, scoop out the insides (close to the skin) and reserve. Season the hollowed-out shells with salt and pepper. Place upside down on paper towels to drain.

2 quarts water

1 cup orzo

6 medium yellow beekfsteak tomatoes

Salt

Freshly ground black pepper

1 medium yellow onion

2 garlic cloves

2 tablespoons extra-virgin olive oil

¾ teaspoon ground cumin

¼ teaspoon cayenne

8 ounces lamb sausage in bulk or ground lamb

¼ cup tomato puree

1 large egg

½ cup pine nuts (pignoli)

½ cup chopped mint leaves

½ cup chopped flat-leaf parsley

½ cup freshly grated Parmigiano-Reggiano (optional)

Dilled Yogurt Sauce (page 370), as an accompaniment

4. Peel, trim, and chop the onion. Peel, trim, and mince the garlic.

5. In a large skillet, heat the olive oil over medium-high heat. Add the onion, garlic, cumin, and cayenne and cook, stirring, until the onion is wilted. Add the lamb sausage, stirring to break it up with a wooden spoon, and cook just until it loses its pinkness. Add the reserved insides of the tomatoes and the tomato puree. Cook, stirring, about 10 minutes. Add salt and pepper to taste and remove from the heat to cool.

6. In a large bowl, combine the cooked sausage mixture, orzo, egg, pine nuts, mint, parsley, and Parmigiano, if using. Stir well to thoroughly combine.

7. Fill the tomato halves with the sausage-orzo stuffing, mounding it gently on the top. Place the tomatoes in the baking pan and bake for 30 minutes. Best served within 1 hour of finishing, accompanied by Dilled Yogurt Sauce, if desired.

SERVES 6

Pork Loin Larded with Garlic and Black Pepper in Tomato-Wine Sauce

Ricardo grew up in a conservative household, in the middle of the last century, in Mexico, which didn't make it easy to learn his mother's cooking secrets and recipes. But, truly, persistence and chicanery paid off.

This is one of Ricardo's mother's recipes. Someone asked about the whole peppercorns buried in the pork. Should you pick them out? Of course not! Eat them—they will be soft and pungent.

1 boneless, center-cut loin of pork, 3½ pounds

8 garlic cloves

20 black peppercorns

2½ teaspoons salt

20 ripe plum tomatoes, 3¾ pounds

1 large yellow onion

¼ cup extra-virgin olive oil

1 cup dry white wine

1 tablespoon dried oregano

1 teaspoon dried thyme

1 cup chicken broth

12 flat-leaf parsley sprigs tied with kitchen twine

1. Place the pork loin on a cutting board.

2. Peel, trim, and cut the garlic cloves into ½-inch chunks.

3. With a slim paring knife, make an incision in the pork, about 1 inch deep. Insert a piece of garlic and push it in deeply with your finger. Make another incision and press a peppercorn into it. Continue to stud the meat, turning it frequently, so that it is "larded" all over with the remaining garlic chunks and peppercorns. Season the loin with 1 teaspoon of the salt, rubbing it into the meat.

4. Wash, trim, and coarsely chop the tomatoes. Peel, trim, and finely dice the onion.

5. Preheat the oven to 350 degrees F.

6. In a large skillet, sauté the onion in the olive oil over medium heat, stirring, until translucent. Add the wine and cook until it almost evaporates. Add the tomatoes, oregano, and thyme, stir to combine, and cook for a few minutes, until the tomatoes release some water. Stir in the chicken broth and cook, stirring occasionally, for 10 minutes more. Bury the parsley in the sauce and add the remaining 1½ teaspoons salt.

7. Place the pork loin in a shallow roasting pan and pour the hot tomato sauce over it. Cover tightly with aluminum foil, place it in the oven, and braise for 2½ hours to 3 hours, bathing it every now and then with the sauce. The pork should be very tender, and the sauce mushy and thick. Remove from the oven, and let the dish come to room temperature.

8. When ready to serve, remove the pork from the sauce and slice it thick, about 1½ inches per slice. Use a sharp knife because the meat will be almost falling apart. Return the slices to the roasting pan. Remove and discard the parsley. Scrape the sides and bottom of the pan and spoon the sauce over the pork. If the sauce is too thin at this point, transfer the pork to a platter and reduce the sauce over medium heat to the desired consistency. This may be served as soon as it is finished, while it is still hot, or it can be held at room temperature for serving within 1 hour of finishing.

SERVES 6

The Accents Table

DRESSINGS, SAUCES, RELISHES, AND DIPS

We already know that foods served at room temperature are at their most flavorful. We also know that there are plenty of occasions when more flavor is desirable, and sometimes even warranted. Take Roasted Breast of Turkey (page 340), for example. Sliced and served plain, it is—and there is no other way to say this—colorless. With Pancetta and Black Olive Sauce (page 365) or Classic Pesto (page 362) or Pear Chutney (page 371) as an accompaniment, it is no longer plain; it has been made different and, suddenly, it appeals. Flavor comes in big packages or small. The Accents chapter is about flavor, big flavor, that more often than not is added in small measurements and transforms a dish.

When you are making sandwiches or panini, remember the power of a flavored mayonnaise over plain. Try a condiment like Roasted Red Grapes and Shallots (page 373), not with an entrée, but on a cheese tray. Use a vinaigrette as a marinade. Stir Classic Pesto, not into pasta salad, but into hot soup. Be as improvisational and creative as that. It is easy and fun. You put your own twist on a dish. It is something we do at Mangia every day.

When it comes to flavors and textures, frequently opposites attract. Mix and match the sweet with the salty, crunchy with soft. Start small, and be judicious if you are unsure. Putting a spicy relish on roast chicken instead of barbecue sauce only works if spicy is what you and your family or guests like. Tasting is the only sure way of knowing if an idea works.

If you are serving a meal buffet style, we would suggest having at least two or three accents on the table as a general rule. The more, the merrier. Always serve accents in attractive bowls, cruets, or pots, and never serve store-bought mustard or ketchup—among the best-known accents of all—in an original container.

Accents lead to discoveries. There is a cache of discovery in this chapter.

DRESSINGS, SAUCES, RELISHES, AND DIPS

Mangia's Vinaigrette

   House Mustard Dressing

   Oregano Vinaigrette

   Rosemary and Roasted
      Red Pepper Vinaigrette

   Roasted Tomato Vinaigrette

Anchovy Dressing with Capers

Ancho Chile Mayonnaise

Herb Mayonnaise

Croutons

Classic Pesto

Parsley Pesto

   Parsley Pesto with Capers

Tapenade

Pancetta and Black Olive Sauce

Nancy's BBQ Sauce

Sweet-and-Hot Pepper Relish

Pickled Vegetable Relish

Mustard Applesauce

Dilled Yogurt Sauce

Pear Chutney

Red Onion Jam

Roasted Red Grapes and Shallots

Roasted Garlic

Eddie's Roasted Garlic Dip

Baba Ghanoush

Hummus

Teaberry Gelatin

ON VINAIGRETTE

There are two basic ingredients for all vinaigrettes: oil and vinegar. The general rule of thumb for the proportions is 3 parts oil to 1 part vinegar. In the markets, nowadays, there is an endless variety of infused oils, and just as many flavored vinegars. Before using any of those, think for a moment about whether you like such flavors and how you are going to use the dressing. For example, if you are contemplating using tarragon vinegar, decide whether the flavor of the tarragon will meld with the other flavors on the table. You would not want to serve it with Asian peanut sauce. Truffle oil, another example, brings the musky aroma of truffles to the mouth and should be used wisely in combination with other foods, or by itself on bread.

Use garlic and salt sparingly in a vinaigrette. Add dry mustard, fresh herbs, or fresh lemon or lime juice in place of vinegar. Shallots, Roasted Garlic (page 374), fresh ginger and cilantro, ground cinnamon and chili powder may each be added, but remember, any of these should be just an insinuation, not a statement, on salad greens.

When using vinaigrette to dress vegetables, consider the flavor, texture, and even the color of the food you are dressing, as well as its capacity to absorb the flavors of the dressing. Eggplant and potatoes are notorious for absorbing dressing and diminishing its impact.

As for dressing a salad: Add the vinaigrette just before serving. Grind black pepper over the salad at the table, not before. Remember that lettuce greens that have not been completely dried will dilute the dressing. And when you add your vinaigrette, do so in small amounts, tossing after each addition. It is better to have vinaigrette left over than an overdressed salad. A properly dressed salad should have only a slight shine of dressing.

Mangia's Vinaigrette

When making vinaigrette, always use quality olive oil and vinegar. Vary the vinegar here, if you like. Red wine vinegar has more intensity than white wine vinegar and is good matched with more assertive herbs, such as oregano. Sherry vinegar, derived from the fortified wine, is a little stronger in character than red or white wine vinegar. Sherry vinegar has a golden hue and burnished flavor that complements roasted peppers, especially. Champagne vinegar is finer, still, with a lighter body and color. And then there is balsamic vinegar. Made from the juice of the Trebbiano grape, it has a distinctive sweet flavor and caramel color that come from aging in oak barrels. There are balsamic vinegars as rare as fine wines, with commensurate prices as well. A collection of vinegars allows for an interesting repertoire of vinaigrettes. We recommend having red and white wine vinegars, as well as balsamic, on hand as a matter of course.

1 small garlic clove

¾ cup extra-virgin olive oil

¼ cup red wine vinegar

½ teaspoon salt

1. Peel, trim, and mince the garlic very fine.

2. In a small bowl, whisk all the ingredients together well. Let stand at room temperature for at least 1 hour before using. Keeps, covered, in the refrigerator for 1 week.

MAKES 1 CUP

Variations

House Mustard Dressing

We have used champagne vinegar in our house dressing from the day Mangia opened in 1982. If you don't have any, use good-quality white wine vinegar instead.

1 cup Mangia's vinaigrette (page 355), made with champagne vinegar in place of the red wine vinegar

1 teaspoon Dijon mustard

1 extra-large egg

In a small bowl, whisk all the ingredients together until creamy. Keeps, covered, in the refrigerator for 2 to 3 days.

MAKES 1 1/2 CUPS

Oregano Vinaigrette

This dressing is very good when served as a dipping sauce with fish sandwiches or as a sauce on simply roasted or grilled fish entrées.

1 cup Mangia's Vinaigrette (page 355)

2 tablespoons chopped fresh oregano

In a small bowl, whisk the ingredients together well. Keeps, covered, in the refrigerator for up to 1 week.

MAKES 1 CUP

Rosemary and Roasted Red Pepper Vinaigrette

This makes a tasty marinade for pork, tuna, and vegetables.

1 cup Mangia's Vinaigrette (page 355), made
with sherry vinegar in place of the red wine vinegar

1 tablespoon minced roasted red bell pepper (see page 193)

½ teaspoon dry mustard

½ teaspoon fresh rosemary leaves

¼ teaspoon sugar

Combine all the ingredients in a blender and puree. Transfer to a bowl for serving or storing. If you make this dressing ahead of time, whisk it before using. Keeps, covered, in the refrigerator for 1 week.

MAKES 1 1/4 CUPS

Roasted Tomato Vinaigrette

Try this sprinkled over slices of goat cheese and serve as an appetizer.

4 roasted plum tomato halves (see page 197)

½ teaspoon ground cumin

1 cup Mangia's Vinaigrette (page 355) made with
sherry vinegar in place of the red wine vinegar

2 tablespoons chopped mint

1. In a medium bowl, mash the tomatoes well, until the pulp separates from the skin. Discard the skins.

2. Add the cumin and the vinaigrette in a stream, whisking constantly with 2 forks. Add the mint and whisk well. Keeps, covered, in the refrigerator for 1 week.

MAKES 1 1/2 CUPS

Anchovy Dressing with Capers

This is for anchovy lovers—and we are, so we make a lot. Don't be tempted to halve the recipe: Mashing anchovies takes time and, anyway, there are any number of wonderful ways to use this. Besides salads, spoon it over boiled potatoes, roasted vegetables, steak or roast beef sandwiches, croutons (before you toast them), or reheated pizza.

6 anchovy fillets packed in oil

1 teaspoon salt

1 teaspoon dried oregano

½ teaspoon Roasted Garlic (page 374)

1 cup extra-virgin olive oil

¼ cup red wine vinegar

3 tablespoons drained capers

1. In a medium bowl, mash the anchovy fillets with a fork. Add the salt, oregano, and Roasted Garlic, and stir until the mixture forms a paste.

2. Pour in the olive oil in a stream, whisking constantly, until all the oil has been added. Whisk in the vinegar and capers. Keeps, covered, in the refrigerator for 1 week.

MAKES 1½ CUPS

Ancho Chile Mayonnaise

Ancho chile peppers are poblano peppers that have been dried. Each has its own flavor, one quite different from the other. In different parts of Mexico, where the ancho chile is used profusely, cooks have different opinions about how to treat it. Some like to toast it, some fry it, and some rehydrate it, as described below. The real question, though, is its condition before you soak it in hot water. We find that the most important factor is the quality of the ancho chile you buy. It should be new, plump, and shining, even when dried. Chiles that are old and very dry do not have full flavor.

4 cups water

2 dried ancho chile peppers

1 cup mayonnaise

1 tablespoon fresh lime juice

Serve this mayonnaise with grilled swordfish, cold roast chicken, or cold roast beef.

1. In a medium saucepan, bring the water to a boil.

2. Wash the chiles well, stem them, and place in the boiling water; boil for 1 or 2 minutes. Cover the pan, turn off the heat, and let the chiles steep until they cool to room temperature. They will feel velvety and pliable.

3. Remove the chiles from the water, reserving the water. Seed the chiles. Put them in a blender, add a little of the water that was used to soak them, and blend to make a thick paste.

4. Scrape the paste out of the blender into a bowl, add the mayonnaise and lime juice, and stir well to combine. Refrigerate for 1 hour. Keeps, covered, in the refrigerator for up to 1 week.

MAKES 1 1/2 CUPS

Herb Mayonnaise

You can use any combination of fresh herbs you wish here. The points to remember are (1) only the leaves should be used; (2) they should be well minced; (3) avoid using large quantities of the strong-flavored herbs, such as rosemary, sage, or thyme. Choose milder-flavored ones, like parsley, basil, or dill. You want the mayonnaise to be fragrant, not pungent.

1 cup mayonnaise

⅓ cup minced fresh herbs of choice

1 scallion, minced (white and green parts)

1 teaspoon Dijon mustard

1 tablespoon champagne vinegar

In a small bowl, stir together all the ingredients until well combined. The flavor will develop if you let it stand briefly before serving. Keeps, covered, in the refrigerator for up to 3 days.

MAKES 1 1/2 CUPS

Croutons

We love croutons at Mangia and make several different kinds. These are the ones we use in our Caesar Salad (page 209). Snack on them, add them to soups, toss a few into other green salads. The concern with croutons is not how to use them, but how to keep them in store. They are addictive.

1 small loaf country bread, about 2 pounds

½ cup extra-virgin olive oil

½ teaspoon salt

½ teaspoon freshly ground black pepper

1. Preheat the oven to 350 degrees F.

2. Cut the bread into 1-inch cubes. Put them in a bowl and add the olive oil, salt, and pepper. Toss to coat.

3. Spread the bread cubes in a single layer on a baking sheet and bake for 30 minutes, turning once, or until golden. Store in an airtight container for up to 3 days.

MAKES ABOUT 4 CUPS

Classic Pesto

If you grow your own basil at home, then you can whir up a batch of this whenever the spirit moves you. It is the flavor of summer, especially when served with home- or locally grown tomatoes.

1. Rinse the basil leaves and pat dry. Peel and trim the garlic.

2. Put the basil, garlic, pine nuts, Parmigiano, salt, and pepper in a food processor and puree. With the motor running, pour the olive oil through the feed tube and blend until the sauce is emulsified and has the consistency of mayonnaise. Transfer the pesto to a bowl. If you are storing it, pour a thin film of olive oil over the top; then cover with plastic wrap. Keeps, covered, in the refrigerator for 1 week.

2 cups firmly packed basil leaves

2 garlic cloves

3 tablespoons pine nuts (pignoli)

½ cup freshly grated Parmigiano-Reggiano cheese

½ teaspoon salt

¼ teaspoon freshly ground black pepper

⅔ cup extra-virgin olive oil

MAKES 1 1/2 CUPS

NOTE: To freeze pesto successfully, it must be made differently. In the food processor, puree the basil with only the olive oil. Transfer the puree to a freezer container and freeze for up to 6 months. To use, thaw in the refrigerator. Place the puree in the food processor, add the garlic, pine nuts, salt, and pepper, and process until blended. If you need to add more olive oil to thin the puree, add up to ⅓ cup. Spoon the sauce into a bowl, and stir in the Parmigiano until blended.

Parsley Pesto

This can be used in countless ways, and unlike Classic Pesto it can be made year-round because of the availability of parsley. We like this best on sandwiches and panini. The variation with capers is tasty with turkey or pork, in particular.

2 cups packed flat-leaf parsley leaves

3 garlic cloves

2 tablespoons walnuts

1 teaspoon salt

½ teaspoon freshly ground black pepper

½ cup extra-virgin olive oil

1. Wash and pat the parsley leaves dry. Peel and trim the garlic.

2. Put the parsley, garlic, walnuts, salt, and pepper in a food processor and process until finely chopped. With the motor running, pour the olive oil through the feed tube into the machine in a slow stream, and blend to a smooth emulsion.

3. Transfer the pesto to a serving bowl. Keeps, covered, in a container in the refrigerator for 1 week.

MAKES 1 ½ CUPS

Variation

Parsley Pesto with Capers
Make Parsley Pesto, as directed; then stir in 3 tablespoons of drained capers.

Tapenade

You can use tapenade in sandwiches, as a dip, or to dress grilled fish, spread on toast as an appetizer, or swirl into vegetable soup. The powerful flavors of Provence—olives and garlic—plus oil-packed anchovies, give it its singular Mediterranean *esprit*.

2 cups niçoise olives, pitted

6 anchovy fillets packed in oil

1 garlic clove

Juice of 1 lemon

½ cup extra-virgin olive oil

1 tablespoon drained capers

In a food processor or blender, put the olives, anchovies, garlic, and lemon juice. With the on/off button, start pureeing the mixture, adding the olive oil gradually, and pulsing the machine, until you have a paste as thick as mayonnaise. Scrape the Tapenade out of the processor into a bowl, and stir in the capers. Keeps, covered, in the refrigerator for 1 month.

MAKES 2 CUPS

Pancetta and Black Olive Sauce

The bold flavors of Southern Italy—
anchovies, black olives, and pancetta—
make this sauce a superb foil for simple
roast turkey (page 340). This is also good
on pasta and as a topping for pan-seared
cauliflower. Or use it as you would
Tapenade (page 364)—as a dip or a
spread for sandwiches and panini.

4 ounces pancetta

1 red onion

1 cup pitted kalamata olives

4 anchovy fillets packed in oil

1 tablespoon extra-virgin olive oil

½ cup dry white wine

1 cup chicken broth

½ cup chopped flat-leaf parsley

1. Cut the pancetta into ¼-inch dice.

2. Peel, trim, and finely dice the onion. Finely chop the olives. Chop the
   anchovies into small pieces.

3. In a skillet, sauté the pancetta in the olive oil over medium heat, stirring,
   until it releases most of its fat, but do not let it brown. Drain off half the
   fat and add the chopped onion and anchovies. Cook briefly to combine,
   cover, lower the heat, and let the onion sweat for about 8 minutes, until
   softened.

4. Add the wine and cook, uncovered, over medium heat until it evaporates.
   Add the olives and chicken broth, cover, and cook about 15 minutes.
   Remove from the heat and let cool. Before using, add the parsley and stir
   well to combine.

5. Spoon the sauce into a bowl, and serve it as an accompaniment. The sauce
   keeps, covered, in the refrigerator for 2 days.

Nancy's BBQ Sauce

This is a sweet sauce, with some tang from the apple vinegar and little heat from the cayenne. Use it on pork, hamburgers, steak, barbecued beans, or shrimp. This is the sauce we use on our bestselling Barbecued Chicken with Toasted Fennel Seeds (see page 332).

1. Peel, trim, and finely chop the onion. Peel, trim, and mince the garlic.

2. In a large skillet, sauté the onion in the olive oil over low heat, stirring, until translucent. Add the garlic and cook until lightly colored, taking care not to let it brown.

1 medium onion

2 garlic cloves

3 tablespoons extra-virgin olive oil

1 can (14 ounces) crushed tomatoes

½ cup cider vinegar

½ cup firmly packed dark brown sugar

½ cup Worcestershire sauce

¼ cup Dijon mustard

1 teaspoon ground cumin

1 teaspoon ground ancho chile powder

½ teaspoon cayenne

½ teaspoon sweet paprika

¼ teaspoon ground cinnamon

¼ teaspoon ground cloves

3. Add the remaining ingredients and mix well to combine. Cook over medium heat, stirring every now and then, for 20 minutes, until slightly reduced and thickened. Let cool.

4. To store, transfer the sauce to a jar or container, cover, and refrigerate for up to 1 week.

MAKES ABOUT 1 QUART

Sweet-and-Hot Pepper Relish

Red and yellow bell peppers combine with harissa, a Tunisian hot chili sauce, to make a lively, rustic sauce that is especially good with meaty fish steaks, like tuna or swordfish. Or try it with chicken, zucchini, or string beans. If you don't have harissa, there is an easy solution: dried hot pepper flakes. In other words, heat is an integral part of this relish. Don't just leave it out.

2 large red bell peppers

2 large yellow bell peppers

1 garlic clove

½ cup finely diced red onion

¼ cup extra-virgin olive oil

1 teaspoon harissa or ½ teaspoon dried hot pepper flakes

1½ cups crushed tomatoes

¼ cup drained capers

3 tablespoons balsamic vinegar

¼ cup chopped basil, firmly packed

Salt

Freshly ground black pepper

SERVE WITH: Pan-Fried Tuna Steaks (page 315).

1. Core, seed, and cut the peppers into ½-inch pieces. Peel, trim, and mince the garlic.

2. In a medium skillet, sauté the garlic and onion in the olive oil over medium heat, stirring, until the onion begins to soften and starts to brown.

3. Add the diced peppers and harissa. Reduce the heat to low, and cook, stirring occasionally, for 15 minutes. Gently stir in the crushed tomatoes and capers, and cook for 10 minutes more, or until slightly thickened.

4. Stir in the vinegar, basil, and salt and pepper to taste. Remove the pan from the heat. Let the relish cool before serving. To store, transfer the cooled relish to a jar, cover, and store in the refrigerator for up to 4 days.

MAKES 2 CUPS

Pickled Vegetable Relish

Here vinegar serves to soften and flavor a combination of colorful vegetables. Use this as you would any relish, for spark, on sandwiches, roasted meats, and grilled or poached seafood.

1. In a medium saucepan, combine the water, vinegar, sugar, salt, cloves, mustard seeds, allspice, and fresh ginger. Bring the mixture to a boil and simmer for 20 minutes to blend the flavors.

2. Prepare the vegetables: Core and shred the cabbage. Peel, trim, and slice the onion; peel and cut the carrots into ¼-inch dice. Core, seed, and dice the pepper into ¼-inch pieces. Put all the vegetables in a large, heatproof ceramic bowl.

1 cup water

1 cup cider vinegar

¾ cup sugar

2 teaspoons salt

6 whole cloves, crushed

1 tablespoon mustard seeds

½ teaspoon ground allspice

1½ teaspoons sliced fresh ginger

1 small head white cabbage, 1½ pounds

1 medium onion

2 medium carrots

1 medium red bell pepper

SERVE WITH: Poached Halibut (page 308).

3. Pour the boiling liquid over the vegetables. Let cool completely; then cover and refrigerate overnight. The next day, drain off any excess liquid from the relish, and adjust the seasonings. Transfer to a serving bowl. The relish keeps, in a covered glass container in the refrigerator, for up to 2 weeks.

MAKES ABOUT 4 CUPS

Mustard Applesauce

This applesauce is chunky and has character and a certain clout. Like most of our accent condiments and sauces, we use this in different ways: with beef, chicken, pork, or veal; as a sandwich spread; or alongside green salad, or a soft cheese.

1. Peel, core, and cut the apples into wedges. Peel, trim, and dice the onion.

2. In a medium skillet, sauté the onion in the butter over medium heat, stirring, until the onion starts to turn translucent. Add the wine and cook until it is almost evaporated. Increase the heat to medium-high and add the apples and honey. Sauté, stirring constantly, until the edges of the apples begin to brown, about 10 minutes.

3. Stir in the mustard and salt, cover, and cook for 15 minutes, until the apples are softened, but still chunky. Remove the pan from the heat and let cool before serving. The applesauce keeps, covered, in the refrigerator for 1 week.

MAKES ABOUT 3 CUPS

6 Granny Smith apples

1 yellow onion

4 tablespoons (½ stick) unsalted butter

½ cup dry white wine

3 tablespoons honey

3 tablespoons grainy mustard

1 teaspoon salt

SERVE WITH: Roasted Filet of Beef with Peppercorn Crust (page 344).

Dilled Yogurt Sauce

There is no better accompaniment to Yellow Tomatoes Stuffed with Lamb Sausage and Orzo (page 346) than this cooling, refreshing sauce. It is also tasty spooned into pita pockets stuffed with crisp mixed greens.

1 garlic clove

1 container (8 ounces) plain yogurt

¼ cup snipped dill

1 tablespoon extra-virgin olive oil

2 teaspoons fresh lemon juice

The best way to chop dill is not with a knife on a cutting board. Use scissors to snip the fronds into small pieces.

Peel, trim, and mince the garlic. Put in a medium bowl. Add the remaining ingredients and stir until well combined and smooth.

MAKES 1½ CUPS

NOTE: The sauce does not keep.

Pear Chutney

This is perfectly wonderful with duck, or another poultry. You might also swirl it into a curried soup for an intriguing bit of additional flavor and body. You could also serve it with soft, ripe cheese, like Brie.

1. Peel, trim, and chop the onion fine. Peel, trim, and mince the garlic. Thinly slice the lime. Peel, core, and cut the pears into 1-inch chunks.

2. In a large saucepan, sauté the onion in the olive oil over medium heat, stirring, until translucent. Add the garlic and cook until lightly colored, but do not let it brown. Add the brown sugar and vinegar, stir to combine and to dissolve the sugar, and bring the mixture to a boil.

3. Add the pears, lime, raisins, fresh ginger, cloves, pepper flakes, cinnamon stick, and orange juice and stir to combine. Cover the pan, reduce the heat to low, and cook, stirring now and then, for 30 minutes. Remove the pan from the heat and let the chutney cool to room temperature. Stir in the nuts and chopped mint. The chutney keeps, covered, in the refrigerator for 1 month.

1 small white onion

2 garlic cloves

1 lime

6 firm pears, preferably Bosc

2 tablespoons extra-virgin olive oil

½ cup firmly packed light brown sugar

2 tablespoons cider vinegar

3 tablespoons golden raisins

1 tablespoon finely chopped fresh ginger

½ teaspoon ground cloves

½ teaspoon dried hot pepper flakes

1 cinnamon stick, 2 inches long

½ cup orange juice

½ cup coarsely chopped, toasted, and skinned hazelnuts (page 57) or unsalted roasted cashews

¼ cup chopped mint leaves

SERVE WITH: Seared Duck Breast (page 343).

MAKES ABOUT 2 CUPS

Red Onion Jam

Cooked onions, especially red onions, sweeten and caramelize and taste totally different from raw onions. This is great used as a spread on sandwiches or panini or served as a condiment with roasted meats and green salads. Some even like it on pasta.

1. Peel and trim the red onions, then slice them very thin.

2. In a large sauté pan, heat the olive oil, add the sliced onions, and sauté them over medium heat, stirring often to prevent them from burning, until they are translucent. Sprinkle the brown sugar over the onions and cook until they begin to caramelize, about 10 minutes.

3. Stir in the orange juice, vinegar, and pepper and blend well. Reduce the heat to low, and cook the onions, stirring now and then, for about 25 minutes, until the juice is reduced and the consistency of the mixture is like loose jam. Let cool to room temperature before serving. Keeps, covered in the refrigerator, for 1 week.

MAKES ABOUT I CUP

4 large red onions

2 tablespoons extra-virgin olive oil

2 tablespoons firmly packed light brown sugar

1 cup orange juice

¼ cup balsamic vinegar

½ teaspoon freshly ground black pepper

SERVE ON: Pecan-Crusted Chicken on Pullman Bread (page 156).

Roasted Red Grapes and Shallots

Here is a great addition to a holiday table. Or use it on a more regular basis with roasted chicken or lamb. You can roast the grapes and the shallots at the same time, as long as you watch the individual cooking times; they are different.

18 shallots

¼ cup extra-virgin olive oil

Salt

Freshly ground black pepper

1 pound seedless red grapes

¼ cup sherry vinegar

3 tablespoons chopped tarragon

1. Preheat the oven to 400 degrees F.

2. To roast the shallots: Peel the shallots. Coat them with 3 tablespoons of the olive oil, season with salt and pepper to taste, and spread them in a single layer on a baking sheet. Roast for about 30 minutes, until golden and soft to the touch. Remove and let cool on the baking sheet.

3. To roast the grapes: Remove the grapes from the stems, and in a medium bowl, toss with the remaining 1 tablespoon of olive oil. Spread the grapes out on another baking sheet and roast them until they swell and the skins are just about to burst, about 10 minutes. Let cool on the baking sheet.

4. Put the roasted shallots in a large skillet and add the sherry vinegar. Bring the vinegar to a boil over high heat and cook about 5 minutes, stirring with a spoon to make sure that the shallots are evenly glazed, until the vinegar is reduced and thickened.

5. Add the roasted grapes and tarragon to the skillet. Season with salt and pepper to taste, and stir gently to combine. Remove the pan from the heat and let cool before serving. To store, transfer to a container, cover, and refrigerate for up to 2 days.

SERVES 6 AS A RELISH

Roasted Garlic

Fresh garlic is pungent and sharp. Roasted garlic is just the opposite—sweet and mellow in flavor, silky in texture. Because it has a more subtle flavor, it becomes a lot more cooperative as an ingredient. We think it is a must in some of our sauces and salad dressing. We swirl it into soups as a finishing touch. It's even great smeared on bread.

1 medium garlic bulb

1. Preheat the oven to 350 degrees F.

2. Leaving the root end of the garlic intact, with a sharp knife, cut off the top one-third of the bulb. Wrap the remainder in aluminum foil and roast for about 45 minutes, or until soft to the touch. Remove and let cool at room temperature in the foil.

3. Remove the foil and, holding the cooled garlic by the root end, squeeze the roasted flesh out of the cloves into a small bowl. Keeps, covered, in the refrigerator for up to 1 week.

A MEDIUM ROASTED GARLIC BULB YIELDS
ABOUT 2 TABLESPOONS OF FLESH

Eddie's Roasted Garlic Dip

Eddie is one of the chefs at Mangia, and one day, out of the blue, he whipped this up. It is sensational as a dip for artichokes or as a sauce for roasted turkey or pork.

In a small bowl, stir all the ingredients together until well combined. The dip keeps, covered well, in the refrigerator for 3 days.

MAKES A GENEROUS 1 1/2 CUPS

1 1/2 cups mayonnaise

2 tablespoons Roasted Garlic

1/4 cup chopped cilantro

1 teaspoon chopped jalapeño pepper

1 teaspoon ground cumin

1 tablespoon lemon juice

Baba Ghanoush

The addition of yogurt sets this baba ghanoush apart and makes it Mangia's. As anyone who loves eggplant knows, this is a wonderful dip for wedges of pita or for vegetables. It is also very successful served as an accompaniment to lamb or chicken.

We roast the eggplants over the gas burner on the stove top. If you'd rather not do that, you can roast them in the oven. We prefer the charred flavor that only comes when you use the open flame.

2 medium eggplants, 1½ pounds each

½ cup fresh lemon juice

2 garlic cloves

¼ cup tahini (Middle Eastern sesame seed paste)

¼ cup chopped flat-leaf parsley

2 tablespoons extra-virgin olive oil

Salt

½ cup plain yogurt

1 package pita bread

1. To roast the eggplant over a gas burner: Place each eggplant on the burner of a gas stove and turn the heat to medium. Char the eggplants, turning them with tongs, until the skin is uniformly blackened and ashy. This should take from 20 to 30 minutes. Remove and let cool.

   To roast in the oven: Preheat the oven to 375 degrees F. Prick the eggplants in a few places with a fork and place on a baking sheet, lined with parchment paper, if desired. Roast for about 45 minutes, or until soft. Let cool.

2. Peel the eggplants and discard the skin. Shred the flesh, and remove the seeds. Put the flesh in a bowl and sprinkle with 2 tablespoons of the lemon juice.

3. Peel, trim, and mince the garlic.

4. In a food processor, combine the eggplant, garlic, remaining lemon juice, tahini, parsley, and olive oil and process until pureed. Taste for salt and add to taste. Add the yogurt and process for 30 seconds to incorporate.

5. Transfer the spread to a wide, shallow serving bowl. Accompany with pita bread, cut into wedges for dipping. Keeps, covered, in the refrigerator for up to 3 days.

MAKES ABOUT 2 CUPS

Hummus

Besides being a great dip and spread, Hummus also makes a tasty stuffed pita sandwich, with the addition of cucumber, red onion, and tomato slices.

For an interesting twist on this traditional recipe, see our black bean version on page 129.

1. In a food processor, combine all the ingredients, but add only 1 teaspoon of the paprika; process to a thick smooth paste. If the consistency is too thick, add water, a little at a time, to thin the dip as desired.

1 can (16 ounces) chickpeas, drained and rinsed

¼ cup tahini (Middle Eastern sesame seed paste)

¼ cup plus 2 tablespoons fresh lemon juice

2 tablespoons extra-virgin olive oil

1 teaspoon minced garlic

1 teaspoon ground cumin

1 teaspoon cayenne

1 teaspoon salt

2 teaspoons sweet paprika

2. Transfer the hummus to a wide, shallow bowl, sprinkle with the remaining 1 teaspoon of paprika, and serve with pita breads, cut into wedges. Keeps, covered, in the refrigerator for up to 3 days.

MAKES ABOUT 2 CUPS

Teaberry Gelatin

This is retro and wonderful, and nothing at all like the flavored gelatin molds with fruit that you ate as a child. A refreshing mix of fruit teas and fresh berries, it is as pretty as can be and delicious as part of a summer buffet. Just the conversation it generates makes it worth trying!

12 cups water

3 bags Red Zinger Tea

3 bags Lemon Zinger Tea

3 bags raspberry tea

2 bags black currant tea

1 cup honey

4 ounces unflavored gelatin

½ pint fresh blueberries, plus additional for optional garnish

½ pint fresh raspberries, plus additional for optional garnish

½ pint blackberries, plus additional for optional garnish

1. In a large saucepan, bring 10 cups of the water to a boil.

2. Put all the tea bags in a large, heat-proof bowl or wide-mouth pitcher. Pour the boiling water over them and let steep 20 minutes. Remove the tea bags and stir in the honey until dissolved.

3. Pour the 2 remaining cups of (cold) water into a small bowl. Stir in the gelatin and let stand for several minutes until thickened. Add the gelatin to the tea, stirring to blend.

4. Pick over, rinse, and dry all the berries.

5. Rinse a 12-cup mold, such as a bundt pan or ring mold, in cold water. Place the mold in a large bowl of ice cubes. Ladle 1½ cups of the tea mixture into the mold. Let stand until it starts to set, 10 to 15 minutes, then scatter some of the berries over the mixture. Pour in another 1½ cups, let set, and follow with more berries.

6. Continue to make layers with the tea mixture and berries, always letting the gelatin set before adding another layer of berries, until all of the tea mixture and fruit have been used. Remove the mold from the ice bath, cover carefully with plastic wrap, and refrigerate until the salad is completely set. Allow at least 4 hours, or let it set overnight.

7. To unmold, lower the bottom of the mold into a bowl of hot water; let stand 1 or 2 minutes to loosen the gelatin. Invert the mold onto a serving platter and garnish with additional berries, if desired. To store, cover loosely with plastic wrap and refrigerate for up to 2 days.

SERVES 6

NOTE: Red Zinger and Lemon Zinger teas, made by Celestial Seasonings, are available in most supermarkets.

smoked, fresh corn soup
with, 90–91
stewed, with tomatoes, green
olives, and raisins, 330–31
and wild rice soup, 84–85
wings, chipotle chile, 339
chicken breast(s):
chunks, roasted, with sesame
dressing, 337–38
herb-stuffed, roasted, 335–36
poached, with mock Cajun
sauce and sliced red
onions on whole-wheat
bread, 182–83
chicken salad:
basil-Parmesan, 333–34
with hazelnut sauce on ciabatta bread, 158–59
chicken soup:
with chorizo, potatoes, and
peas, 86–87
with mushrooms and sun-
dried tomatoes, 82–83
Puebla, 88–89
chickpeas with broccoli rabe
and roasted shallots,
294–95
chiles, *see specific chiles*
chipotle chile:
chicken wings, 339
salsa, black bean salad with
tomatoes, feta cheese and,
287–88
chocolate:
bread with crystallized fruit,
54–55
bread with dried cherries,
55
chip cookies, Mangia, 58–59
white, cherry cookies, 64
chorizo:
potatoes, and peas, chicken
soup with, 86–87
salsa, jumbo shrimp with,
on olive rolls, 184–85
stewed with onion and red
and yellow peppers on
semolina bread, 154–55

chowder, salmon, with fresh
corn and bacon, 76–77
chutney, pear, 371
seared duck breast with,
343–44
ciabatta bread:
chicken salad with hazelnut
sauce on, 158–59
sautéed broccoli rabe with
golden raisins, pine nuts,
and Pecorino Romano
on, 172–73
Spanish tortilla with
poached tomatoes on,
175–77
cider, apple, chilled butternut
squash soup with, 106–7
cinnamon:
and clove cookies, 59–60
pecan oat scones, 17–18
coconut muffins, 32
cod, poached, with Catalan
sauce, 306–7
coleslaw, barbecued pork loin
with, on baguette bread,
162–63
cookies, 56–71
corn:
fresh, and bacon, salmon
chowder with, 76–77
muffins, three-berry, 27–28
and oven-burst cherry
tomatoes and cilantro-
lime dressing, 213
roasted, wild rice and,
279–80
and roasted potatoes with
poblano chile, 211–12
soup, fresh, with smoked
chicken, 90–91
soup, spicy, with poblano
chiles and cream, 92–93
country bread:
French ham, Vermont
Cheddar, green apples,
and walnut aïoli on,
152–53
Italian, roasted shell steak

with caper sauce on,
164–65
Parmigiano-baked portobellos with roasted red pep-
pers on, 137
roasted eggplant, tomatoes,
and peppers with gor-
gonzola cream on, 174–75
smoked mozzarella with
baby spinach and roasted
tomatoes on, 138
couscous with Moroccan vegetables, 242–44
crab, soft-shell, with bacon,
tomato, and garlic aïoli on
a brioche bun, 149–50
cranberry pumpkin scones,
19–20
cream:
basil mascarpone, chilled
zucchini soup with,
116–17
gorgonzola, roasted egg-
plant, tomatoes, and pep-
pers with, on country
bread, 174–75
spicy corn soup with
poblano chiles and,
92–93
tomato sauce, pancetta, and
basil, penne with, 256–57
crème fraiche, avocado, red
onion, tomato, and Bibb
lettuce on Pullman bread,
ham with, 151–52
croutons, 361
anchovy, and Parmigiano
shavings, grilled radicchio
with, 226–27
Parmigiano, tuna Niçoise
salad with, 316–18
cucumber(s):
avocado, scallion, and lime
salad, 214
soup with yogurt and dill,
chilled, 99–100
tomatoes, and feta cheese,
penne with, 264–65

and fresh tomato salsa,
grilled whole baby zuc-
chini with, 236–37
mayonnaise, 360
mayonnaise, bacon, tomato,
and arugula on focaccia,
grilled tuna club with,
141–42
-stuffed chicken breasts,
roasted, 335–36
honey:
bran muffins, 35
and ginger carrot soup,
96–97
hummus, 378
black bean, with red onions,
farmer's cheese, and ancho
chile sauce in pita bread,
129–31

jalapeño peppers, *see* pepper,
jalapeño
jam, red onion, 372
pecan-crusted chicken with,
on Pullman bread, 156–57

lamb sausage and orzo, yellow
tomatoes stuffed with,
346–47
leek(s):
and pasta soup with goat
cheese, 102–3
sautéed, cherry tomato, and
pine nut salad, 231–32
sautéed, pesto, and oyster
mushrooms, fusilli with,
247–48
lemon:
-peppered shrimp with
green rice, 327–28
and poppyseed mascarpone
muffins, 36–37
-sautéed greens, and
Pecorino Romano cheese,
farfalle with, 245–46
lentil(s):
with garlic sausage and sage,
298–99

with peppers and goat
cheese, 300–301
soup, Moroccan, 118–19
lettuce, Bibb, avocado, red
onion, tomato, and crème
fraiche on Pullman bread,
ham with, 151–52
lime:
-cilantro dressing, corn and
oven-burst cherry toma-
toes and, 213
cucumber, avocado, and
scallion salad, 214
and ginger, sweet potato
soup with, 104–5
loaf cakes, 48–53

mangoes and jalapeño peppers,
saffron rice with, 277–78
mascarpone:
basil cream, chilled zucchini
soup with, 116–17
muffins, lemon and poppy-
seed, 36–37
muffins, strawberry, 38–39
mayonnaise:
ancho chile, 359
herb, 360
herb, bacon, tomato, and
arugula on focaccia, grilled
tuna club with, 141–42
meat entrees, 344–49
meat loaf, mustard, with
sautéed mushrooms on
brioche bread, 160–61
Mexican gazpacho, 101
mezzi rigatoni with parsley
pesto and roasted peppers
and red onions, 258–59
mint:
and brown sugar sauce,
roasted butternut squash
with, 228
pesto, fresh tomato salad
with, 229
wild rice with oven-burst
grapes, almonds and,
281–82

Moroccan:
dressing, orange, whole
roasted beet salad with,
205
lentil soup, 118–19
vegetables, couscous with,
242–44
mozzarella:
fresh, tomato, and cracked
black pepper on focaccia,
167
prosciutto, and olives,
charred red bell peppers
stuffed with, 221
smoked, with baby spinach
and roasted tomatoes on
country bread, 138
muffins, 24–41
mushroom(s):
sautéed, on brioche bread,
mustard meat loaf with,
160–61
and sun-dried tomatoes,
chicken soup with, 82–83
see also specific mushrooms
mustard:
applesauce, 369
dressing, house, 356
meat loaf with sautéed
mushrooms on brioche
bread, 160–61

Niçoise, roasted tuna, on
French baguette, 143–45
Niçoise salad, tuna, with
Parmigiano croutons,
316–18

oatmeal granola cookies,
61–62
oat scones, pecan cinnamon,
17–18
octopus with red pepper salsa,
320–21
olive(s):
bread, chèvre with grilled
radicchio and roasted red
peppers on, 132–33